The Changing Office Environment

NATIONAL BUSINESS EDUCATION YEARBOOK, NO. 18

Editor: MARGARET H. JOHNSON
University of Nebraska at Lincoln
Lincoln, Nebraska

Published by:

National Business Education Association
1906 Association Drive
Reston, Virginia 22091

THE CHANGING OFFICE ENVIRONMENT

Copyright 1980 by

NATIONAL BUSINESS EDUCATION ASSOCIATION
1906 ASSOCIATION DRIVE
RESTON, VIRGINIA

$12.00

LIBRARY OF CONGRESS CARD NO. 80-65210
ISBN 0-933964-19-6

Contents

PART III
HUMAN RESOURCES

PART IV
OFFICE COMPETENCIES, OCCUPATIONS,
AND CAREER OPPORTUNITIES

PART V
CURRICULUM CHALLENGES OF THE
CHANGING OFFICE ENVIRONMENT

Part I
PERSPECTIVE

CHAPTER 1
Growing Need for Office Personnel

ELAINE F. UTHE
University of Kentucky, Lexington

A successful business provides goods and/or services that are salable in the marketplace. These goods and services must be developed economically and efficiently and then marketed within an optimal time and in sufficient quantity to make a profit. The business office *facilitates* the other functions of the company and then *documents* its profits and losses through record-keeping. Offices in government, education, and other areas serve the same facilitating function; while profit and loss may not be an ultimate objective in these offices, certainly information processing and recordkeeping are vital components.

Thus, the office functions as the communications center. It is a supporting function—and is an overhead expense. Consequently, the office workers must be efficient, productive individuals. Every business—whether large or small—engages in a full range of office functions; in the small company the office force may consist of only one person who performs all the functions. In larger offices, the office functions may be divided among many individuals in several departments. In either case these workers prepare and maintain records of all types, and they facilitate internal and outgoing communications. As both the recordkeeping and communications functions increase in quantity and complexity, there is an ever-increasing demand for more office workers.

The growing need for office workers has two different facets: need for *more* workers (quantity) and need for better *workers* (quality).

PREDICTED NEED FOR NUMBERS OF WORKERS

Office workers will be needed in greater numbers in future years—and this need will exist at all levels of responsibility and for many different types of jobs. The demand will be created in three ways: (a) numbers needed to replace those retiring, leaving the labor force temporarily, fired or promoted, and changing careers; (b) numbers needed for new openings caused by expansion; and (c) numbers needed for emerging jobs.

Estimated needs. The Labor Department predicts that over 20 million office workers will be needed in 1985—an increase of 34 percent from 1974.[1]

---

[1]Carey, Max. "Revised Occupational Projections to 1985." *Monthly Labor Review*, November 1976. p. 13.

Some office jobs will decrease in numbers, while others will increase more than the 34 percent.

For example, over six million secretaries will be needed in 1985—this is an increase of nearly 50 percent over the number employed in 1974. The increased demand for more secretaries in the future may cause an even further drop in hiring standards than now present.

The demand for almost all other types of clerical office personnel will also rise according to predictions—notably, typists by 35 percent, billing clerks by 56 percent, estimators and investigators by 36 percent, mail handlers by 35 percent, and receptionists by 38 percent.

A few jobs will be in less demand: namely, the demand for stenographers will decrease by 24 percent, keypunchers by 20 percent, and telephone operators by one percent. These decreases will be due to changes in technology—specifically, the improvement of equipment—and more such changes may arise in the near future.

Over 475,000 computer specialists will be needed in 1985—an increase of 55 percent over those employed in 1974. However, the number of low-level jobs (such as keypunching) will decrease—again the technological changes cause most of the decrease. The increase in small desk-top computers used in business by the "ordinary" office worker or small business will also have an effect on the types of computer specialists needed. Desk-top computers will handle routine types of office jobs rapidly and will use standardized programs developed by experts; the user will operate the computer but will not create entirely new programs for it.

Over 10 million individuals will be employed as managers, officials, and/or proprietors in 1985—a 22 percent increase over 1974. Bank officers and financial managers will increase by 47 percent; office managers by 40 percent; health administrators, 67 percent; and sales managers, 30 percent. Therefore, supervisory skills must be developed in potential supervisors in order to ensure competence when openings occur. Because of the increase in demand for more clerical and secretarial workers, the demand for clerical supervisory personnel is predicted to rise to nearly 300,000 people by 1985.

Trends and issues. A number of factors have already influenced the present demand for greater numbers of office workers and will continue to have influence for the future also. For example, successful businesses tend to expand in size and to cover wider geographic areas; thus the number of products and/or services increases. These expansions increase the demand for records and communications; the greater the expansion, the more complicated these systems become.

Governmental regulations—which continue to grow—force companies to maintain new types of records and to maintain more details on present records, notably, in terms of taxes, affirmative action, consumerism, sex equity, and retirement plans, to name a few.

The decreasing birth rate trend will continue; even now, the number of teenagers entering the labor market each year is slowly declining. Furthermore, the career opportunity horizon for young girls is no longer confined to office work, teaching, and nursing as in past years. The pool of young female office workers is becoming smaller, while the demand for greater numbers of workers is increasing; there does not seem to be a corresponding pool of young male workers to fill many of these clerical jobs.

The number of women in the labor force is growing yearly and will probably continue to rise in the next decade. In 1950 approximately 33 percent of the women in the United States were working. By the mid-1970's over half of the female population—53 percent—were employed. There is a larger percentage working at each age level now, and more women are working for more years. The Bureau of Labor Statistics indicates that 40 percent or more of the 16- to 17-year-old and over 55 percent of the 50- to 64-year-old women are working. Furthermore, the percentage of working women in the other age brackets was even higher in the mid-1970's—18-19 years old, 59 percent; 20-24 years old, 65 percent; and 25-54 years old, over 55 percent.[2]

More of the working women have small children at home and are combining a career and marriage. Also, more women are returning to work or beginning careers even though they have been out of school and the labor market for several years; some have few skills to offer or find that their skills have deteriorated.

The sex equity issue will influence both the size of the pool of potential office workers and the types of training programs offered in the future. That is, the proportion of women in some occupations in relation to the proportion in the total labor force shows lack of sex equity. The total labor force is 41 percent female, yet 98.5 percent of the secretaries and typists are female and only 26.9 percent of the accountants are female.

These issues and trends, as well as many others, will affect the future need for office workers. Several will also affect the quality of the workers who may be available, as discussed in the next section and throughout the remaining chapters.

CONTINUOUS NEED FOR WELL QUALIFIED WORKERS

Employers constantly seek the best qualified office workers available on the market for the amount of pay; however, in recent years this search has not necessarily been a successful one. Although surveys conducted over several decades show consistently that office workers lost their jobs because of lack of ability to get along with others rather than lack of skills, the trend seems to be that potential workers may have deficiencies in both areas. In fact, in recent years employers have hired as "secretaries" individuals who do not possess the traditional secretarial skills. Many receptionist/typist positions of former years have been upgraded to the job title of "secretary" without a corresponding change in tasks, duties, responsibilities, and qualifications.

Confusion also arises when job titles are used to distinguish other factors than differences in tasks, duties, responsibilities, and qualifications. For

---

[2]U.S. Department of Labor, Bureau of Labor Statistics. *U.S. Working Women: A Chartbook.* Bulletin 1880. Washington, D.C.: Government Printing Office, 1975.

example, some companies use the job title of "administrative assistant" for the male worker and "executive secretary" for the female even though the work and responsibilities are the same. Generally speaking, there has usually been a considerable pay differential too.

Changes in the bookkeeping and accounting area are also occurring. More of the routine bookkeeping procedures are computerized, especially in large companies. Small businesses often employ a computer service to complete their accounting functions for them. The accounting functions are sometimes divided into narrow segments, such as accounts receivable clerk, so that the worker can specialize and do an easy routine rapidly. The worker seldom has an understanding of the overall accounting system in these cases, and the work therefore becomes boring.

The buying-selling transactions using plastic credit cards have multiplied many times over in the past decade, and the resulting paperwork has created a need for more workers to deal with these credit transactions.

The search for well qualified workers will continue as employers seek those with better typewriting, shorthand, calculating, and other office skills, those with a good knowledge of business functions, those with good attitudes, and those with decision-making abilities. Employers will continue to search for those who can manage their own time and supervise the time and work of others. The search for productive workers and imaginative leaders will become more intense as the decade passes. More technological improvements will also be sought to increase the efficiency of the office and to make it more responsive to the needs of business.

Need for office skills. In recent years fewer individuals have been truly qualified for and fewer are actively seeking office positions. Consequently, companies often hire an underqualified person who can perform some of the needed functions. For example, companies that hired only those who could write shorthand at 120 words per minute a few short years ago often require only 80 words per minute today. The same corrosion in standards also exists with typewriting skills—a drop from 60-75 words per minute to 50 for some companies, and a drop from 50 to 40 for others. This loss in skills affects the total production of office services; the lack of support services for executives has not been documented but would probably be extensive.

Shorthand skills are extremely important in the business world, and those individuals with good dictation and transcription skills are in great demand. In fact, a survey of top and middle management by *Fortune* indicated that 71 percent of the top managers and 52 percent of the middle-level managers dictate directly to a shorthand-writing secretary.[3] The managers also dictated to a recording unit at other times and when away from the office.

In recent years, however, shorthand enrollments at all educational levels have declined; less than 50 percent of the first-year students enroll in second-year courses. Shorthand systems (including alphabetic ones) have

[3]Management Attitudes Toward Office Productivity and Equipment Suppliers." *Fortune,* 1976. p. 8.

been developed and others revised to lighten the memory load so that individuals with less ability can learn shorthand; but even so, many students do not succeed in becoming successful shorthand writers or transcribers.

Why? Shorthand teachers must often teach basic English skills—spelling, punctuation rules, capitalization rules, etc. As a result, students who finish first-year shorthand may or may not have a salable skill. And yet, if the students who enrolled in first-year shorthand had average ability, good English skills, and good typewriting skills, they could succeed in acquiring marketable dictation and transcription skills within that one year—at 100 words per minute or more. These standards cannot be met, however, when the shorthand teacher must teach English, shorthand, and typewriting within the shorthand course.

Furthermore, the shorthand program that takes two years to develop marketable skills often discourages students with good English skills from enrolling. More individualized shorthand instruction is needed so that those who can spell, punctuate, and capitalize correctly may concentrate on learning shorthand rather than reviewing skills in which they are already proficient.

Typewriting skills acquired by beginning workers tend to be declining rather than rising in recent years, or so it seems to employers. Causes are difficult to pinpoint and may be multiple in number. Some of the decline may be attributed to the fact that the "better" students often seek jobs in other areas than office work; some may be due to lowering of instructional standards because of competition for students among elective courses. Part may be due to the philosophy of the quarter system (or semester system) in which students elect courses with insufficient guidance; students often choose a course because a good friend did, the course is easy, or it meets at a convenient time. An additional hazard of the open-selection concept exists in skills courses because the student selector is not aware of the amount of time needed to build a skill and does not enroll in consecutive terms.

Students in schools with an open-campus concept enroll in only sufficient courses to graduate so that they can leave the school early each day for a part-time job—and part-time jobs are still relatively plentiful. However, the students select a temporary and low-level job with the immediate goal of earning money. Many of them should stay in school in vocational courses, such as business courses, until they have acquired office skills with a reasonable degree of competency.

Need for specialty skills. The continuous need for office workers with better qualifications—or different ones—goes on and sometimes shifts directions. For example, the advent of the text-editing memory typewriters created an entirely new job title in the *Dictionary of Occupational Titles.*

The need for "specialty" secretaries is increasing—that is, many employers seek individuals with some special training in such areas as technical, medical, and legal areas. Word processing centers employ individuals who have good typewriting skills, particularly those with relatively high rates of keystroking speed and good transcription skills.

The large companies seek individuals with expertise in areas other than secretarial skills, also. Personnel are needed in data processing, reprographics, records management, and mailroom systems—and each area can be a highly complex, sophisticated one. New technology is constantly developing in these areas. Three types of personnel are needed—system planners, operators, and troubleshooters. The system planner must be an expert in the field, be creative in planning, and be able to train others in operating the system; the planner must be able to work with users to determine their needs and be able to communicate with them about the output. The operators must have the skills to run the equipment and must be accurate in providing input; they must be able to produce work at top speed. The troubleshooter (who may also be the system planner) is needed to solve internal problems with the system, to overcome or counteract human error, and to cope with complaints effectively.

Need for decision-making abilities. Office work is seldom a routine—it involves making decisions, some minor, some major. Each worker needs some facility in managing time so that important tasks are completed by the deadline. Every worker needs some training in developing good work habits and motion simplification as well as in setting work priorities. In order to make such decisions, the office worker must understand the functions of the office, the way in which the work flows, the importance of accuracy, and the philosophy of a team approach.

Professional attitudes toward work and one's job responsibilities are essential if the office team is to accomplish its goals efficiently. Pride in work and consideration for others (customers or co-workers) must be present.

Neither decision-making abilities nor professionalism develop by themselves; they are enhanced by training, by application, and by reinforcement.

Need for supervisory abilities. Supervisors have two basic needs: an understanding of the work objectives and an understanding of people. With these two factors—plus a lively imagination and a keen sense of dedication —supervisors are able to meet the need for profit and to find the means to keep employees happy and productive. As the need for office workers increases—and the supply grows smaller—the supervisor will need a keen talent for balancing work demands with individual's abilities.

The office manager—or team of department heads—has many responsibilities in today's business office, ranging from data processing, word processing, and telecommunications to personnel areas. The manager must deal with politics in the office and with time management of the human resources in that office. This individual needs a broad management view and must take an organizational outlook in managing the office. Leadership abilities are essential, of course; creativity and a futuristic viewpoint aid in managing the office team.

The growing need for office personnel—and the desire for well qualified ones—challenges business education. We must produce more and better qualified office workers.

Although technology advances continue to make office work easier in some respects, all machines are operated by human beings and therefore humanistic skills will continue to set production levels. Furthermore, as office technology becomes even more complex in some areas, there will be even greater demands for the "troubleshooter" individual—the one who understands the entire system and who can correct human or machine errors.

Need for updating for workers. If 20 million office workers are actually working in 1985, as predicted, many of them will probably be working with outdated office skills. Why? The number of new graduates from training programs will be steadily decreasing; therefore, more workers will be found from those who have been out of the labor market for some time, have little or no office training, or have had an insufficient amount of it to be productive. Even those who have been employed during this time will need updating as technology advances.

CHALLENGES TO BUSINESS EDUCATION

The employment predictions just reviewed—and the current trends affecting them—give rise to many challenges for and questions about business education for the next few years.

We must produce (a) a greater number of office workers, (b) workers with different specialties, (c) workers at different levels of the administrative ladder, and (d) workers for technology not yet in existence. At the same time, we must produce productive workers with professional attitudes.

Business educators must plan programs that are flexible and up to date. These programs must be efficient in producing the best quality of worker in the least amount of time, and they must produce individuals who have both good office skills and good human relations skills.

Teaching methods must be devised that work well with individuals and provide opportunities for all types of workers. Standards must be maintained and the training time must be flexible. Standards are an elusive concept—should one standard be adopted to measure every student's progress? Or should individual students leave programs with different levels of skills (and records that convey the level of achievements to both the student and the employer)? Are competency statements rather than grades one way to answer the "standards" question?

Programs will be needed to train tomorrow's manager of administrative services to assume different responsibilities. The growing need for office personnel will cause problems because of a lack of individuals entering the field. Recruitment will be a problem. Technology, as well as constraints from outside forces, will dictate the need for differing qualifications for this level of supervision.

Problems will continue to exist with using human resources so that individuals are deployed to the best advantage for both the company and the individual. New careers, new personnel techniques, and varying supervision techniques should be enhanced by the office environment itself. All these factors must be considered in finding and keeping office personnel.

The knowledge of current and future technology relating to office functions is a continuous challenge. Both businessmen and educational personnel must share in the responsibility for developing office competency requirements, and then in matching individuals to job needs. As competencies are set and shared, educators must translate them into curriculums and programs, as well as teaching-learning competencies.

In addition to futuristic looking programs and teaching methods, teachers must constantly strive to update their own knowledge and skills about the office functions and the needs of the business world. The best teaching method that supplies old-fashioned ideas is simply not acceptable. Consequently, there is a constant need for in-service teacher training as well as sound preservice training.

THE FUTURE

The future holds many challenges for business education. Issues and concerns relating to the disadvantaged and handicapped, sex equity legislation, and career education represent only a few of those we face—and others may emerge later.

Should changes be made? What is good in present programs and what needs changing? How should these changes be made? How should we proceed to ensure reaching new goals?

Creative thinking, futuristic attitudes, and expert knowledge of the present situation are needed if changes are to be productive. The next chapters provide a basis for thoughtful analysis for continuous updating in business education.

CHAPTER 2

Tomorrow's Manager of Administrative Services

University of Iowa, Iowa City

The fact that an entire yearbook designed primarily for business educators has been devoted to the subject of the changing office environment suggests several important points. One is that an extremely close kinship exists between education and the office, a kinship that will doubtless continue long into the future. A second point refers to the fact that many important changes are occurring in the office, changes that not only will affect future office operations and employee behavior, but also the programs in office education offered by the business departments in the high schools, community colleges, and universities throughout the world.

In the 1980's the office takes on new responsibilities and performs many new and exciting tasks as it expands into uncharted areas. At the same time, it requires many of the old as well as a whole host of new qualifications of its work force. In this time period—called by many the postindustrial age or the age of information—the simple office of the past steps aside to make room for its more complex counterpart directed by a new breed of manager. Within the total area of the office there is developing a new environment, along with broader qualifications needed for its management, both of which this chapter will explore. However simple this new environment seems, this discussion should be approached with the caution suggested by Zahner's Law, which states: "Everything is more complicated than it looks to most people."

CHANGING OFFICE CONCEPTS

To understand the new office manager requires, first of all, focusing on the organizational concepts underlying the manager's responsibilities. For this reason, a brief historical sketch is provided to trace the development of the office which has resulted in the new type of office function—administrative services—and the new type of manager needed to direct it.

A historical sketch of the office. Recently, the earliest office or administrative center on record was unearthed by Italian archeologists digging in Syria. Dating back to 2400 B.C., an incredible set of 15,000 clay tablets was found and traced to the little-known kingdom of Ebla, whose king employed some 11,000 administrators and civil servants to manage his offices. The Ebla records predated paper by many centuries and were inscribed on tablets stored on wooden shelves lining the royal file room. Doubtless this early office performed functions similar to those of the modern office; it was an information center responsible for processing the daily intelligence for controlling the growth and administration of the Ebla kingdom.

Through the centuries similar office functions were found, all sharing the manual production of information. Lundberg's 1975 study at Columbia University suggests that the early office, prior to 1870, was dominated by males equipped with quill pens and ink pots. Correspondence was penned by professional writers trained as scribes. There were no telephones, no lights, no secretaries, no office machines, no banks or insurance companies. Lundberg goes on to trace the past century of office work, dividing it into four time periods, each of which bore some unique features that distinguished it from the other stages. The first period (1870-1910) saw the incursion of large numbers of females into the office where all work was performed by hand. During the second period (1910-1930), scientific management, which had previously been directed toward work in the factory, was applied to office work with the large scale introduction of machines (typewriters, adding and calculating machines, and duplicating machines) as a substitute for the pen-and-ink work of earlier days. The stressful third period (1930-1945), which included the depression of the 1930's and World War II, brought increased emphasis on greater productivity and more efficient use of human resources. The fourth period (1945-1970) involved postwar problems and, from the mid-1950's on, the introduction of computerized data processing and an increasing succession of related hardware and software items, each growing more sophisticated in its impact on the office. It was during this last period, too, that the impact of systems thinking for understanding the overall operation of the office was developed.

A sequel to the Lundberg study would doubtless show that the decade of the 1970's involved even wider application of the computer to the office and increased integration of other machines with the computer to perform office work. Other chapters in this Yearbook confirm this fact, with their discussions of micrographics, reprographics, mini- and microcomputers, and the marriage of the telephone industry with the world of computers in the new telecommunication functions. Each of these machines shared something in common with the others—it performed one or more *related* functions for processing information. Thus, the concept of a family of *information processing machine systems* was born, and the place where the machines were used—the office—became the *information center.* Many of the reasons for this information-intensive feature of the 1970's will be treated in remaining sections of this chapter.

The office management concept. For many years—probably the first 50 years of the nineteenth century—good office management meant careful, thorough recording of information. With this basic notion in mind, the effective office manager was considered to be one whose entire operation was accurate, economical, neat in appearance, and applied the most efficient procedures for performing the office work. A premium was placed on high levels of clerical skills. Such an office had a narrow impact on the organization. While its services were available to the entire firm in which it resided, these services were almost exclusively devoted to collecting and processing data (largely typing, calculating, and duplicating) and, of course, for maintaining neat, usable files. The interrelationships among each of these information functions, as well as the identification of other equally necessary functions, were not widely emphasized. Instead, functional responsibilities in the office remained as isolated activities with little or no recognition of the interdependence that each function had on the other. As such, the basic *raison d'être* for the whole office function was missing.

The administrative services concept. In some cases abruptly, but in most cases gradually, the computer changed all that about the office. With its power to handle infinite quantities of data and to transport such data over telephone lines to any part of the world, the computer unified the separate functions of organizations. Too, it unified—at least conceptually—the previously separate functions in an office. Systems analysts demonstrated effectively to top management that purchasing is related to sales and vice versa; that finance and accounting are related to all other functions; that production has a similar relationship; that the collection and recording of data in the office is basic—and hence related—to the processing, distribution, and later storage of that data. Furthermore, the unique role that the office plays in the modern organization became clear as greater reliance was placed on its product—information—to *serve* the decision-making needs of management. Thus, an evolution of thought from the narrower office management concept to a broader administrative office serving the entire organization emerged.

This new view "saw" the office as a facilitating or helping agent provided to assist top management and all other parts of the enterprise. The broader term "administration" was used to describe the services provided by this expanded office function. Other names frequently suggested for administrative services were administrative management, administrative office management, administrative services management, and administrative systems. Where the field is restricted to the information life cycle, as suggested by Murdick and Ross, the term information services or information management is used. A more realistic term, perhaps, is administrative support systems or management support systems (the terms "administration" and "management" are used synonymously in this context) since the information-related functions of the modern office *support* the primary functions in the organization. An illustration of this concept, slightly modified from that originally developed by Lemasters and Stead, appears in Figure I.

In this context, the purpose of the office as an administrative services function is to provide specialized knowledge on the entire information cycle for the whole firm; to respond to the physical needs of employees regarding space, machines, and the like; to help ensure the security of the organization;

and in a closely related way, to care for the maintenance needs of the work force. This greatly expanded concept of administrative services includes not only the traditional office functions of records management, forms control, office supplies, mailing services, office environment, and office systems procedures but even has been broadened to include food services (cafeterias and vending operations), graphics, photographic and printing services, and reprographics. In some firms, the responsibility for car pool and parking operations is also added.

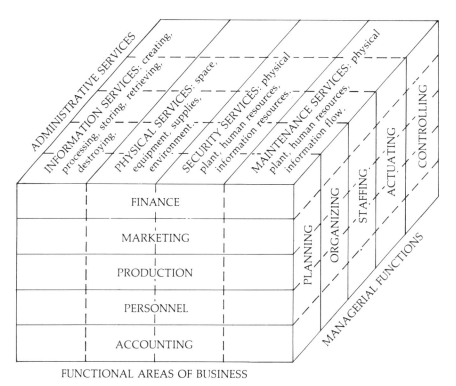

FUNCTIONAL AREAS OF BUSINESS

FIGURE I. A conceptual view of the administrative services function

As the world becomes more and more dependent upon services, top management in all fields has responded to the pressing needs for these services to assist in the administration of the main functions of their organizations. Often new positions, such as vice-president of administration or vice-president of administrative services, have been established to coordinate this pervasive and rapidly growing function. In turn, business schools in colleges and universities have followed suit, expanding their less comprehensive, traditional office management curriculums to include the entire administrative services spectrum, but more closely tied in with finance, marketing, production, personnel, accounting, and other related business administration and computer functions. The better programs in education include new courses with greater depth in business and economics, resisting the temptation of "putting new labels on old jars." Thus, true administrative services in no way should be considered a euphemism for modern-day secretarial education!

An organizational chart showing the placement of a typical administrative services division appears in Figure II. Each of the subfunctions in this figure (data processing, systems analysis, and the like) provides for the key administrative needs of the functional areas cited in Figure I.

On a national scale, the American Management Association (AMA) has taken up the challenge of in-service education of management personnel in this new area of work. In a series of recent administrative services workshops held around the country, the AMA has included these wide-ranging topics:

1. Organizing, planning, setting, and measuring short- and long-range goals
2. Developing and utilizing interpersonal skills, including effective communication, motivation, and delegation techniques

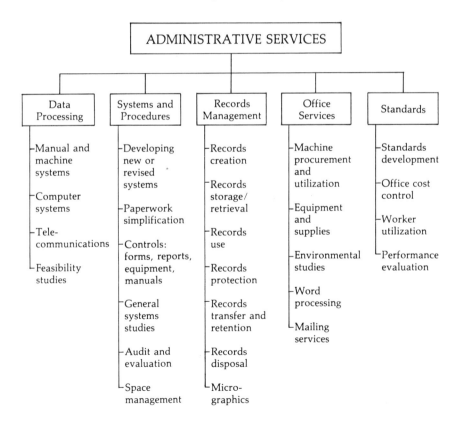

FIGURE II. Administrative services in a typical large-scale organization

3. Selecting and developing personnel which involves setting standards of performance, training new employees, and helping them improve their performance on the job
4. Preparing and controlling the operating budget
5. Managing telecommunications
6. Managing mail and messenger service
7. Applying micrographics to information storage and retrieval systems
8. Planning and designing office space
9. Evaluating and selecting office furniture and equipment
10. Developing and maintaining records management programs
11. Administering forms control programs
12. Managing secretarial services
13. Managing in-plant printing and reprographics
14. Providing job enrichment opportunities for employees
15. Maintaining security in the office.

From a quick study of this list of topics, it can be seen that many of the traditional office services have been retained (items 3, 6, 8, 9, 10, 11, and 12 are examples), but with new "twists," geared to modern organizational needs. The remaining topics show that the complex organization of today requires additional services, and that modern management must provide these services to survive.

Where has the office gone? "The past is prologue" is a fitting introduction to the development of the modern office. As discussed in this chapter, the office has evolved historically to a point where its functions have company-wide impact, where its operations are based upon more and more mechanization, and also where its management requires increasing skills and competencies far broader than those required of the office manager of the past.

Visionaries today talk about an "office of the future" concept that has already arrived. Such an office is described as a place where management interacts with a company's information network. The purpose of this office is to speed up the flow of information, while at the same time reducing office operating costs and providing its workers with a meaningful work experience. Its technologies, such as word processing, data processing, reprographics, micrographics, and communications, are all integrated to provide better service and are restricted mainly to large organizations.

However, in more practical terms that relate to small and large offices alike, the office has evolved into a function made up of many interdependent, complementary units. In this conceptual view the office is considered as:

1. An economic unit producing value. As such, it is a type of factory employing economic resources (people, space, and capital—to name three) and designed to produce a service.

2. A human-social unit of supervisors, typists, secretaries, workaholics, low- and high-motivated persons, minority and majority persons with the usual types of human problems.

3. A geographic unit—located somewhere in space and designed to serve its firm as a decision center where information is produced and utilized for making management decisions.

4. An ecological unit concerned with noise, seeing, and comfort and convenience problems and with understanding ergonomic issues, that is, the effects of the environment on the productivity and attitude of workers.

5. A technological unit of machines and new systems and their interrelationships.

6. A communication unit for sending and receiving messages.

RESPONSIBILITIES OF THE ADMINISTRATIVE SERVICES MANAGER

The previous discussion has pointed out that a new type of office manager—the administrative services manager—is emerging to handle a growing list of responsibilities. In the large firm where complex operations require a great deal of specialization, each function may be headed by a manager who directs a separate department. Data processing, word processing, and records management are examples of such functions. In the smaller firm, on the other hand, where little specialization is possible, the office manager will probably be responsible for all of the functions discussed in this section but on a less specialized scale.

The actual responsibilities assigned to the administrative services manager will vary from firm to firm. In general, however, they can be divided into two types: (1) *functional service responsibilities* dealing with each of the different functional areas under the manager's jurisdiction; and (2) *managerial process responsibilities,* those operational activities necessary to manage effectively each of the content areas specified in (1) above.

Functional service responsibilities. Whatever operations are assigned to the office ultimately become the functional content of the office and thus the responsibility of the manager of that office. When the office expands to become an administrative center, the administrative services manager assumes responsibilities over these functions:

1. All office services, which include procurement and utilization of office equipment and supplies; mailing and reprographic services; correspondence management including word processing; and electronic communications as well as market research related to each of these topics

2. Data processing, which includes machine systems methods and design, feasibility studies, conversion, installation, and follow-up studies

3. Records management, now broadened in scope to include manual and machine record life cycles (creation, storage and retrieval, use, protection, transfer, and retention and disposal); micrographics; record security and privacy; forms management; reports management; and records systems analysis

4. Administrative systems and procedures studies which involve developing new or revised systems, simplification of office work, environmental controls, space and work flow analysis, standards development, and performance evaluation of all aspects of administrative systems

5. Related information services, such as technical library functions (business and engineering are two common examples) and the supervision of graphics which includes photography, printing, and audiovisual operations

6. Security controls covering the prevention of loss of records, equipment, and company assets as well as the unauthorized use of any of these organizational resources.

As mentioned previously, firms that expand the responsibilities of administrative services managers even further include such important areas as company insurance coverage, administrative operation of the company fleet, and food services for employees.

Managerial process responsibilities. While the previous responsibilities for the administrative services manager are considered as specialized functional service duties for this new type of executive, there is another set of responsibilities that are implicitly assigned to most managers, especially those operating in the private sector. These responsibilities are regarded as *managerial process responsibilities* in that they accrue to the management of all of the functional service fields discussed earlier. Put simply, this responsibility means that any manager or supervisor—whether in a profit-maximizing setting or not—is implicitly responsible for certain activities. These responsibilities include:

1. Understanding fully the total responsibilities of the unit being supervised, including its relationships to other units in the organization.

2. Developing realistic goals for the units in line with organizational policies.

3. Planning and organizing the assigned resources in line with the approved goals.

4. Directing employment activities and administering company personnel matters in line with company policies and procedures.

5. Supervising, evaluating, and motivating all personnel reporting to the manager.

6. Setting appropriate productivity standards in accordance with employee participation in order to maintain high levels of output. This requires a comprehension of the relationship between people and machines (when one can be substituted for the other), and of the role of attitude and motivation in achieving organizational goals. Ethics and value systems also interact in this process.

7. Seeking effective information on an ongoing basis that provides sufficient knowledge to keep abreast of the demands of the job. This requires continual updating of general and technical knowledge, most commonly acquired through self-education or in-service programs.

8. Understanding fully how decisions are made and the role of the office as an information "producer" to furnish information upon which such decisions are made. Implied in such decision making is full appreciation of the role of probability, risk, and uncertainty in most of the company operations. Note how probability and uncertainty work on such everyday office activities as machine breakdowns, worker illnesses, the mood swings of certain employees, and poor service repair. From the knowledge of the organization over

time, a manager develops a valuable historical perspective from which "flows" sound professional judgment.

9. Developing controls, which includes setting measures by which the unit's performance is evaluated and rewarded. Thus, all managers are responsible for ensuring that each employee clearly understands how much *was* produced as well as how much *should have been* produced by each worker.

10. Communicating effectively, an all-important and all-pervasive responsibility extending throughout the firm as well as outside the firm. Tomorrow's manager of administrative services will view the totality of communication processes and systems including human-oriented verbal and nonverbal forms as well as technological systems in which machines and people interact (communicate).

11. Keeping an ever-watchful eye on the "bottom line," profit. Too often administrative operations have been considered as unrelated to the profit-making process. Modern managers, to be effective, must understand that the dollar wasted in the office is the same size and of equal importance to the dollar wasted in the plant; and with white-collar administrative staffs increasing faster than other segments of the work force, the administrative services manager will be on "constant alert" to control and reduce costs of operations, and to apply cost/benefit thinking to these operations. As the wag has stated, "Money is the root of all evils, and a person needs roots." The manager of administrative services has a big stake in the generation of sufficient profits to maintain operations. A common rule of thumb often applied to administrative costs may help to visualize the seriousness of the problem: For every dollar spent on administration, as much as $20 in product sales are required. With increasing inflationary pressures on management, the ultimate question is not can we do it, but can we afford it?

These 11 responsibilities, a studied glance will show, contain a certain element of specificity, of tangibility. The background for each one can be developed from the accumulation of knowledge obtained from management education combined with relevant work experience. Each responsibility is measurable to a reasonable degree. Thus, most people with a sense for management can, in fact, understand the importance and purpose of these responsibilities.

On a more ethereal, mystical level are additional responsibilities that have their roots in a manager's philosophy of work. The role of work in the manager's life plan, how well such a manager perceives and translates these perceptions into effective work strategies, and how responsive such an individual is to subtle forces on and off the job are perhaps even more basic responsibilities than the easy-to-identify list just discussed. Out of a list of many, two such subtle responsibilities expected of effective modern management seem to take priority.

The first of these subtleties deals with the general topic of bureaucracy. To many, "administration" and "bureaucracy" are one and the same. The former term has been assigned respectability in organizational life while the latter is used in a pejorative sense by most people. The reason is obvious; most of us have had infuriating encounters with offices in which considerable time was lost in filling out the wrong forms, in which required deadlines were not clearly communicated and hence not met, or in which a host of pencil-pushers with no apparent background for a problem were responsible for rendering an "objective" decision on our future. The administrative services manager is and will continue to be a bureaucrat and hence must sense that poor administrative systems are self-perpetuating and that the largest office staff, which seems to be operating efficiently, may not be justified in the best interests of the total firm.

Several laws, including Parkinson's Law of Administration and the Peter Principle, address this problem. The insightful manager has a continuing responsibility to question whether his or her own organization as a type of bureaucracy is accruing too much power over the operations of the firm. Simplification of such operations is possible, but it requires a bold quality that is not commonly found. Such a manager must be a strong "upstream swimmer" who can effectively counter the strong, relentless tide of more and more administration.

A second responsibility relates to the growing social conciousness that must accompany the more technical aspects of management. In contrast to the responsibility of past generations of managers who had a specific job to do within their firms, modern managers must demonstrate their concern for, and take an active part in, achieving positive societal goals. While both an interesting and a frustrating idea, it nevertheless is one that can no longer be ignored.

Many examples come to mind. Today's management talks freely and warmly about its labor force, calling workers its greatest asset. At the same time it regards them cooly and dispassionately as a cost, depending upon the technical and financial concerns of the moment. In his interesting book, *Small Is Beautiful,* Schumacher discusses technology and economy and states that both will have to be treated as if people mattered. This is, of course, not an easy choice, for inflationary pressures call for costs to be minimized and capital's use to be optimized and conserved. The monotony of the large office discourages creative and emotional expression in many people. Self-fulfillment and self-realization may not surface in such a setting, with the result that a breakdown in group performance occurs. However, the effective manager will consider such innovations as reorganization, variable working hour plans, and second-career options for valuable employees. The term for this kind of social consciousness van Dam calls "social technology," where technology assumes a "human face."

Thus, the effective manager of administrative services operations must necessarily wear many "hats." Humanistically, the needs of the work force must be better understood and their talents better employed. Technologically, the manager must be concerned with proper application of machines to those necessary processes that are unrewarding to people but are cost-effective so far as the total operation is concerned. And herein lies a potentially dangerous problem. Organizations in the age of information reward mechanical efficiency and push for more and more machines to replace people as a measure of efficiency and cost effectiveness. Yet, the effective manager may need to take the position of the auto driver who entered a one-way street counter to the traffic flow. When the police officer was about to fine the violator, the driver cleverly asked, "Constable, does it occur to you that the arrow may be pointing in the wrong direction?"

QUALIFICATIONS NEEDED BY
ADMINISTRATIVE SERVICES MANAGERS

At first glance, finding a person who can handle effectively all the responsibilities cited for tomorrow's administrative services manager may seem to be an impossible task. Certainly it is a challenging one, for such positions include these three important skills: technical skills, human skills, and conceptual skills. While not all of these skills will be found in any one individual, certainly a proper mixture must be determined for the specific position to be filled.

A manager of the administrative services function must, first of all, be able to deal effectively with organizational problems. These involve goal setting, effective planning and organizing, and a flexibility to adjust to changing conditions. For example, with the introduction of new telecommunication facilities that bring together a widely scattered corporate empire, the span of control (that is, the number of people reporting to an executive) has been expanded over the comfortable six to eight persons traditionally considered effective. As the director of service operations with companywide responsibilities, such a manager must be service- or user-minded, which means that the needs of other departments and the interests of the total organization must be sensed and met. Called for, in this case, is the ability to articulate the administrative services functions (what is available to whom, etc.) and to coordinate the use of these resources within the firm. Thus, maintaining sound relationships with heads of other departments utilizing administrative services as well as relationships with both top management and subordinates is a primary qualification. In the January 1978 issue of *Management World*, Harold T. Smith identifies 20 critical competencies for managers as determined by a survey of 457 members of the Academy of Certified Administrative Managers, 62 percent of whom responded. (This group is made up of experienced administrators who have passed the five-part examination sponsored by the Administrative Management Society and hence certified as to their knowledge-level competence in administration.) The top four managerial competencies, listed as super critical in terms of importance rating, were abilities to (1) listen actively; (2) give clear, effective instructions; (3) accept responsibility for problems; and (4) identify real problems. The remaining 16 competencies related largely to related communication and human relations skills. Due to the overriding importance of these two skill qualifications—technical and human—along with the ability to conceptualize, each of these qualification areas will be briefly discussed below.

Technical skills for the administrative services manager. First and foremost, the manager must be able to communicate effectively. Besides possessing the skills of writing, speaking, reading, and listening, such a

19

manager must be able to conduct meetings, flowchart, give clear-cut instructions, and ask effective questions. In addition, a sound knowledge of information systems and telecommunication technology is paramount along with a general comprehension of the role of operations research for planning and control purposes in the firm.

The manager need not be an expert machine operator; rather he or she should understand the functions of office machines and understand the role that storage-retrieval machines, micrographic devices, word processing and data processing equipment, and telecommunication play in the firm. Closely related are skills in coding information, in formulating standards that measure worker performance, and in the procedural skills needed to set up an effective work system. A related technical skill, in a sense, is the ability to budget, to conduct feasibility studies, and to determine cost effectiveness.

Human skills for the administrative services manager. The list of such skills is infinite. High on the list are such qualifications as perceiving problems between people; effective counseling, disciplining, and motivating employees; and creating a relaxed yet motivated environment in which work is effectively delegated and evaluated. In the end, the administrative services manager heads a unit that offers service and advice to other departments; thus, the human ability to suggest tactfully and to interact positively with other departments is of critical importance.

Conceptual skills for the administrative services manager. Studies, such as Sheriff's study at Iowa, have shown that as an individual moves up the managerial ladder that person has a *decreased* need for technical skills but at the same time an *increased* demand for conceptual skills. Examples of conceptualizing skills follow:

1. Viewing the organization as a whole and the office as one of its parts
2. Designing and creating new work systems to meet new organizational needs
3. Perceiving clearly and accurately complex relationships and issues and translating them into sound operating programs
4. Recognizing and prioritizing problem areas and critiquing alternative methods of resolving problems.

Closely intertwined with conceptualization are related analytical skills (to identify problem parts and their interrelationships) and a logical mind. (Thus, a college degree with broad preparation in business and economics, organizational behavior including communication, and mathematics should be a minimal educational qualification.) On the one hand, the manager must be objective and deal with factual information; on the other, such an administrator must be subjective and closely attuned to the feelings of the work force. In the final analysis, the ability to balance the two may well be the ultimate qualification for success.

SOME CONCLUDING COMMENTS

In an editorial appearing in the August 1976 issue of *Modern Office Procedures*, John Dykeman calls the traditional definition *and* concept of the office archaic. Rather than a place in which the affairs of a business or professional person are carried on, as Webster has defined it, Dykeman suggests that the office has become an umbrella that covers all administrative functions in an organization, regardless of where they are performed. And since the primary function of this administrative arm is service, it follows that the person responsible for managing administrative services must possess a broad set of qualifications as outlined earlier. However, the keystone in this future organizational structure will be information, so the executive in administrative services must know how to manage all aspects of the information process.

Already there are dozens of multifunctional systems available to handle a growing number of office tasks. In the future, more and more of these systems will be tied together. However, just as there is no ready-made, off-the-shelf, plug-in panacea for all organizations, neither is there any one set of responsibilities or qualifications for the administrative services manager.

To move directly from the "old" office operation to the "new" administrative services concept is like trying to jump from the ground floor to the top of the stairs; it's unrealistic. Rather, the qualified manager will take the steps that are here now. Such a person, as Kleinschrod so effectively remarked, must stay above the administrative landscape and see and understand the problems, the opportunities, and the relationships among them. Such a person who has the authority to do something about them can adequately design and build, from all the available components, the flexible, responsive administrative services system for that organization.

CHAPTER 3

Constraints Affecting the Business Office

JIM N. BRUNO
Administrative Management, New York, New York

In the contemporary business office, employees are finding that they need to work with new equipment, and because of this they need to develop new working skills and cultivate new working relationships. In short, the office is changing. Employees, and management as well, fear changes that tamper with organizational procedures and hierarchies. Fear of change is the major constraint to development in the office.

Of the many factors currently causing change, four promise to have the greatest impact in the very near future: (1) Business has a need to handle more information each day. (2) Clerical employees, and often the executives they support, are not as productive as they need to be to handle the increasing amount of necessary business information. (3) Employees are becoming disenchanted with clerical and secretarial positions and are looking for more satisfaction and opportunity to grow in their jobs. (4) Top management historically has viewed administration as a support function for sales, production, and finance. As such, administration evolved as a "cost of doing business," often thought of as a necessary evil.

OFFICE WORK

The office is the place where administration, i.e., the management and handling of information, takes place. According to recent estimates, the average business spends 40-50 percent of its total operating costs on administration.[1] To give the reader an idea of the importance of information in today's business world, almost half of the total U.S. work force is employed in an information-handling capacity. These employees earn 53 percent of the wages paid in the United States.[2]

What are all of these people doing? What types of information are they handling?

INFORMATION

Legislation, with its ensuing regulations at the city, county, state, and

---

[1]"The Office of the Future, an In-Depth Analysis of How Word Processing Will Reshape the Corporate Office." *Business Week*, June 30, 1975. p. 49.

[2]"Communications Industry Replaces Manufacturing As Keystone of U.S. Economy." *Commerce America*, August 15, 1977. p. 16. (Washington, D.C.: U.S. Department of Commerce.)

federal levels, is literally burying business in paperwork. In 1976, according to the Commission on Federal Paperwork, government-forced paperwork cost the private sector $32 billion, or 130 million employee hours.[3] One heavily regulated public utility, Wisconsin Power and Light, reported that its costs for regulatory reporting increased 6,200 percent in the 10 years between 1967 and 1977.[4]

Every business has a host of regulations and regulatory commissions to worry about. Acronyms for government-enforced regulations and their regulatory bodies can fill a book, and the average business in the United States must be aware of, and comply with the regulations of, at least the following:

—Internal Revenue Service (IRS)
—Occupational Safety and Health Act (OSHA)
—Employee Retirement Income Security Act (ERISA)
—Equal Employment Opportunity (EEO)

In addition, there are state employment security (unemployment insurance) and worker's compensation laws as well as industry regulatory bodies such as:

—Federal Communications Commission (FCC)
—Federal Trade Commission (FTC)
—Federal Aviation Administration (FAA)
—Food and Drug Administration (FDA)

For a perspective of how much information handling is called for to report to these agencies, let's look at an example for just one—EEO.

Should a business's personnel files be audited by the government because of a discrimination suit, the following documentation may be necessary:

1. The number of hires in a given year
2. The number of promotions by ethnic group within the organization, giving information on old position and new
3. The total number of applicants in a year, giving names, minority group identification, sex, education attained, tests given, dates tested, test scores, and whether or not hired
4. List of minority workers currently employed giving information on position hired at and current position as well as name, minority group, date of last promotion, and education
5. Terminations in past year, giving name, minority group, sex, job classification, rate of pay at termination, date, and reason for termination
6. Number of discrimination complaints in past year
7. The total number of employees in each job classification by ethnic group and sex.

[3]"Paperwork Commission Offers Recommendations To Ease Burden, Cost." *Nava News* 31:5; September 23, 1977. (Fairfax, Va.: National Audio Visual Association.)

[4]Schwartz, Malcolm R. "Look Before You Leap: Planning in a Tight Economy." *Impact: Information Technology* 1:4; April 1978. (Willow Grove, Pa.: Administrative Management Society.)

When an EEO complaint is made, the government looks for policy patterns to prove discrimination. It is business's obligation to provide the records which prove or disprove such patterns exist. The documentation this demands is swelling the office workload.

Other needs for information also burden administrative environments. A changing economy calls for fast, accurate business decisions. Top managements need to be constantly aware of their organizations' financial position. Slow reactions to a change in economic conditions can be costly in terms of higher interest rates, shrinking or changing markets, and new competitors.

Managerial decisions are based on knowledge of the forces affecting a business. The more accurate and timely the knowledge, the better the decision. At a time when the information workload has been burdened by regulatory documentation, top management finds it needs a better response time to economic and business conditions. These two informational needs are forcing businesses to look at new ways of handling information.

OFFICE PRODUCTIVITY

Administrative work is predominantly performed manually, with the work being done, for the most part, by clerks and secretaries reporting to supervisors. The office has been slow to automate. In comparison to agriculture and industry, the prime users of automated techniques, business administration lags far behind in capital expenditures for equipment. The theory in most office environments is "bring in more people to handle increasing workloads."

Office automation promises to better handle swelling information demands while minimizing the need to hire additional people. In essence, this means increasing office productivity. The following example shows how.

In the spring of 1978, the Dartnell Institute of Business Research released the figure of $4.77 as the cost of the average 150-word business letter dictated to a secretary.[5] By simply automating the dictation part of the business letter cycle, the average cost drops to $3.74, a $1.03 savings per letter. In addition, automating dictation frees up the secretary's time to do other things. Ideally, the secretary can handle additional work during this time, which in effect allows the executive to delegate more. Automation, in its simplest form in this example, allows the executive and the secretary to increase their productivity without having to work harder.

CHANGING ATTITUDES ON CLERICAL WORK

The Administrative Management Society reports that clerical wages have been keeping pace with inflation, averaging a 7 percent per year increase over the past five years. Yet, clerical salaries are threatening to increase at a rate higher than inflation. The Work In America Institute predicts a shortage of secretarial and clerical workers in the future because

---

[5]Minor, R. S. "Cost of Average Business Letter Set at $4.77." Chicago: Dartnell Institute of Business Research.

women, who comprise most of the clerical work force at the moment, are seeking more fulfillment and status from their jobs. They are less than enthusiastic about finding satisfaction in the traditional jobs that have been open to them. This is especially true for younger women just entering the job market. They are seeking careers with opportunity rather than merely jobs for a paycheck. Minority group job applicants, as well, have had their career aspirations elevated. The job a person does for a living is a means of status among peers and in the community. Unskilled positions available in office environments simply are not enticing.

Without dwelling on the sociological reasons for people's balking at traditional office work, it suffices to say that as the labor market dries up, clerical and secretarial salaries will be forced higher at an even greater rate. By adding the cost of inducements such as better wages and fringe packages to the already high cost of administration, it is easy to envision traditional administrative information handling costs soon exceeding 50 percent of the cost of doing business.

Managements are being forced to look for new and better ways of handling administration. Interestingly, while labor intensive administration is keeping pace with inflation, and threatening to increase in cost faster than inflation, recent electronic technology is lowering the cost of office equipment. While postal rates are increasing annually, the costs of electronic document distribution and computer logic and memory are decreasing.

REACTIONS TO TECHNOLOGY

Electronic technology is maturing to the point that it may be able to help solve increasing cost problems while promising almost instantaneous communication of information. Top management is especially attracted to the communication aspects of technology because it promises faster information on which to base managerial decisions. This directly affects the success they have in doing their jobs.

Developments in technology, cost, and management's need to know portend monumental changes for the office environment, its procedures, and most important of all, its people. New skills are already in demand for occupational categories such as word processing operators.

The contemporary business office is at the threshold of becoming the working environment for a team of highly skilled specialists. How rapidly it transforms itself depends upon how its people react to change. Within each organization, some will lobby for change, while others will do everything in their power to restrain it. Each organization will find that its work force reacts differently. Through this, the new office—with its skilled employees, its sophisticated equipment and procedures—will evolve.

To the casual observer, the impact of automation is usually anything but mild. Within the office environment, electronic technology promises to alter everything from the simplest gadget, the pencil sharpener, to the most sophisticated mainframe computer. How this technology is brought into the office will dictate employees' reactions to it.

One lesson administrators are learning fast is that administrative work is unlike industrial or agricultural work. Administration's primary product, information, is intangible. It is not easily quantifiable for it changes, having no set value. Costing procedures developed in industry do not apply in administrative environments where often no two jobs are alike.

Likewise, task simplification for assemblyline production usually is not effective. This was painfully evident in the evolution of word processing where organizational and procedural changes were introduced with the new equipment. Manufacturers originally sold word processing to users as a means of automating the typing function. Manufacturers were quick to point out, and wrongly so, that to be most effective, the secretarial job needed to be split into its elementary functions—typing and administrative support. Typing was classified as all forms of keyboard work. Administrative support was classified as all nontyping secretarial duties. To maximize the efficiency of task simplification, manufacturers and vendors urged users to establish word processing centers to handle typing and administrative support centers to handle all other duties. In an attempt to sell the word processing reorganization concept to the secretaries whose jobs were being changed, new career paths, culminating in word processing management positions, were promised.

The first jolt came when the traditional secretary/executive team was split. Working relationships were destroyed. Managers as well as secretaries balked. The second, and almost fatal, jolt came when former secretaries were placed in word processing centers and told to type seven or eight hours a day. Now called word processing operators, the secretaries in the centers viewed their environment as a typing pool—a demotion. Manufacturers and word processing managers were so adverse to this description of what was done that to this day the word "pool" is taboo. Yet, this is not to say it does not exist.

In 1972 and 1973, when the word processing/administrative support split was rigidly adhered to, many experiments in word processing failed dismally. Eventually the realization that each organization was different came into focus, and other organizational configurations such as satellite centers[6] and secretarial clusters[7] evolved. These were a step back towards the traditional secretary/executive team, allowing secretaries to work for fewer executives. Once again, personal rapport between executives and their supporting employees developed. The lesson that pure work simplification in an administrative environment could lead to employee discontent was well learned.

Word processing survived. As of 1977, estimates have placed the industry gross at over $700 million. This figure is expected to grow to well over $2 billion by 1982.

---

[6]Satellite centers are small word processing typing groups strategically located within an organization, usually by department and specializing in work of department. May be in addition to or instead of centralized word processing group.

[7]Secretarial clusters are groups of word processing operators and administrative assistants handling work for executives within close proximity. Often clusters specialize in work of specific administration department. May be in addition to or instead of word processing/administrative support centralized groups.

SPECIALIZATION

Word processing is but one form of administrative specialization. Offices today are a conglomeration of administrative specialty areas such as records, reprographics, telecommunications, data processing, and word processing, all in support of business's three primary functions.

Office equipment developments have generally been restricted to particular administrative specialty areas. Until recently, seldom has technology gone beyond the borders of a discipline in an attempt to coordinate the work of two or more specialty areas. Computer technology was, perhaps, the only development that affected administrative subdisciplines such as reprographics and records in addition to doing its main job of processing information. Management saw fit to deal with computers, the anomaly in the office environment, by taking them out of the office and placing them in their own closed environments.

In addition, a number of other factors came to bear on data processing which further alienated this administrative specialty from the mainstream of administration. Computer operation demanded highly skilled operators and programmers. Specialized training was necessary. Along with the specialized knowledge came computerese, a unique language or jargon computer people use to communicate with each other. While this verbal shorthand might enhance communication between data processing specialists, it tends to block communication between specialists and other office and other office employees not knowledgeable in the area.

The office found itself divided into specialty domains with managers highly knowledgeable in their specialty areas becoming the nobility in the feudal office structure. At best, interdepartmental communication and cooperation became strained. Duplication of administrative work has become common, adding to the administrative cost burden.

COOPERATION

Electronic technology is making possible more than just quicker input, processing, storage, retrieval, and communication of information. Recent developments are allowing for the sharing of information between administrative specialty areas. Distributed processing, through the use of intelligent terminals (minicomputers at remote locations), allows for rapid conveyance and processing of information between departments without the need for memos, intra-office deliveries, and in some instances, paper itself. Invoices that were heretofore created in quadruplicate, with copies going to sales, finance, production, and then records, may now be generated on display screen word processing minicomputers. They can be entered into memory in finance and records and communicated to production for order fulfillment without the use of paper. While this is possible now, in reality, numerous obstacles impede the use of such a system, not the least of which is bringing the departments involved together to plan for such a drastic change in systems, procedures, and even personnel.

For a cooperative planning effort of this magnitude to succeed, strong leadership and commitment at upper levels of management is needed. Perhaps a new, high level position, information manager, is in order. The ideal information manager will view administration as more than mere support. The manager will understand, as well, why the information is needed. Thus, administration will grow in importance, gaining planning capabilities for the organization en route.

GENERALIST VS. SPECIALIST

Administrative specialties will continue to exist, and some, such as word processing and telecommunications, will grow in importance. Yet generalism—the possession of working knowledge in all administrative areas—will be the key factor allowing the administrator in charge to manage the specialty teams to get administration's job done.

As top management comes to view administration for the timeliness and importance of the information it provides, they will give administration more responsibility in overall organizational planning and decisions. From an upper management vantage point, administrators will be able to view the entire administrative needs of the organization with organizational instead of departmental goals in mind. Duplication of effort will be minimized as mere "bandages" need no longer be applied to problems department by department.

It is possible to minimize the effect of exclusive administrative domains, but only when top management recognizes such domains as impeding their organization's growth and well being.

OTHER AREAS OF CONCERN

There are numerous day-to-day equipment and people problems that need to be overcome before the office can take advantage of the technology that exists. Some are as follows:

Fear of equipment. Because of the sophisticated skills needed to operate many computers, noncomputer people tend to fear the electronic components and their keyboards. Computers have been unforgiving of human error, and a slight error in logic could be magnified manyfold in an area such as accounts receivable. To make computers easier to work with, manufacturers are developing systems that need no special knowledge of programming languages. They are, at last, attempting to make equipment which is compatible to people and the needs of an organization rather than trying to force people and organizations to adapt to the peculiarities of the equipment.

In addition, people just entering the office job market are not afraid of working with computers. They do not fear keyboards and display terminals because they began working with electronic equipment while in school. As these people move up in the business world, they will be more willing to operate a minicomputer or display desk station than are their predecessors who tend to still insist that they are above working with the equipment. The day is not too far off when electronic office equipment will come to be viewed as tools of administration, perhaps as common as the pen or pencil is today.

Standardization. Jargon differentials between specialty areas tend to slow down the communication process. Different administrative languages are causing a Tower of Babel effect in the office where effective work is being stymied by people's inability to communicate with each other. This is especially true in communications between specialists and generalist managers. Often managers renege on their responsibility by delegating too much authority to a subordinate specialist who appears knowledgeable in the technical field. Frequently it is easier to delegate than to learn.

In addition to standardizing technical languages, a need also exists for developing standards that assure compatibility among different "brands" of equipment systems. Then equipment will not have to be turned over every time the workload changes or grows. Manufacturers are reluctant to make equipment which allows add-ons by other manufacturers. Because of this, in part, changing administrative requirements cause some organizations to look for entire new lines of equipment as they outgrow the old. Leasing instead of buying has minimized the effect of equipment which no longer fills the need of an organization, but this is often an expensive route. Frequently businesses look to time sharing and outside services to fulfill their needs, but again there are not ideal solutions.

Unionization. Currently less than 10 percent of the clerical work force is unionized.[8] If the office environment follows the lead of industry and simplifies worker tasks to increase the efficiency of automation, then job dissatisfaction resulting in white collar unions may well take place. Needless to say, managements would like to see the 10 percent figure remain static or shrink.

Training the work force. Current specialty employees are getting most of their training from manufacturers, vendors, and in-house cross training of employees. Little is being done by schools to prepare students for specialized administrative entry positions. On the other hand, business management graduates are getting specialty training within functional fields such as finance and marketing. Yet, they are not getting the generalist overview necessary to manage a sophisticated administrative information complex.

Administrative managerial responsibilities are evolving to the point where administrators are being asked for input on corporate decisions and directions. They are being asked to manage information complexes comprised of knowledgeable people, detailed procedures, and sophisticated equipment. This is quite different from the responsibilities of the office manager of the thirties or even the fifties.

Administrators need not know how a piece of equipment operates, but they should know what it can or cannot do, how well, and how the equipment and its operators fit into the organizational work flow. Armed with this knowledge, administrators then can be effective organizational leaders.

---

[8]*Office Salaries 1978-79.* p. 38. Willow Grove, Pa.: Administrative Management Society.

Today's administrative specialists find themselves weak in their dealings with people and organizational matters while the administrative generalists are weak in their systems and equipment knowledge. In order for either of these types to manage integrated information complexes, they will first have to master their deficiencies. Or, perhaps, a new type of manager is being called for, a type that needs to be cultivated in our schools and our organizations.

In summary, the major changes happening in business are currently happening within the office environment. This change is away from manual administration and towards automated systems and procedures. But, automation in the office is not the same as it was in industry and agriculture; task simplification is not working. In addition, with organizationally pertinent information as the end product, office change needs to be flexible, varying from organization to organization.

The major constraint to change, especially automated change, is people's reaction to it. People are currently slowing the automation process down because of their fears of the new office environment it promises and their roles in it. The slowdown is good for business for it allows organizations to experiment and develop proper solutions to their problems.

Highly sophisticated, integrated administrative systems are neither the answer to all of administration's problems, nor will they cause the employee revolution many fear. The need by business to document what it does will still exist. Electronic technology only makes it easier to do. Furthermore, administrative work is being performed adequately at the moment. Yes, duplication of work and needless documentation do exist, but for the most part, the work is getting done. Business has the time it needs to allow for a steady evolution from what is to what will be. This should radically defuse adverse employee reaction.

Part II

OFFICE FUNCTIONS AND SERVICES

CHAPTER 4

Systems Concept

FLOYD LANGFORD, JR.
Louisiana Tech University, Ruston

Today's economic and business atmosphere is one of ever-rising labor costs and increasing demand for information of all sorts. Office systems and procedures are going through a revolution. Businesses are experiencing a dire need to stay abreast of the leading-edge technologies, techniques, and their proper application in order to remain competitive. The current aphorism pertaining to information systems is "The Future Just Arrived." BIOSOMA is today's popular acronym, meaning the coming together of man, society, and machines.

Society today is an information society. Information is a corporate resource; it is what office operations produce. Information must be relevant, timely, accurate, complete, available, and usable. Technology is a tool used by people to get the information job done. Systems, too, are tools. Systems do not do anything; people do. The ability to convert business information into sound judgments is distinctively human. People, equipment or technology, procedures, and space are the components of a system; and they are interacting, interrelated, and interdependent.

Business decisions are only as good as the information brought to bear in the decision-making process, and the information is only as good as the system will allow it to be. Information processing is a system whether it is viewed in that manner or not. It is usually a network of systems or subsystems. All office employees and many other employees are information workers—part of a system. The technological and procedural elements of a system may be manual, mechanical, automated and electronic, or a combination of any two or all three of these.

Corporate information systems today are rapidly becoming more swift, timely, and accurate. Business strategy is developed through consensus on the basis of analyses and planning made possible by sophisticated systems providing sophisticated information to all levels of decision making. The very survival of a firm—markets, labor relations, product and service innovations, the safety of investments, sources of funds, acquisitions, and liquidations—requires an organization of information.

HUMAN INFORMATION ENVIRONMENT

At all levels of management there is increasing familiarity with information systems, allowing each manager to become more involved than ever before with his area's information function as a resource base. Organizational status, managerial style, and organizational structure will need constant evaluation. The information systems function is moving from a remote, staff/service position to one more deeply involved in the business of the corporation. Consequently, managers at all levels and in all areas are demanding greater control over the information activities. Because of changes in communications technology and related developments, the technical aspects are becoming increasingly "transparent" to the end user. Thus users more and more are dictating their needs. An efficient and effective information system not only provides useful information to management at all levels but is also usable by management.

Information uses. Top management wants to know the profit and loss effects of capital investments and on-going expenses of information systems. A concern of top management is whether or not the information system is helping the corporation gain its immediate profit goals and long-term objectives. Top management wants (1) the most relevant information (2) at precisely the right moment (3) to produce an infallible management decision (4) at the least possible cost. The end product is delivering decision-oriented information to management. Such information is used (1) to run the business, (2) to measure performance day to day, (3) to track progress toward longer term strategic goals, and (4) to alert management to any changes in the internal or external fundamentals. Meeting these needs requires involvement and participation of personnel from top management to operating personnel.

Information objectives. An information system that is commonly defined, generally accepted, and widely used throughout an organization bears in mind the organization's (1) long-term goals, (2) internal structure, (3) budgeting and planning processes, and (4) communication and data processing capabilities. Therefore, objectives of an information system are to provide (1) information to exercise control over operations, (2) early warning of developing problems, (3) enough specific data on nonroutine problems to indicate remedial action required, (4) necessary market and economic background to interpret financial data correctly, and (5) adequate information to allocate human and financial resources effectively.

Information criteria. Criteria helpful in fulfilling established purposes and objectives may be elected from among the following. The first is uniformity, which means that definitions, formats, allocation policies, and transfer pricing methods should be consistent. A second criterion is timeliness. Information delivered after the decisive time period has passed or before it is relevant is both costly and useless. Merging the accounting systems with the information systems is a third criterion. This integration helps to avoid duplication of effort and to assure information integrity and relevance. Flexibility is a fourth criterion. The information system design needs to lend itself to shifting from geographic dimensions to particular products or special types of customers. A fifth criterion is conciseness. Too much information is just as ineffective as too little. The cost of exhausting all possible sources of information is prohibitive; therefore, priorities are essential. No amount of information will assure perfect judgments. Cost/benefit analysis will likely determine priorities and cut lines. If a manager has to wade through reams of documentation when the decisive time has come, the information system has defeated its own purpose. Last, an often overlooked criterion is that of user and operator interviews. A system with maximum potential will not work unless users and operators will work with it. An information system is as much the operator's system as any one else's.

ORGANIZATIONAL INFORMATION ENVIRONMENT

An issue of major import is the ease with which an information system can build a bureaucracy. There is a temptation to produce endless outputs of useless information. A highly recommended remedy is to determine relevancy of information at the lowest possible organizational level, preferably where the information is captured. Analysis should also occur at the lowest appropriate level and be passed upward for action without further analysis.

Integrative/interactive systems. Effective interaction among line managers, corporate managers, and specialized unit operating personnel is the integrative force that brings about a total corporate information system, which has an impact on the way a company conducts its business. Integration seems to be the key factor for an efficient and effective information system. Computer experts such as programmers and system analysts think differently than do executives. Whereas executives tend to seek alternatives and possibilities in a dynamic and changing world, computer experts seek firm definitions and fixed problems which can be solved. Too, information designers generally have limited knowledge of detailed business system requirements. Using departments become quickly annoyed.

A continuing problem is one of limited objectives. The use of old computer technology imposes a limited capability. Frequently, solutions are limited to finance, inventory, and marketing problems. This limited concept takes into consideration neither the management processes, administrative functions, nor office operations. Coordination of information needs with technological trends is an important consideration.

Centralization/decentralization. Centralization or decentralization is often an issue. There is no clear-cut choice between the two alternatives. In fact, entire corporate structures are being reviewed in the information system updating process. Considerations are based on such areas as profitability goals, market segments, products, and customer services. Decentralized workstations may capture and integrate information of several kinds. However, centralized control assures the overall integrity of information generated in this manner.

Information is gaining recognition as a valuable resource on the same level as capital and labor. The time has come to get away from information as being underpriced, underutilized, and underrated. Information architectures are being redesigned to meet the new needs of organizations. Companies reorganize their decision-making processes to adjust to political, economic, social, and market swings. The information system will be required to deliver a broad spectrum of research-based information even beyond that available within the corporation.

SYSTEMS AND PROCEDURES

It is essential to think in integrated systems and in networks since they reflect an organization's business. Business is comprised of a series of transactions that interrelate with one another. These transactions are processed by means of the information network. Integrating the organization's information technologies into interfacing processing modes is becoming just as important as interfacing the company's business transactions. The right information, at the right time, in the right place, in the right form, is critical. Too, a major goal in offices is to cut costs and increase productivity. Vast amounts of clerical and executive inefficiency stem from the need to process information, get it from one place to another, and from one form into another. Systematizing and integrating technologies in the information flow cuts inefficiencies and assures executives of information access.

Integrative/interactive systems. A centralized information base provides the same information for differing functions, thus eliminating redundant entry and reducing input errors. Data base modules in a total business system might include personnel, finance, business operations, administrative services, inventory, sales control, etc. The personnel module might include the functions of payroll, personnel status, stock and savings plans, pension plans, skills inventory, insurance reporting, and applicant resources. The finance module might include general ledger, accounts receivable, accounts payable, etc.

A centralized data base information system collects and integrates data from different business functions and stores the collected data at one location. Information may be distributed throughout an organization both vertically and horizontally. Integration is effected by the use of a single information library.

In a centralized and integrated system each piece of information is used only once. For example, an employee's name is entered only one time instead of its having to be repeated in the many subsystems in which it is referenced. Thus, duplication is avoided, errors are greatly reduced, and updates are simplified. At the touch of a button, accounts receivable can be viewed at a glance for comparison with last month in order to determine which accounts require action. Funds available for acquisitions and mergers and for credit requirements can be projected. Salary, job classifications, and length of service comparisons can be made. Surveys of job skills can be made for filling job requisitions. For example, if a Fortran programmer is needed with IBM 370/158 experience, in a salary range of $18,000 to $20,000, and possibly some foreign language capability, the skills inventory prints out a set of names of candidates within moments.

A network of interfaces can eliminate procedural red tape and provide executives with timely information available within their own domains and in a form they are likely to be familiar with and probably chose themselves. Fingertip information capabilities of systems permit executives to be doing that which they are best at and are being paid to do—making and implementing decisions. Not to be overlooked is maximum equipment utilization. In a completely interactive system all equipment is accessible to all users. Placing processing power in the hands of the people who need the results eliminates having to communicate already processed hunks of information from one place to another, which is very costly.

A significant benefit of information integrations is that they can be put together piece by piece, thus enabling management to meet new needs, make adjustments, and solve new problems as they are recognized. As needs expand, additional capability can be built into the system easily. This change is possible because the information is held in common and the equipment is all interactive, eliminating the need to revamp applications or file-management programming. The new segment is immediately an integral part of the network. The system's benefits can be brought to every company subgroup through communications interfaces. Manufacturing branches, sales offices, distributorships, etc., can become part of an integrated network. Also, the cost of each new segment of the network can be justified on the basis of what that element by itself will be doing in the organization's workflow.

Another advantage of interactivity is that if a department is meeting its printout needs and has time left over, the printer can do tasks for other departments. Too, when an applications processor unit goes down, the application may be run on any other available processor. On-line interactive capability, operable by users rather than just computer programmers, makes it possible for personnel to get needed information without waiting for computer report printouts. Users may modify either inputs or outputs, query the computer, and modify programs. Conversational or structured formats are offered accessing personnel through on-line interactive or data collection terminal entries.

Systems technology. The possible combinations of functional components for information systems are many. However, the three most basic elements in an information system are (1) input/output, (2) information-base storage, and (3) communications/distribution. Different technologies or different approaches within the same technology can perform similar functions, depending upon the size and operations of an organization.

Input/output includes data processing, text-word processing, optical character recognition (OCR)/code scanning, phototypesetting, dictation/voice input, and photographics/micrographics. Included in information-base storage may be hard-copy documents, micrographics, and magnetic storage (tape, disk, bubble, etc., and advanced memory devices). Communications/distribution may include data communications, facsimile, telex/TWX, microwave/satellite, voice-level communications, fiber optics, laser technology, and reprographics. An integrated information system will include at least two of the three functions.

Technologies involved in an integrated information system are data processing, word processing, micrographics, communications systems, machine dictation/voice input, facsimile, optical character recognition (OCR), copiers/duplicators, and phototypesetting. Technical equipment considerations for an information network are (1) modularity, (2) compatibility, (3) upgradability, (4) ease of use, (5) availability, (6) flexibility, and (7) confidentiality. A modular system allows additional units of the same type to be added for more power without affecting the operating system. Compatibility lets the user follow any path through the network that works most efficiently, using various combinations of available technologies. The pieces in an information system will likely need to be rearranged for changing work-concentration and evolving company goals. When the time comes to upgrade the low-end equipment, the high-end equipment needs to be easily and quickly integrated into the system in order to render a minimum of disruption. Ease of use means the system can be easily mastered by the average employee. With regard to availability, network design should permit a user to gain access and complete transactions most of the time. Flexibility allows an information network to reflect the organization's own personality—in other words, suiting the solution to the problem and not the other way around. Confidentiality may be gained by use of levels of authorization codes or passwords and by giving certain departments local-access-only storage for their own information.

Teleprocessing/telecommunications. Telecommunications is simply nothing more than the moving of information from one point to another. This response usually means converting digital electronics to analog and back to digital via modems, which means modulation/demodulation. This is necessary because speech signal variations are gradual and distortions only bothersome; digital signal variations are rapid and transmission interference is catastrophic. Telecommunications is constituted by wire networks, microwave circuits, and satellite links.

Big information processing jobs are done on a large central computer (CPU). Small tasks are done locally on mini- or microcomputers, which may remotely access the central data base through the mainframe computer. This process today is known as distributed processing. A controller operating between the CPU and the modem converts the high-volume computer flow to the slower flow of the communication lines. Since dial-up lines are slow and leased and private lines are expensive, multiplexers allow several terminals to share a single line while it appears to the user that each has his own line.

Information is sent through the modem and over the lines to a terminal via the concepts of codes, modes, and protocols. Telecommunication codes are of two types: (1) Extended Binary Coded Decimal Interchange Code (EBCDIC), a combination of eight bits for each character, and (2) an American Standard Code for Information Interchange (ASCII), a seven-bit code. Timing of the transmittal and receiving devices must be synchronized, or the information will turn to garbage.

There are two ways to synchronize transmission and reception: (1) asynchronous mode, whereby each separate character is individually synchronized—but, at the same time, the volume of data that can be pumped through the line is limited; and (2) synchronous mode, synchronizing each message, allowing more information to be transmitted—but an error causes the entire message to be retransmitted.

Communications protocols are analogous to policy statements. These statements define the structure, contents, sequencing procedures, and error-recovery techniques for transmission of information between two points. The standard protocol for synchronous mode communications is Binary Synchronous Communications (BSC), which defines the sequence of characters needed to establish (1) a connection between two devices, (2) the message format, (3) terminating sequence, (4) error responses, and (5) error-handling techniques.

Business requirements determine whether communication is interactive or batch. Interactive terminals are constantly connected to the CPU. Communications are constant and are in either structured or conversational mode. Batch means a once-a-day transfer of information.

Society is due for an explosion in its capabilities for gathering, manipulating, and disseminating information via modern telecommunications technology. Aside from the telephone itself, seven types of electronic mail transmission systems employ telecommunications technology. These are (1) data communications systems (a major portion of the system), (2) communicating word processors, (3) Telex and TWX, (4) facsimile, (5) mailgrams, (6) telegrams, and (7) message switching services.

DATA COMMUNICATIONS. Data communications offers the capability of transmitting computer-stored data from one location to another, from memory to memory, not printed out on paper or shown on a screen. Another term for data communications via electronic mail is distributed data processing.

COMMUNICATING WORD PROCESSORS. Communicating word processors merge the technology of the computer and communications equipment. Text-editing units may communicate between two or more remote sites or intrafacility. Options make it possible to transmit copy to a phototypesetter or communications with other intelligent machines such as copiers. Data processing and work processing both use the same electronic technology. Therefore, the intelligent terminal, an input-output device, joins the two into an information processing and communications network. Nothing will be copied; there will be no paper at the front end. The keyboarding will record electronic impulses. As cost and size of memory continue to drop, word processing equipment becomes powerful data storage equipment. Consensus exists that word processing equipment is the catalyst of tomorrow's information processing networks. Word processing equipment is the centerpiece for the integration of the pieces into a cohesive, systematic information handling network.

TELEX AND TWX. Telex and TWX are both carried by Western Union and employ the use of teletypewriters. Of the two codes used, TWX transmits at a higher speed and is billed on a minute rate, while Telex is billed on a pulse rate of one pulse per character.

FACSIMILE. Facsimile is a process of the original message's being scanned by a light-sensing device, and transmitted line by line over special communications lines to a receiver which recreates the image.

MAILGRAMS. Mailgrams are a joint U. S. Postal Service and Western Union operation. The network transmits messages electronically among U. S. Postal Service offices via Western Union computers. Messages are delivered in the next day's mail. Special services such as stored listings and text for immediate and repeated access are offered. About the only advantage remaining for using telegram services are the tapes kept by Western Union which serve as letters of record.

MESSAGE SWITCHING. Message switching offers switching among terminals in a private network, store-and-forward message systems, and packet-switching networks. Communications companies set up and run private switching systems on an industry by industry basis. Such networks are SICOM for the banking and securities industry and ARINC for the airline industry. Western Union's Infocom is a public, third-party network available for medium-sized users.

The use of computer-based message systems (CBMS) for store-and-forward is the fastest growing area of telecommunications electronic mail. It is more user oriented and more productive. A CBMS offers the operator a personal message terminal allowing the user to access incoming messages at a convenient time. Messages may be disposed of electronically, filed, or passed along. The equipment maintains an audit and eliminates or reduces the need for files. Utilizing a keyboard terminal, an employee logs on by answering the CBMS questions of name and authorization code. After recognition and upon command, a listing of the incoming messages will print out by subject and name of sender.

The two packet-switching companies that are FCC-listed common carriers serving the United States are Tymnet and Telenet. Both offer connection for a wide array of terminal equipment. Packet switching is a sharing concept, with interconnected minicomputers placed at strategically located centers. These nodes or minicomputers are continually in communication with each other and with the supervisor, permitting traffic to be rerouted in the event of high volume or trouble. The customer dials the local packet network, and enters name and password; the node then signals for a communications path to the destination. Once the path is established, the user terminal is on-line to the host computer.

Data processing and word processing will be more widely available locally with distributed processing. However, certain local information will need to be reflected in the central data base; and to achieve local jobs, there will be a need to access the central data base. Input and output often will be the telecommunications network. The productivity of the office depends heavily on the investments in data processing, word processing, and telecommunications. Effective and economical integration of technology and information will be achieved through telecommunication networks.

Text/management network. A text management and processing system may be comprised of text processing, retrieval, and a delivery system. The system may draw from multiple sources in an on-line mode, then edit and format the text off-line at operator convenience. Available in the system is the ability to produce reports in a variety of forms, such as hard copy, copy, microfiche, camera-ready typeset galley, or input into a computer mainframe in either batch or interactive modes for storage, retrieval, and editing at a later date. The beauty of this is that all the foregoing is in machine-readable form. Other possibilities that can become part of the system are OCR input and digital transmission of microimagery over voice-grade phone lines.

COMPUTER CONNECTION. A tie-in with data processing through a special language expands the system even further. A designated program can be loaded into a word processor enabling the equipment to communicate with a computer. The connecting link to the computer is a modem and voice-grade phone line. Commands are keyed in on the word processor, which initiates and performs a computer search. The desired information is selected and recorded. Editing and modification can then be done in an off-line mode.

Combine the word processor with a telephone and additional data bases may be accessed and used to input and retrieve information. In this manner, large amounts of text from various sources may be selected and captured with a minimum of keystrokes. Bulk information may then be tailored to the needs of the requester through the use of the word processor, at a tremendous time and cost advantage. A completed document may be kept in a number of forms, all machine-readable: magnetic local media, hard copy, copy, magnetic central media, or microfiche in OCR-B font.

COMPUTER OUTPUT MICROFILM (COM). Computer output microfilm can be interfaced with the text management and processing system. The information on the magnetic media is transferred from the word processor to a nine-track tape converter drive, which produces a computer-compatible computer tape. The tape is then fed to a computer output microfilmer with a computer on the front end. This unit generates microfiche, which can be used as a final product, stored until needed, duplicated and distributed, or converted to copy. Microfiche written in OCR-B type font are universally machine readable, and copies made from the fiche can be input into another word processor or data processor by using an OCR input device.

PHOTOTYPESETTING. Phototypesetting is another interface that may be integrated into the text management and processing system. Word processor magnetic media and computer output microfilm computer tape may both be converted and formatted for input into a phototypesetter. Typeset galleys of documents are made ready for a print-shop camera from original output of a word processor.

FACSIMILE. Interface another technology, that of facsimile. The equipment receives a microfiche, scans, and transmits the information over phone lines to a receiving station. If the output is in OCR-B font, the receiver is provided with machine-readable output. The information on the microfiche may be displayed on a CRT at the receiving station, or a copy may be made in OCR-B font for future input if needed.

OPTICAL CHARACTER RECOGNITION (OCR). Optical character readers, sometimes called page or document readers, permit the entry of text or data into a processing system with a typewritten page as the original medium. The system includes a six-step process: (1) an author generates a draft, (2) a typist prepares a rough typewritten copy, (3) the author edits, (4) the reader scans and records on magnetic media, (5) the text-editor operator prepares correct copy, and (6) the output disposition is selected.

Output capabilities, aside from storage for future display and usage, are phototypesetting, word processing applications, computer data entry, minicomputer storage and output, and telex paper tape for telecommunications transmittal. For phototypesetting, OCR technology is capable of producing both magnetic media and paper tape. OCR enables the word processor to output via a printer, or if the word processor is a communicator interconnected to a computer and an intelligent copier, the possibilities expand. One such capability is computer output in the form of microfiche. If OCR-B font is used, the microfiche may become facsimile input for transmission. Order entry, time accounting, and financial report input and analysis are types of OCR output that can be data entered into a computer or a minicomputer. Entry into a computer is made via a data processing terminal or a combination word processing/data processing terminal. OCR output can be entered directly into a small business computer. Telex tape output from an OCR will transmit the exact image of the typed page, whereas teletypewriter-prepared telex tape does not. OCR equipment also has the capability to convert magnetic medium from one type to another.

Starting with word processing equipment it is possible to interface and integrate into a system a number of technologies including data processing, photocomposition, computer output microfilm (COM), optical character recognition (OCR), and facsimile. Thus, implementing text processing, retrieval, and a delivery system, a text management network system is composed of several systems or subsystems.

Communicating text processors can talk not only with one another but with other communicating equipment such as the Telex/TWX network, computers, and the Mailgram system. A forecast has been made that facsimile equipment will soon accept electronic input from text processing magnetic media including cards, tapes, and diskettes. The system will be tied into a network by a computer-based PABX. The computer-based PABX will handle image-oriented equipment such as facsimile, videophones, intelligent copiers, communicating text-editing equipment, teleprinters, and data processing. Too, voice-oriented systems such as the telephones, remote access answering machines, and dictation equipment will be a part of the total text processing/management network.

Word processing and data processing combined. Combining word processing and data processing is accomplished by means of a shared-logic or time-sharing system. Text preparation of documents and correspondence is achieved and simultaneously all pertinent data is recorded to provide information for day-to-day and long-term management decisions. The data is compiled and analyzed for management reports.

Data processing functions that can be performed using text-editing equipment and minicomputer or microprocessor intelligence or a CPU make it possible to compile reports on many phases of a firm's business. Daily records of business transactions may be stored and manipulated to indicate rankings, values, and identities. The file is continuous and can be accessed to compile data for weeks, months, quarters, and years. Ranges can be specified including time spans, amounts of money, and disposition of business activities. Geographic, product, and customer analysis and comparisons can be performed. Business deadlines and schedules are other data processing functions obtainable in a system merged with word processing. Payroll, accounts payable and receivable, ledgers, financial statements, and inventory are typical data processing functions combined with word processing. Finally, some of a firm's public relations functions can be automated. Conventional office techniques become automated. Entry of only essential information automatically generates correspondence, legal documents, file cards, file labels, shipping papers, bills, order documents, customer acknowledgments, invoices, shipping labels, and selected public relations documents.

Distributed information processing. A distributed information processing system in an automated office represents a confluence of technologies. Operating around a particular local data base may be local CRT's teleprinters, printers, and card readers. The local CRT's are used primarily for inquiry, batch transaction entry, data entry, edit, and verification. Also utilizing the local data base may be remote terminals on leased lines and dial-up ports of both teleprinter and terminal types.

The local data base interfaces with the host CPU, which may also be on line with a COM processor for micrographics capabilities. However, an intelligent terminal configuration on the local level can perform many logic functions independent of the CPU.

Distributed information processing systems commonly mean interconnecting networks of minicomputers, intelligent terminals, intelligent peripherals, and one or more central computers. However, the distributed concept can also mean independent minicomputer systems or independent small systems dispersed throughout departments or divisions. Each of these systems may perform only the functions required for its own business unit without physical interconnection among the systems.

A major advantage of a distributed system is that it enables downloading or dispersing processing and storage requirements. In some instances, the need for a large CPU is eliminated, while in other instances there is considerable mainframe overhead relief. Also in cases of a CPU crash, local processing can continue to operate. Another distinct advantage is that local managers have their own information processing capabilities with assigned responsibility and accountability. The network enables users to share resources and peripherals so that a request for information can be entered from any terminal in the system, and the network's intelligence locates and delivers the information in the desired format.

The integration of office information systems continues to advance as integration of incompatible devices is made possible by PABX/CBX's. This telecommunications technology is equipped with message switches, MPU-based interface boxes that front-end each processor, and network controllers with switching capability.

Distributed systems are multifunctional, share file capabilities, and incorporate the advantages of both stand-alone and shared-logic word processors. The stand-alone word processors continue to operate if the mini goes down. Word processors can share printers and other peripherals, as well as the large disk memory of the mini. Communications, storage, and file manipulation powers of the minicomputer node can be shared by the word processing terminals, making it possible to network electronic mail, OCR, photocompositors, and intelligent printers into the configurations.

IMPROVEMENT OF METHODS AND PROCEDURES

Providing data to management, via current manual and automated information systems, remains cluttered with duplicate input forms. Procedures, that should guide, instead, confuse. Useless data fills the files, and reports bury rather than highlight critical management information. Information is often unreliable and difficult to summarize and evaluate, and exchange between levels of management is complicated.

Planning and organizing. There are three basic reasons why information systems are not as effective or efficient as they could be. First, data processing managers and vendors both contribute to a hardware-software orientation for information systems as opposed to management-decision orientation. Second, executives impose information requirements without determining the impact on lower levels. Third, traditional organization structures preclude a total systems approach.

Elements of a system include the forms used to capture input, the machine for processing, the uses of the products, the ultimate disposition, and the procedures needed to achieve the system's objective. Information is generated, recorded, transmitted, processed, analyzed, used, stored, and destroyed. A system's information flow is interrelated in that recording affects transmission and processing and, in turn, analysis and use.

The array of technological tools is bewildering. Some of them are electronic data processing, word processing, photocomposition, telecommunications, micrographics, reprographics, and filing systems.

Management provides the analytical and conceptual techniques and disciplines for information systems. These include operations research, industrial engineering, systems analysis, records management, forms control, reports management, and statistical techniques.

Piecemeal organizational solutions confuse and contradict, and make an integrated information system extremely difficult. Information technologies are usually dynamic, particularly when they are merged. Records management, forms management, reports management, and statistical management are elements of information systems; therefore, organizational separation of these functions results in confusion and conflict. An integrated systems approach will be permitted only through organizational structures that recognize the unity and interdependence of information flow from people/technology generation to people/technology disposition. An information system depends upon the familiarity with the capabilities and limitations of all information technologies and related managerial techniques.

Documentation. The basic element of management information systems is good documentation of methods and procedures. Inadequate documentation results in incomplete, incorrect, and unclear information. The benefits of good documentation are that it increases processing efficiency, reduces processing costs, improves management control, eliminates confusion and frustration, and improves employee morale. A lack of documentation produces inadequate procedures and an absence of standardization that, in turn, prohibits the monitoring of procedures and, hence, the ability to evaluate performance.

A documented management summary assists management in determining whether sequencing is wrong or inappropriate and makes procedural deficiencies apparent. Information documents should help, not hinder. They should contain useful information in useful formats, instead of irrelevant information in formats that make information access difficult.

Whether documenting manual or automated procedures and systems, the following guidelines are offered. Avoid long explanations which hide needed information in a mass of words. Place considerable attention on careful segmentation of information. Use tables and forms frequently. Place a detailed table of contents at the beginning of each set of documents for a program or a system. For procedures, a "playscript" format concisely explains the sequence of what is to be done and who is to do it.

The primary document for management planning is a summary of each system. One succinct paragraph stating the objectives of the system should suffice. A one-page flowchart, which shows the relationships between the parts of the system, with short explanations, complements the summary paragraph.

Suggested criteria for documentation standards follow: (1) accuracy as determined by an information review of several people; (2) completeness, an all-questions-answered approach; (3) conciseness, few words, forms and tables for quick information location; (4) clarity, specific words, defined jargon, and simple sentence structure; (5) ease of reference, detailed table of contents, thorough index; (6) ease of use, frequent subheadings, introductory scope paragraphs, examples, samples; and (7) ease of maintenance, segmentation into small groups for addition and deletion ease.

Improvement of methods and procedures emanates through documentation. The end result is making work more efficient and pleasing, reducing cost and confusion, and serving as a morale builder for people and their organization.

SUMMARY

In summary, the key challenge of office systems is the recognition that the growing trend toward the interconnection of technologies through telecommunications imposes a requirement for coordinated planning. To introduce coordinated planning into an area that has never used such techniques before has organizational, political, and people implications of extraordinary magnitude.

Separately developed technologies are being interconnected through telecommunications—word processing to reprographics, reprographics to micrographics, etc. Thus, there is a need to learn not one, but a number of technologies, at least on a conceptual level, to bridge the barriers. In the past, the office has been a large group of diversities, each concerned with its own specialties and largely unaware of the impact of activities upon all the components of a system—people, technology, and space. Advanced developmental systems, such as a combination of word processing, electronic message box, photocompositor/typesetter, electronic storage and document distribution, "arrived" today.

CHAPTER 5

Data Processing

WILLIAM O. DRUM

Rincon High School, Tucson, Arizona

Data processing is nothing new in the office world. However, the methods of performing it are rapidly changing and so must the curriculum in business education. The word *data* refers to a collection of numbers, letters, words, etc., and to change it into useful information *data processing* must take place. Data processing refers to manipulation of data by some device. These devices may range from paper and pencil to a sophisticated electronic computer.

METHODS OF DATA PROCESSING

Regardless of the method used in processing data the cycle is the same—input, manipulation, and output. At the input stage data is originated. It must be recorded on an acceptable input medium, at which time it is coded and checked for accuracy. Manipulation involves sorting or arranging the data in specific order to facilitate calculations and for future use. The necessary calculations are performed and the data is summarized into a concise form, thus grouping the data into meaningful information. Output data is communicated—by distributing the useful information to the point of use—or is stored for future use.

Manual data processing. The tools in a manual data processing system are pencils, pens, ledgers, journals, etc. Even in a manual system steps can be taken toward automation (elimination of repetitive steps). Some of these steps involve the use of carbon paper, snap-out forms, embossed plates, pegboard systems, or edge-notched cards.

Mechanical data processing. Mechanical systems use machines, but the functions are performed manually. Typewriters, electronic calculators, accounting machines, and cash registers are examples of some of the equipment used in a mechanical system. Many of these machines have mechanisms that enable them to simultaneously produce paper or magnetic tape that can later serve as input into computer equipment.

Electromechanical data processing (unit record equipment). Unit record equipment requires data to be recorded in a machine-readable form—usually punched cards. Control panels wired by the operator are necessary on this type of equipment. Once the data has been recorded and the control panels have been wired, much of the human effort is eliminated as the equipment is automatic. Ever since Herman Hollerith developed the punched-card system used in the 1890 U.S. census, office operations have been revolutionized. Unit record equipment involves the use of the following punched-card devices: keypunch, verifier, sorter, collator, interpreter, calculator, reproducer, and tabulator (or accounting machine). However, with today's technology and the development of the large scale electronic computer for the big business and the mini- and microcomputers for the small business, to include much training on unit record equipment in the business education curriculum would be a waste of time.

Electronic data processing (EDP). Electronic systems contain some of the concepts of processing found in the unit record systems—data is recorded on an input medium and much of the human effort is then eliminated. Unlike the unit record systems, the computer has a memory; processing is accomplished by electronic impulses rather than moving mechanical parts, instructions are given in the form of a program rather than a wired control panel, and thousands of operations are performed per second.

The electronic computer has developed over a period of time. In fact it may have had its beginning with the ancient Chinese abacus. Charles Babbage is considered the father of the computer with his "analytical engine" in 1833. His ideas were sound but the machine was never built, as the technology of that day was not as sophisticated as it needed to be. The Mark I, the first electromechanical computer, was designed by Professor Howard H. Aiken of Harvard University and built by IBM in 1944. Most of the early machines were of a scientific nature, but in the 1950's IBM began to manufacture electronic computers for business use. By the mid-1960's many of the earlier unit record installations had been replaced by electronic equipment in larger businesses, and today with the microprocessor chips, it is possible to obtain a low-cost system for even the small-business user.

WHAT IS A COMPUTER?

To most people a computer is visualized as a giant electronic monster with blinking lights that has some sort of mysterious power and wisdom. In reality, nothing could be further from the truth. Essentially, a computer is made up of input units, output units, and a central processing unit.

Input units feed or introduce data into the system. Instructions are also fed into the system through the input units. Some of the input media are punched cards, punched tape, disks, optical characters (OCR), magnetic ink characters (MICR), direct input (keyboards), and audio input.

Output units produce records and reports for people to use or record the results on a new medium which can be used to satisfy further automated processing needs. Some of the output media are printed lines, punched cards, punched paper tape, magnetic tape, video (CRT), microfiche, and audio.

The central processing unit (CPU) controls the processing routines, performs the arithmetic functions, and maintains a quickly accessible memory. In effect, it is an electronic filing cabinet, completely indexed and capable of storing large amounts of data. The CPU basically consists of three parts:

1. The control unit directs the operations of the entire system.

2. The storage unit stores the instructions of the program that is running, the data that is currently being used, and results of intermediate calculations. (This unit is also referred to as main memory or core storage.)

3. The arithmetic/logic unit performs calculations and makes decisions. Attached to the core storage usually will be some type of auxiliary storage which will be discussed later.

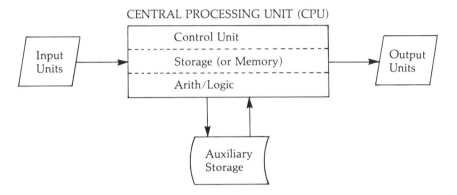

CENTRAL PROCESSING UNIT (CPU)

One might think of a computer as resembling a factory. The INPUT is likened to raw materials coming in. The CPU is the factory where the processing is done. When the raw materials arrive (INPUT), the supervisor (CONTROL) directs them to be stored in the warehouse (STORAGE). Later, the supervisor (CONTROL) directs them to be sent to the assembly line (ARITH/LOGIC), where processing will be accomplished. From there, the product goes back to the warehouse (STORAGE) until it is needed. At that time the supervisor (CONTROL) directs it to be shipped out.

There are two basic types of computers: digital and analog. A digital computer uses numbers or symbols that can be represented in an "on or off" condition and performs its calculations by counting. Business computers are digital and represent the large majority of computers. An analog computer measures rather than counts and is mainly used in scientific applications.

PREPARING INPUT FOR THE COMPUTER

Many input devices may be attached to a computer using the various input media listed above. Some of these input media which are found in the modern office will be discussed in more detail.

Punched cards. The standard punched card contains 80 or 96 columns of data and is prepared on a keypunch machine. If the card is interpreted or a printing punch is used (one that prints as well as punches holes), the card is man-readable as well as machine-readable and may therefore be used as a document. It is easy to add a record to a file of cards or to remove one. However, cards have several disadvantages that have caused them to be less popular than they once were. Each record is limited to 80 or 96 characters, and large decks of cards can cause storage problems. The use of punched cards is a very slow method of getting information into a computer even with a high speed card reader, since it is mechanical. To ensure accuracy of the data that is punched in cards, the cards need to be run through a card verifier. The operator of the verifier feeds the cards through the machine, keying in the data from the source document. This process checks the accuracy of the holes in the cards and will indicate any errors.

Punched paper tape. While this may be prepared directly on a teletype or paper tape punch, it is usually a by-product of another machine such as a typewriter, cash register, or adding machine. The record length is not limited as in cards, but it is difficult to make corrections, additions, or deletions to a file.

Magnetic tape. This medium overcomes many of the disadvantages of cards and may be prepared directly on a key-to-tape machine operated similarly to a keypunch. The record length is not limited, and errors may be corrected simply by writing over. However, it does not have the advantage of being man-readable. A reel of tape is inexpensive, may be reused, and is much less bulky than cards. One reel of tape can store the equivalent of a 100-foot high stack of cards. It could be read into a computer in about four minutes as opposed to about four hours for that many cards. Tape is often used as an inexpensive method of off-line storage and for backup. Tape's biggest disadvantage is that it is a sequential medium and all records must be accessed and processed sequentially.

Optical characters (OCR). Hardware has been developed that will read special fonts of type, ordinary upper case printing, hand printing of a certain style, and marks or lines in predetermined locations. The bar codes now widely used by department stores, supermarkets, and libraries fall into this category as they are read by an optical scanner which converts these symbols into electronic impulses to be stored in the computer.

Magnetic ink characters (MICR). This medium is used almost exclusively by banks. Magnetic ink characters in special type fonts are imprinted on checks and deposit tickets. These are then read by a high-speed reader-sorter into the computer's memory.

Direct input. This medium allows the user to communicate directly with the computer by keyboard, either on a terminal with a keyboard similar to a typewriter or a special device such as a touchtone telephone. While this would be a slow method of inputting large quantities of data, it allows the user to work in a real time environment getting immediate response to inquiries and being able to update records at once.

RECEIVING OUTPUT FROM THE COMPUTER

Output (meaningful information) comes in a variety of forms in the modern office.

Printed lines. For large volumes of hard copy output, the line printer is most widely used. A line printer produces reports, letters, statements, etc. on continuous form paper at speeds ranging from 100 to 2,000 lines per minute. There are two major types of line printers: impact printing and electrostatic or nonimpact printing. Impact printing which uses an inked ribbon and paper is the most widely used. The electrostatic printer may be faster but uses a special light-sensitive paper and is therefore much more expensive. It also will not allow for printing multiple copies.

Computer output microfilm (COM). An alternate method of hard copy output, which is much faster than a line printer, is having the computer generate an output magnetic tape. This tape is then converted to reels of microfilm or microfiche, which are much more convenient to store than large volumes of printed material. A 4″ x 6″ microfiche would contain the equivalent of 208 or more full pages of printed output. If hard copy is later needed, photocopies of any individual page may be made.

Punched cards. Just as the standard 80- or 96-column card can be used as input, it can also be used as output. Many computers are equipped with a piece of hardware called a card reader/punch. This is both an input and output device. Output cards are often used for renewal notices, checks, or utility bills. Usually these cards must be run through another device called an interpreter that will put printing on them if they are to be used as a document—the holes are satisfactory for other machines to read but not for people to read.

Video (CRT). The cathode ray tube, which resembles a television screen, is now being widely used in many offices to receive data from the computer or for communications. Together with the keyboard discussed in the direct input section, it enables the user to communicate directly with the computer. Inquiries can be made into files which are kept updated at all times. In cases where hard copy is needed a different type of terminal may be used, such as a teletype. These terminals produce the output on paper rather than on the screen.

Voice I/O. Voice output is used in some applications to give responses to inquiries such as the balances of accounts, stock quotations, etc. These usually are prerecorded responses from which the computer may select. However, computer-generated responses are currently being experimented with and developed. Also work is being done with devices that will accept voice input. It is expected that great improvements will be made in this area in the future, and this will be a widely used input/output medium.

Magnetic tape. Just as data may be read into the computer from tape, it may be written out on tape. It must be converted to some other form if it is to be used by man, or else it is used as input in future applications. If it is converted, this may be an off-line operation.

STORING DATA IN THE COMPUTER

Data enters the computer from one of the input media as previously discussed and comes from the computer in the form of one of the output media. However, inside the computer it is in an entirely different form. While this conversion takes place automatically, most students find a computer's language fascinating, and it is helpful to learn some of the advantages and disadvantages of the various storage devices.

Data is represented by electronic impulses which are either present or absent. Something may be magnetized or not magnetized, or in the case of cards, there is a hole or there isn't one. Since the two possible conditions always exist, a two-digit system (binary) is used. Many computer codes are in existence, such as six-bit BCD, EBCDIC, or ASCII; and other numbering systems, such as octal and hexadecimal, may be employed as an alternate means of representing binary numbers. (Because of space limitations, it is not possible to discuss these codes or numbering systems in this chapter).

Core storage (main memory). As previously mentioned, the program that is currently running and the data record that is being processed must be in the main memory or core storage. The memory often consists of tiny, doughnut-shaped rings about the size of a pin head placed on intersecting wires. When current is sent through these wires, the cores become magnetized. Each core represents a binary digit (called bit for short). A combination of six or eight bits represents one character (this is referred to as a byte or one addressable position of core storage).

Because core storage is completely electronic and there are no mechanical parts, it is the most efficient type of storage. Each address (or byte) is directly accessible. That means that nothing has to rotate or move to read the contents of that location or to write new data in a particular location.

Core storage is the most expensive type of storage, however, and because of that the amount of it is limited. The amount of core storage determines the kinds and sizes of the programs that can be run on the particular system. To hold large volumes of data and libraries of programs, other types of storage are usually available. The most widely used types of auxiliary storage are magnetic tape, magnetic disk, and magnetic drum.

Magnetic tape. This medium has previously been discussed as input and output. Magnetic tape is also used to store data or programs. They are recorded as magnetic spots, usually on seven- or nine-track tape. The code is much the same as that used in core. Usually attached to the central processing unit will be one or more tape drives. When a reel of tape is mounted on one of these drives, it is said to be "on line" and can be read into core or can have new data written on it. Reading from tape does not destroy what is there, but writing does. A reel of tape has a protection ring that can be removed so it can be read but nothing can be written on it. Magnetic tape is a very inexpensive, compact storage media; about 14 million characters may be stored on a reel. The big disadvantage is that it must be read sequentially. Therefore, it is very time consuming to locate records unless they are being processed sequentially. In many applications tape is used for backup purposes. Backup files are stored in vaults or at remote sites for security. These backup files are copied weekly or sometimes even daily. A tape librarian may be employed whose job it is to keep these organized.

Magnetic disk. One of the most widely used types of auxiliary storage is the magnetic disk. A disk is a round metal surface coated with magnetic recording material on both sides. Six or more of these are usually mounted on a cylinder with enough space between for a read/write head to move in and out reading or recording data. The data is recorded as magnetized spots on tracks using a code similar to that in core. Disks are referred to as a random access device, meaning that any record can be obtained directly without reading all the records in sequence to get to it. The read/write heads are on an arm that moves between the surfaces which are rotating at a very high rate of speed. Data can be transferred from the disk to the main memory at rates over 150,000 characters per second. While disk storage is much more expensive than tape, in most cases the speed overcomes this disadvantage.

Disks may be permanently mounted, in which case they are on-line at all times, or may be removable. Recently, a new type of disk called floppy disk or diskette has been introduced. These are very popular on the mini- and microcomputers. They are also used as input devices into larger systems. They are replacing cards as input in businesses whose data entry departments are using key-to-disk equipment rather than the older keypunch machines. The floppy disks are flexible and are stored in envelopes. The entire envelope is inserted in the disk unit, and the disk surface is rotated inside the protective covering.

Magnetic drum. For large volumes of data that must be on-line at all times, such as airline reservations, drum storage is often used. A magnetic drum is a large cylinder that is coated with material that can be magnetized similar to disk or tape. The drum is divided into tracks with a read/write head positioned over each track. As the drum rotates, the read/write head can sense data that is recorded in that track or can write data there. This head is also a random access device, and it is possible to get to any record almost immediately. The only delay would be the rotational delay, which is minor. Data can be transferred from the drum into main memory in large volumes and at very high rates of speed.

PROGRAMMING THE COMPUTER

One quickly learns that computers do exactly what they are told. The process of giving instructions to a computer is known as programming, and one who does this is referred to as a programmer. There are several steps in the development of a program.

Analyzing the problem. First of all there must be a thorough understanding of the problem. This consists of determining where the data will come from and in what form. A record layout will have to be planned. Then the output must be planned and the layout for that will have to be prepared. The programmer may be given these detailed specifications that have been prepared by a systems analyst, or he/she may have to meet with the department or person desiring the program and design it himself/herself.

Planning the logic. The next step is to determine the steps necessary for the computer to solve the problem. This may be done by preparing a flowchart, or more recently, pseudocodes are being used. A pseudocode is simply a form on which the necessary steps to solve a problem are written in English statements. It allows the programmer to organize the logic before attempting to code the program in a symbolic language.

Coding the program. After the logic is worked out, the program must be coded in a programming language. The two most popular business languages are COBOL and RPG. The most widely used mathematical languages are FORTRAN and BASIC. However, since microcomputers are becoming so numerous in the office and small business, BASIC is also being used for business applications as it is quite often the only language available on these systems. Newer, extended versions of BASIC have been developed that lend themselves to business applications more efficiently than the earlier versions, which were primarily equation-solving languages.

Compiling the program. After the program is coded, it must then be entered into the computer. This may be done by recording it on cards, floppy disks, tape, or entering it on-line from a terminal. The source program is then converted into machine language known as the object program. If errors are detected by the compiler, these must be corrected before this conversion will take place. This is known as debugging.

Testing the program. Once the program has been compiled, it must then be tested with data. It may be necessary to make changes to the program and recompile it until the desired results are obtained. When testing a program, not only samples of typical data normally expected should be run but also data with errors and exceptions so that all possibilities may be tested and it can be determined whether the program will crash.

Documenting the program. When the program has been tested and debugged, it is then loaded into a library of programs and stored for future use. Unless the program is properly documented it will be of little value, for no one will be able to use it. The documentation consists of the following:

1. A description of the problem
2. A flowchart of pseudocodes
3. File descriptions (input and output layouts)
4. A source listing of the program
5. Test cases and sample results
6. A complete list of instructions needed to operate the program.

MICROCOMPUTERS IN THE OFFICE

Microcomputers, products of the last three years, probably will have a greater impact on the office and the small business than any other development. They are putting tremendous computing power within the reach of any budget. Systems with CRT's are available for less than $1 thousand, and small systems complete with diskette storage and hard copy printers can be obtained for $3 thousand up. Packaged software of typical business applications—payroll, inventory, accounts payable and receivable, etc.—are available for a nominal cost. Without too much training the user can also develop his own programs. As mentioned before, most of these computers use BASIC as the primary language. However, some manufacturers are now developing and marketing compilers in FORTRAN and even versions of COBOL. This necessitates adding more memory, but most microcomputers can be easily expanded.

In microcomputers the most common type of memory is called RAM

(Random Access Memory). This is used to store user-written programs and data temporarily, but the contents are lost when the computer is shut off. To store the manufacturer-supplied software such as compilers, monitors, and special applications, a certain amount of another type of memory named ROM (Read Only Memory) is needed. This memory is not lost when the power is shut off, and it is not possible for the user to write in this area.

A wide variety of input, output, and storage devices are available for the microcomputer. Most of them come with a CRT/keyboard as standard equipment. Magnetic tape cassette units, floppy disks, printing terminals, and line printers may also be interfaced with many of these. Some of these systems can be tied into a larger system and in effect become an intelligent terminal themselves.

Microcomputers are gaining a foothold in large businesses, too. Some of the problems of having a centralized computer system, as well as the costs of communication, have been reduced by decentralizing and using microcomputers.

HOW SHOULD BUSINESS EDUCATION STUDENTS BE PREPARED FOR TODAY'S OFFICE?

Not all students will be programmers, but all students will be working with the input and output from computers; and some will come in direct contact with input and output devices. They must be able to use them!

The equipment that is available in the classroom will partly determine what the curriculum can be. Many schools now have access to a computer through time-sharing and will have terminals in the classrooms. With the low cost of the microcomputers (and getting lower all the time), it should soon be possible for any classroom to have some type of computer equipment. When a system can be purchased for less than the cost of an electric typewriter, it should be within the reach of most departments.

Many secretaries and clerical workers will be using terminals to get information from the computer and to enter data into it. Therefore, these people need some training on the use of terminals. Small units of instruction can be incorporated in existing secretarial and clerical training courses. Today's accountant is using the computer as a tool. Therefore, accounting courses must include units of instruction utilizing the computer. Again, these students do not need to be taught programming but must learn to use accounting applications.

All business students should take at least an introduction to data processing course. Many texts and materials are available for a course of this nature—some not even requiring the use of equipment.

Topics that should be included in an introductory course follow:

A. Data processing—past, present, and future

B. The punched card—terminology, layout, uses (keypunching if a card punch is available)

C. Preparing input media for automated processing—types, techniques used, study of different codes

D. Understanding electronic computers—input and output devices, central processing unit, internal and external storage

E. Problem solving with the computer—flowcharting, writing programs in BASIC

F. Use of terminals—how to log on and off, how to use existing programs, how to create and modify files, use of monitor commands, use of text editor, and use of utility programs.

In schools where equipment is available, more advanced work in data processing should be offered to those who wish to continue their training in this area. Again, what is offered will depend on the equipment that is available. As previously mentioned, BASIC is the primary language available on microcomputers; if microcomputers are used, more advanced programming concepts than those offered in the introduction course should be pursued. These would include various business applications and use of files and file maintenance.

Since COBOL is the most widely used business language, this should be taught if the class has access to a computer with a COBOL complier. The following concepts should be included:

A. Introduction to structured programming and design

B. Programming input and output operations

C. Addition, subtraction, and report editing

D. Multiplication, division, and use of COMPUTE statements

E. Comparing and final totals

F. Control breaks

G. Multiple level control breaks

H. Table processing.

For those students who really get "turned on" to data processing, advanced work in the form of individualized and independent study can be available. This might include advanced BASIC or COBOL using tables, sorts, multiple files, etc. FORTRAN with business applications, case studies, and special projects can also be provided.

Today's office is rapidly changing, and we as business teachers must be ready and willing to keep pace with the times. It may mean additional training for ourselves, it may mean a drastic revision of our curriculum, it may mean a "sales job" on the administration convincing them of the need for new equipment, and it may take lots of hard work; but it is challenging, exciting and rewarding.

CHAPTER 6
Word Processing

RUTH I. ANDERSON
North Texas State University, Denton

Since word processing was introduced in the 1960's, it has ballooned into a multibillion dollar business with far-reaching implications for both business and office education. Fifteen years ago businessmen and educators alike frequently debated whether word processing was going to be a fad, fashionable today but gone tomorrow, or whether it would become as well established as data processing. Few people gave much thought to the possibility that someday the two areas might gradually merge until it would be difficult to make sharp distinctions between them, yet that has already happened in many firms.

Word processing was introduced as a relatively narrow concept which dealt with typing, the capturing of original data by keystrokes. Emphasis was upon the ease of correcting errors and the rapid error-free playback of the final copy, often referred to as power typing. When captured information was stored and played out later with only variables typed by an operator, the process was called automatic typing.

In less than 15 years, due to the continuing improvements of technology in the word processing field, the original concept has enlarged until today a high degree of formatting and editing is generally regarded as part of the process. Formatting refers to the various automatic machine functions that can be performed by today's word processing equipment, all of which formerly had to be performed manually. These automatic machine functions include visual display, automatic centering, automatic margin adjust, automatic end-of-page, two-column printing, underscoring, decimal tabulation, decimal point alignment, indentation, and right margin adjust. Editing, on the other hand, involves changes or rearrangements that must be made in the text, such as text insertion and/or deletion, on-line editing with a CRT display unit, global search and replay, and automatic search for all occurrences of a given word or phrase and the substitution of another word or phrase in its place.

An even broader concept of word processing is emerging which ties automatic typing equipment into a communications network for input and output. Optical character recognition systems may be tied in. Output from the word processing equipment may go directly to phototypesetting equipment or may be transmitted directly to the office where the final documents are needed. Output may be processed directly onto microfilm or routed to an automatic filing system. All these separate units may be tied together and controlled by an "office computer." In this interpretation of the word processing concept, word processing is part of a total information system rather than an entity unto itself.[1]

WORD PROCESSING EQUIPMENT

Technology in the word processing field is changing so rapidly that it is difficult for business educators to keep pace with the new equipment constantly appearing on the market. It is even more difficult at times to decide which equipment should be considered for training purposes. However, basic criteria which should be considered are:

1. The type of equipment being used in the area in which the students will seek employment

2. Compatibility of the equipment with other equipment now and in the future

3. The cost of the equipment—leasing versus outright purchase

4. The training package furnished by the equipment company

5. The company's training program for the instructor.

When word processing was introduced, training was largely limited to magnetic tape and magnetic card machines. However, as more and more manufacturers entered the market and as technology expanded the concept, the problem of selecting the equipment on which to train a student became more complex. Today there are over a hundred companies manufacturing word processing equipment and supplies; and while many companies do offer highly competitive equipment so far as functions and costs are concerned, there are vast differences in the scope of the functions the equipment will perform and the manner in which the equipment is operated.

The first type of word processing equipment consisted of stand-alone text-editing typewriters. Each unit operated independently. The first machines used magnetic tape for storage; later units used magnetic cards or cassette tapes. Until the past few years, the stand-alone texteditors were considered efficient and high-producing units and were found in most word processing centers. They are still found in many centers which purchased the equipment.

More recently stand-alone display text editors have gained wide acceptance and are generally considered to be superior to the stand-alone units without display. The display units are, of course, more expensive. Many companies are now turning to a systems approach to word processing. In these installations several display units may be connected to an off-line printer with a much faster output than cards or tapes, ranging from 350 to 1,100 words per minute, depending on the type of printer.

RELATIONSHIP OF WORD PROCESSING TO DATA PROCESSING

Although word processing and data processing originally were consi-

---

[1]De Mund, James. *Word Processing.* Fitchburg, Mass.: Business Forms Technical Institute, 1977. pp.4-6.

dered as two distinctly separate areas, technology is forcing the two areas closer and closer together. Both word processing and data processing do talk the same language to a degree. Both deal with storage, access, input, output, and logic. Today many word processing systems offer a degree of intelligence that shows a relationship to data processing—alphanumeric sorting, list processing, formatting, and data management. Optional software packages are even available which will allow some data processing jobs to be run on word processing equipment.

On the other hand, data processing is considered an operational sequence, usually mathematical, performed on facts and figures. Word processing may be considered an operational sequence also, but dealing with the processing of words, not figures, though a few systems can also handle figures on a very limited basis.

WORD PROCESSING STRUCTURES

Just as the concept of word processing has changed and broadened since its early introduction in the sixties, so also has the structure and organization of word processing changed since its inception. Originally the advocates of word processing emphasized the possibilities of increased productivity. Business was desperate for ways to decrease their soaring office costs. Salaries of office workers had been rising rapidly during the 1960's, the volume of paper was staggering, qualified secretaries were unavailable, and marginal workers made costly errors. Because word processing was heralded as a means of increasing the productivity of office workers, it was not surprising that the structure recommended for its installation was the word processing center. Word processing centers made possible the measurement of productivity since the work was highly specialized and supervised. It was indeed possible to measure fairly precisely the amount of work being produced by the word processing center and the productivity of each individual worker.

However, in spite of increased productivity and decreased costs, not everyone was entirely satisfied with this type of organization. Many considered the word processing center to be dehumanizing. Management at times expressed dissatisfaction also. They wanted workers close by, so that problems could be discussed as soon as they arose, secretaries could specialize in their area of the business, and rush work could be delivered promptly. Further, companies often had difficulty persuading their managers and principals to use the word processing center, with the result that in addition to the center these principals had a personal secretary, resulting in increased office costs. Consequently, today in some firms the structure is being changed; and in companies introducing word processing for the first time, the organization is often quite different from the concept of the word processing center.

The trend today is toward work groups, sometimes called satellites. With work groups each department or area of the company has its own group of office workers, some of whom are operating word processing equipment and others who serve as administrative secretaries or assistants. This structure permits each group to become thoroughly familiar with the needs and responsibilities of the area in which they work and to know the principals for whom they are working. They are readily accessible and responsive to each person in the area, a convenience which the principals and managers appreciate. While overall production cannot be so readily measured, many people believe that this approach to word processing is more in line with the needs of business and that it will be the structure most companies will adopt in the future. As word processing continues to advance and word processing is recognized as a systems approach to handling office communications, the work group would seem to be an ideal structure for many large organizations.

The nature of the work group will vary from department to department, even within a single organization. A work group assigned to a highly technical area might be composed of specialists, each dealing with a particular aspect of the technical work of that department. The group might consist of a word processing specialist, a clerk typist, and perhaps two administrative secretaries or assistants. The word processing specialist would handle the word processing equipment. The clerk typist might prepare copy for an OCR scanner or statistical rough drafts, and the two administrative assistants would handle research, dictate correspondence, prepare reports, schedule appointments, etc. Preferably these persons would know shorthand so that they could take telephone messages, record notes when doing research, use shorthand in preparing reports, and in general employ the skill to assist them personally in carrying out their responsibilities. Another work group assigned to a less specialized area might use a generalized approach, with only the word processing operator being a specialist. The others in the work group would be able to handle any job assigned to the group.

WORD PROCESSING IN THE CURRICULUM

Business educators are well aware that word processing is a field that is going to affect their discipline and their students. Many feel that they should be introducing word processing into the business education curriculum but are uncertain just what the objectives or content of such courses should be. Before introducing word processing into the curriculum, the following questions should be considered:

1. How valid is the training of word processing employees on the high school or community college level?

It must first be determined to what extent word processing is being used in the area which the school serves. Even if word processing is widely used, this may not necessarily indicate that the schools should institute word processing courses. Word processing supervisors agree that if students are unable to attain a typing skill of 50 to 60 words per minute (with many requiring a minimum of 60) in less than two years, they would prefer that the students complete a second year of typing rather than one year of typing and one year of word processing. Many also indicate that they would prefer to have the schools correct weaknesses in spelling, punctuation, and grammar rather than teach word processing.

2. Will it be possible to secure enough equipment to provide adequate word processing training?

If it is not possible to secure enough equipment to train students properly in its use, then there is little to be gained by purchasing or leasing the equipment. Students cannot learn to operate sophisticated word processing equipment in one or two periods of hands-on instruction.

3. What equipment should be purchased or leased if word processing is introduced into the curriculum?

The problem of the type of equipment to lease or purchase is becoming increasingly difficult to solve. At one time when most of the word processing equipment found in business offices was produced by one company, this was a simple decision. But today the trend is to diversify and to select various types of equipment to handle the different jobs encountered with each business organization.

4. Should the concept of word processing be taught rather than skill in using the equipment, or should the program include both word processing concepts and machine training?

Schools which cannot afford to purchase or lease word processing equipment may still feel that their business students should know something about word processing. Should a course in word processing concepts be introduced, or should the concept of word processing be included as a unit in secretarial or office practice or in vocational office education? Most teachers agree that their business students should know what word processing is, but there is little agreement as to where or how this information should be presented.

5. Should business be involved with the schools in the training of word processing operators, and if so, to what extent?

Should business assist the schools with their word processing training by providing speakers and demonstrations? Should they encourage field trips to their word processing installations? Or should there be some type of cooperative program in word processing? While this might seem a logical solution to the high cost of the program, it is not often feasible since few businesses have equipment available for students' use nor do they wish to utilize such expensive machines for training in a cooperative program.

6. What should be the content of word processing courses?

The content of the word processing course is not easy to define. A course in the operation of a particular piece of word processing equipment offers few problems since most companies provide training for the teacher and also have excellent instruction manuals for the operators. However, problems designed to test whether students understand the functions they have performed with the aid of the manual are seldom available. While a number of texts are available, they tend to go out of date shortly after they are published. Teachers of this course must revise their materials each time the course is offered.

7. Should word processing courses be substituted for shorthand courses? Do students need both skills, or should they specialize?

It is possible that students who do not like shorthand might do well in word processing, but it must be remembered that the same English, spelling, and proofreading skills are required in both areas. Some persons predict that, should the satellite or small work groups concept replace the word processing center, some of the persons in the work group would find shorthand extremely beneficial for helping them carry out their responsibilities, whether or not they ever use shorthand to record verbatim dictation. Also, considering the demand for secretaries who can take dictation, it is evident that business is still a long way from the total concept of word processing as most equipment manufacturers view it. Indeed that day may never arrive.

8. Should the word processing program include a word processing center offering its services to the school and/or the public?

Whether the word processing program includes the operation of a word processing center may well depend upon the amount of training students receive and the equipment available. It is scarcely fair to students to expect them to produce an acceptable quality and quantity of work when they first begin their training. On the other hand, after they have had a semester's work on the equipment, they might be able to operate a center with little difficulty. If a minicenter is set up, it should be a training program for word processing supervisors as well as word processing operators.

While most dictators agree the term word processing encompasses not only the work performed by operators of sophisticated electronic equipment but also the work handled by the administrative secretarial support personnel, this chapter will be limited to the introduction of programs designed to provide young people with an understanding of word processing and, where feasible, to develop word processing skills.

Once the decision has been made to introduce word processing into the curriculum, a survey should be made of the present course offerings to determine whether word processing might be included in any of these courses or whether a separate course or courses will be needed. Also the type of courses must be decided—whether to offer only a concept course or only instruction in the operation of word processing equipment or both.

Word processing in the secondary schools. Most high schools today find it impossible to implement a word processing program because of the expensive equipment needed for training purposes. However, even small schools can make it possible for their graduates to enter this field if they are well prepared in their basic skills. Students must have a typing skill of approximately 60 words per minute to even secure an interview by the word processing supervisor. Schools already have invested in typewriters; and if two years of typing are required to attain this degree of skill, then students with this vocational objective should take a second year.

No expensive equipment is required for teaching business English, with special emphasis on punctuation, spelling, and proofreading, all skills essential for securing and holding positions as word processing operators.

60

A school with some financial resources but insufficient funds for leasing or purchasing word processing equipment might consider teaching machine transcription, a skill frequently overlooked in the high school curriculum. If offered at all, machine transcription is usually included as a part of an office practice course along with other office machines and clerical and secretarial procedures. Students are fortunate if they receive three weeks of machine transcription, one period a day, which is not adequate for word processing. Students do not automatically transfer their knowledge of grammar, spelling, punctuation, and typing usage rules to the machine transcription process. To produce an acceptable quality and quantity of work from machine dictation requires many hours of practice which few students ever receive. As a result, when high school graduates encounter machine transcription on the job, they dislike it because their skills are inadequate.

High school students planning to enter the field of office work should know what word processing is. A unit on word processing should be included in the office or secretarial practice course or in the vocational office education program. The students should visit companies having word processing installations or observe demonstrations of word processing equipment by a representative of an equipment organization. If questioned in an interview as to whether they would like to work in a word processing center, they should be able to respond intelligently.

A scattering of vocational high schools are offering word processing training at present and doing the job effectively. While these programs vary widely, they should emphasize the following areas:

1. Basic business language for word processing—emphasizes business English, spelling, proofreading, business writing, editing, use of the dictionary, etc.
2. Keyboarding skills—a minimum typing skill of 60 words per minute for five minutes, with no more than five errors
3. Machine transcription—minimum transcription rate of 25 words per minute
4. Magnetic keyboarding—60 words per minute with no errors
5. A mini word processing center or laboratory (optional).

Word processing in postsecondary institutions. Word processing is being offered today in private business schools, in schools that specialize in training word processors, in community and junior colleges, and in four-year colleges and universities. The schools that specialize in the training of word processors are a relatively new development, and those schools having sound programs find their graduates are in much demand. Such schools are found only in the large metropolitan areas.

The community colleges have been active in promoting word processing courses, some of which have been very effective. However, schools which purchase one or two pieces of word processing equipment and enroll 30 students in the class, meeting one hour a day three times a week, cannot hope to do much more than acquaint their students with the basic concept of word processing. If a community college plans to offer word processing, certain changes in the curriculum must usually be considered. All students entering the program should be able to type at least 60 words per minute. The number of credit hours of typing or hours in class is far less important than meeting this basic skill requirement. The students would, of course, also be able to perform basic typing applications proficiently.

All students should complete a course in business English and receive credit for the course only upon demonstrating basic proficiency in the area.

All students should complete one semester of machine transcription, credit again to be based upon the ability to produce an acceptable quantity and quality of material on machine transcription tests administered under timed conditions. In many community colleges this course is entitled Introduction to Word Processing, but in reality it is a course in machine transcription. Students who wish to specialize in legal, medical, or technical areas should receive practice in transcribing material in their areas of specialization.

A course in word processing equipment and a course in word processing concepts should be introduced. The course in word processing equipment should be designed to develop skill in the operation of basic word processing equipment such as the memory typewriter, text-editing typewriters (card and cassette tape), and display units with a CRT screen. The course should be taught on an individualized basis so that maximum use could be made of the equipment. Students would be required to sign up for a specified number of practice hours a week, at least five or six. In this way the equipment would be utilized throughout the day, and the students would have access to it for a sufficient amount of time to develop proficiency in its operation. The specific units of instruction on the equipment would depend upon the amount of equipment available and how much time each student is able to utilize the different types of machines. Most reputable manufacturers of word processing equipment provide excellent self-instructional manuals which are essential in this phase of the word processing program.

The word processing concepts course should thoroughly acquaint students with various facets of word processing. The following topics might be included in such a concepts course:

A. Word Processing—What is it?

Word Processing Today—The Changing Office Scene
The Evolution of Word Processing
Vocabulary of Word Processing
Pros and Cons of Word Processing

B. An Analysis and Evolution of Word Processing Equipment

Generations of Word Processing Equipment
Capabilites of Various Types of Word Processing Equipment
Determination of Needs of Company
Consideration of Cost and Production Factors

C. Conducting a Feasibility Study

Selecting the Word Processing Study Team
Developing Forms and Collecting Information
Analyzing Kinds and Amounts of Work Performed
Comparing Present Production and Costs with Word Processing
Report to Top Management

D. Word Processing Personnel

    Job Descriptions for Word Processing Personnel
    Specific Duties and Responsibilities of each WP Position
    Selection of WP Personnel

E. Training Word Processing Personnel

    Training in Operation of WP Equipment
    Training in Operational Procedures of WP, Work Flow, etc.
    Training in Managerial Supervisory Skills Needed in WP

F. Management and Word Processing

    Development of Communication Skills
    Development of Dictation Skills
    Information on Procedures and Policies of WP in Company

G. Organization of Word Processing

    WP Center
    WP Center and Satellites
    WP Management Support System
    Individual WP Units Throughout Company
    WP Team and AS Team

H. WP Manuals

    Manuals with Prerecorded Letters for Management
    Manuals for CS Secretaries
    Manuals for AS Secretaries

I. Production Standards for Word Processing

    Types of Measurement—Line, Page, Document, Unit Count
    Performance Standards on Various Types of Copy
    Standards for Beginning WP Secretaries vs. Experienced Workers

J. Developing Promotional Opportunities in WP (Career Paths)

    Managers
    Supervisors
    Levels of Correspondence Secretaries
    Levels of Administrative Secretaries

K. The Administrative Secretarial Team

    Organization of AS Secretaries—One to Several Managers; AS Teams, etc.
    Training
    Procedures and Policies

L. Motivation and Supervision of WP Personnel

    Incentive Pay and Bonuses
    Advancement
    Production Goals
    Awards

M. Systems Approach to WP—Relationship of WP to DP

N. The Office of the Future and WP

O. In-Depth Study of a WP Installation

Ideally upon completion of these two courses, the students should have an opportunity to enroll in a word processing laboratory which could be operated in a number of ways. The laboratory might be set up as a mini word processing center with machine dictation and hard copy being submitted to the supervisor. The students would take turns serving as center supervisor. Specific rate schedules would be established for work performed, and students would be paid for their services. Most centers operated by student personnel are open a limited number of hours a day so that all work may be completed by the time requested.

The instructor might choose to set up the laboratory in work groups. In this case, three or four students would be assigned to each work group and would be given projects to complete. Some of the activities in the projects would require the use of word processing equipment. Other activities would be of the administrative secretarial type. The students in each work group would determine which jobs should be completed on the equipment and which should be completed by the administrative assistants in the work group. Students would alternate positions in the work group throughout the course. This plan does not provide the incentive of pay and is more difficult for a student to supervise, but it could prove to be more in line with the current thinking than the mini word processing center.

A community college wishing to offer a one-year word processing program might include the following courses in the program:

First Semester	Hours	Second Semester	Hours
Intermediate Typewriting	2	Office Typing Problems	2
Business English	3	Business Speech	2
Machine Transcription	3	Concepts of Word Processing	3
Office Machines	3	Office Procedures for Word Processing	3
Magnetic Keyboarding	3	Business Communications	3
Introduction to Data Processing	3	Word Processing Lab	3
	17		17

A two-year program is considered preferable, as this permits the student to enrich his educational background with other general education and business courses.

THE FUTURE OF WORD PROCESSING

Today people no longer debate whether word processing is here to stay. Rather they discuss what word processing will look like in the future. In fact, word processing is moving so rapidly the future becomes the present. Today word processors discuss such advanced technology as satellite communications, bubble memory, fiber optic cable transmission, laser impact printers, plasma display, voice creation and voice recognition, and portable keyboards. Business educators are becoming increasingly aware that the office is indeed far different today than it was yesterday and that tomorrow it will be different from today. Word processing and data processing have already joined forces in an effort to increase the productivity and efficiency of the office. The business educator who recognizes the opportunities in this field and decides to train young people for them will find the experience challenging and stimulating, for there are no ruts to follow.

CHAPTER 7

Written Communications

MALRA TREECE

Memphis State University, Memphis, Tennessee

"Nothing endures but change" is a quotation from Heraclitus, written about 500 B.C. Modern technology continues to change the media and methods of transmitting and receiving oral and written messages; and students, teachers, and business people must be aware of these trends and developments. The principles of human communication, however, are constant and universal. "The more things change, the more they stay the same" is an adage that applies, to a great extent, to effective communication in the organization and to successful teaching of communication.

A desirable attitude toward preparing students for effective business writing in the changing office environment might best be described by the educational cliché "back to basics," provided that these basics could be reasonably defined. Such essential instruction would unquestionably include a sound foundation of the knowledges, abilities, and desirable attitudes that will enable students to adapt and grow, develop creativity, and use logic and judgment when approaching new situations. Students should be prepared for today's world, not yesterday's, as well as for tomorrow's. Teachers, however, cannot present all the information or develop all the skills that students will need in responsible employment. Learners must be given the background, plus the motivation, to continue learning throughout their lives.

Business messages at one time were written with a quill pen, and in earlier times, carved on bark or chipped on stone tablets. Now they can be printed and transmitted by computers or beamed all over the world—or into outer space—by satellites. Facsimiles of anything written, typed, drawn, or photographed can be sent by electronic mail, using the voice telephone network. Word processing equipment can communicate directly with typesetting equipment. Each year the various kinds of equipment used to process information become more comprehensive and amazing. Regardless of the method and equipment used in sending and receiving messages, however, the most useful tool of communication is—as it has always been—language. Automated, sophisticated machines cannot be designed or operated without the use of communication between humans, and, especially, the application of human thought.

Although this chapter is primarily concerned with written communication, many characteristics of successful letters, reports, memorandums, and other business writing are indistinguishable from those of effective speech. Both the writer and the speaker are concerned with understanding and acceptance. To achieve these goals, the communicator must have a proficiency in language and an empathy with the receiver of the message, plus knowledge of the subject matter being communicated. Some of the principles of business writing also apply to the effective management of communication, for example, empathy and the positive approach. In addition, the content of written communications may be determined by the method of distribution and the receivers of the message. Thus, the following discussion relates somewhat to all forms of communication and to the management of communication within an organization. Emphasis is upon preparing business students to become proficient communicators, especially efficient and effective business writers.

COMMUNICATION IS A VITAL AND CONTINUOUS PROCESS

A recent Department of Commerce study concluded that the economy of the United States is based on the transfer of knowledge, more so than upon manufacturing; 46 percent of the gross national product is derived from the production, processing, and distribution of information. It is no exaggeration to state that business *is* communication. In addition, communication is an essential element in the personal and professional life of every individual and in the structure and operation of every organization.

All aspects of communication are interrelated. Communication in any form is affected by the many and varied influences that enter into human behavior.

Effective communication is far more than the knowledge of "correct" English and the expected pronunciation and spelling of words. It is more than the ability to construct flawless sentences, to speak confidently and audibly from a public platform, to write clever advertising jingles, to arrange various letter forms, or to apply the rules of parliamentary procedure. All these abilities are important or desirable, but even more important are the communicators' relationships with other persons and their own self-concepts. Effective communication requires knowledge and application of principles of psychology, semantics, logic, and persuasion. It also requires a workable—preferably an expert—knowledge of language, including the meaning of words as they are defined in dictionaries and their connotations and customary usages.

Successful business writers and speakers must have meaningful messages to send forth; that is, they must know what they are talking about. They should have a thorough knowledge of their company's products, policies, services, and procedures. Most important of all, the effective communicator should have a healthy self-respect and a corresponding respect for the receiver of the message.

Just as communication is an almost continuous process in the personal and professional life of an individual, it is the most important and continuous process within an organization. It involves, in addition to human interactions, the efficient management of the mechanical tools of communication: the computer, the typewriter, the telephone, dictating and duplicating machines, and specialized audio and video equipment. Even more important than the management of equipment is the management of human communication within an organization.

ETHICAL COMMUNICATION IS VITAL TO THE FUNCTIONING OF ANY ORGANIZATION

Workers at all levels are motivated by oral and written communication that assures them of the company's interest in them. Management should make sincere efforts to inform and instruct employees about organizational plans, benefits, policies, and newsworthy events. Messages from management to employees, as well as from employees to management, must be sincere and built on trust if they are to be conducive to morale building, productivity, and organizational and individual progress. Honest, open communication downward encourages the same kind of communication to flow upward. Good intent, however, is not enough. Poor skills and techniques can also lead to poor communication and poor communication systems.

The importance of open, honest communication within and from an organization should be brought into every business course, from MBA programs in management to vocational classes for keyboard operators. Employees invest a portion of their lives in the organizations for which they work; they deserve adequate and sincere communication. As much as possible, employees should be given the opportunity to participate in decision-making processes, for whatever affects the organization also affects personnel. At the very least, all workers should be given the recognition and advantages of being informed about organizational policies and procedures and the reasons behind them.

In organizational communication, as in individual and personal interchange of thoughts and ideas, communicators are socially and morally responsible for the content and effect of their messages. Examples of social responsibility, or the lack of it, have been widely discussed in relation to advertising and mass communication, and laws have been passed to prevent deceptive practices and wording. These laws or similar ones also apply to business letters, memorandums, and reports, including those pertaining to credit, hiring practices, and employee rights. Some firms, including most publishing companies, now encourage nonsexist language in all official messages within the organization itself and in publications or informal writing going outside the company. Business, professional, and government organizations are becoming aware of the necessity for competency and responsibility in the use of written and spoken words.

In addition to judging messages sent in the light of social and moral responsibility, reason and judgment must be used in analyzing messages received. A knowledge of the processes of communication will help students and business people to construct their own messages and to analyze those received from other persons.

COMMUNICATION IS AN INTEGRAL PART
OF ORGANIZATIONAL ACTIVITY

Communication permeates every facet of operation and is especially important at the management level. Regardless of the type of organization, the basic principles of communication remain the same; purposes, methods, media, and formats differ somewhat. Clerical jobs, supervisory work, sales and advertising, secretarial responsibilities—all these functions are made up almost entirely of communication activities. Accountants communicate with figures, graphic illustrations, and spoken and written words, in addition to the many and constantly occurring methods of nonverbal communication that accompany all other forms of human interaction. Personnel in any occupation, with the possible exception of production workers and manual laborers, communicate with other persons throughout most of the working day. Although the time spent in oral exchange of ideas and information exceeds that spent in writing, beginning as well as experienced business people seem to feel less confident of their ability to write.

Internal communication moves upward, downward, or horizontally, using these broad terms to indicate levels of responsibility. Messages that move downward exceed those that move upward. These mesages are used to coordinate efforts and activities, to instruct, to direct, or to explain decisions or policies. Upward communication is often in the form of reports, oral or written. Written reports are prepared in various styles and formats; although the trend seems to be toward informality, increasing emphasis is placed upon professionalism and objectivity. Management must have adequate and correct information in order to make intelligent decisions.

Reports also travel horizontally, as from one department to another. Reports can be said to move downward in the sense that results of research studies are reported to personnel below the level of the report writer, but they seldom move downward for the purpose of using the report information in decision making. Insufficient, ineffective, inept, or inefficient reporting constitutes a major problem of organizational management.

Internal downward communication is used to instruct employees, to build and maintain employee morale and goodwill toward the organization and toward management personnel, and to keep the routine and special activities of the organization moving smoothly and efficiently. (Instruction in business writing classes should include messages of various kinds to be used within the organization; this area seems to be given less attention than it deserves because of emphasis on letters going outside the company, or on letters and other writing for the student's personal interests.)

The memorandum format serves as a medium for many and various kinds of business writing, including numerous short reports. The memorandum is by far the most widely used type of written communication between members of an organization, and at times it is sent outside the organization.

In addition to the familiar (and sometimes overused) memorandum, many standardized forms of various kinds are used for written messages within and from the organization. These prepared forms must be used to reduce costs, if for no other reason. Another advantage is that clarity is more likely to be achieved when the reader has learned to expect certain types of information to be presented in similar arrangements. Standardized forms and form letters should be written with even more care than individually dictated letters, as their effects will be multiplied by the great number of readers.

External communication is planned for some of the same purposes as internal communication. The organization must build and maintain goodwill with customers and the public, as it must do with employees. Customers and the general public receive directions and instructions about the use of the company's products and services. The organization receives information from and sends information to customers, stockholders, the public, and government agencies in order to plan and proceed with manufacturing, selling, and promotional activities.

Customer communication includes retail and wholesale selling by personal contact, telephone conversations, letters, and various kinds of advertising and public relations releases. Other purposes of customer communication are instructions about credit, collection, and the adjustment of claims.

EFFECTIVE LETTER WRITING IS STILL IMPORTANT

The business letter continues to be the most widely used form of external written communication. Except for appearance, some letters differ surprisingly little from those written two or three centuries ago. Slow, stereotyped wording was already trite at that time. On the other hand, some modern writers work so hard to eliminate all unnecessary words, sentences, and paragraphs that their writing sounds curt and blunt. An idea that some writers find hard to accept is that brevity and conciseness are not necessarily synonymous. Letters can be sincere without being harshly direct.

Most frequently written letters. The kinds of letters most frequently written by Certified Professional Secretaries, according to a study completed in 1971, are listed below in order of descending frequency. The composing responsibilities of Certified Professional Secretaries are assumed to be typical of business writing in general.

- Inquiry and request letters
- General administrative letters
- Replies to requests and inquiries
- Goodwill messages, including those from the president or top management
- Miscellaneous letters of other kinds
- Letters about employment
- Claim and adjustment letters

- Credit and collection letters
- Sales and sales promotion letters[1]

In addition to these letters, the Certified Professional Secretaries who served as respondents of the study wrote reports, memorandums, minutes of meetings, bulletins, handbooks, announcements, business articles, leaflets, programs, specifications, training material, summaries, and various other kinds of internal and external communications. The extent and kinds of writing differed according to the kind of organization, the department, and the level of responsibility. According to the cited study, and as shown by other studies and simple observation, the range of formats and purposes of written communication is wide. The variety of written messages is likely to increase as the individual moves ahead in a business or professional career.

It would be impracticable, if not impossible, for teachers to approach each kind of letter or other written message as a differing unit, for in addition to the types listed here, there are many others. Even if this comprehensive approach were possible, it would accomplish little, for the varying types of written messages are much more similar than they are dissimilar. Although students need extensive practice in writing—far more than most teachers are able to assign, evaluate, and return—they should not be encouraged to approach writing, or any type of communication, in a mechanistic way. They should be encouraged to develop their creativity and to use their common sense. In order to be creative and to use the problem-solving approach, however, they need a strong background of communication knowledges and skills.

One of the most important considerations when planning letters is the general rule that most letters, as well as memorandums and reports, are best arranged in either the direct or the indirect order, with the choice depending upon anticipated reader reaction. This simple guide, which can be taught in a few minutes, will save countless hours of hesitation in writing and dictating and, overall, result in more effective and persuasive messages. (The arrangement described as "persuasive" is a variation of the indirect order. The chronological order, although appropriate for some material, is not the best choice for usual business writing.)

Basically, the difference between the direct and indirect arrangement is this: The direct (also described as the deductive) arrangement begins with the gist of the message and uses the remaining space to expand upon this central message by giving details, examples, or added information of any kind. The indirect (also described as the inductive) builds up to the gist of the message; for example, a report arranged in this order ends with "conclusions and recommendations." A bad-news letter, which should be arranged in the indirect order, also builds up to the gist of the message—the bad news; but because of the emphasis that is automatically placed upon the closing paragraph or paragraphs of the letter, the emphatic closing position is used for a diplomatic request for action, sales promotion, goodwill, or other "softening" passages to subordinate the bad news. This arrangement

---

[1]Treece, Malra C. *Written Communication Responsibilities and Related Difficulties Experienced by Selected Certified Professional Secretaries.* Doctor's thesis, Oxford: University of Mississippi, 1971. pp. 47-49.

71

of ideas in no way decreases sincerity, and it need not affect clarity. As writers work to attain an appropriate psychological approach, however, they must keep in mind that sincerity and clarity are even more important.

Students should be taught that the direct order is usually preferable unless they see a definite reason for choosing the indirect, such as the necessity for persuasion or explanation. By following these simple guides to the arrangement of ideas, teachers and students need not be overly concerned that one type of written message is different from those written previously. The same principles apply, for example, to refused adjustments as to refused requests or refused claims. Routine, informational communications should ordinarily be approached as if they were good-news messages.

An important advantage of familiarity with the direct and indirect arrangements, in addition to the fact that the appropriate choice ordinarily results in more persuasive and convincing letters, is that the writer saves a great deal of time in planning messages and in the writing or dictating process.

Most frequent difficulties in composing. Difficulties most frequently encountered in business writing, as reported by respondents in the research report cited, are listed in order of importance according to the number of writers reporting these difficulties:

- Being able to compose without wasting time
- Avoiding trite expressions
- Writing concisely
- Achieving the proper psychological approach
- Planning the appropriate report form (for reports for use within and from the company)
- Making meaning clear
- Planning different types of letters
- Building goodwill
- Finding library information (research sources for reports)
- Making message accomplish its intended purpose.[2]

These perceived difficulties, which agree substantially with previous and more recent studies, can serve as a general guide for instruction in written communication. Other major weaknesses of business students, not reported by or expected from Certified Professional Secretaries, are grammatical, spelling, and punctuation errors; limited vocabulary; and ineffective sentence and paragraph construction.

EDUCATION SHOULD BUILD NEEDED COMPETENCIES

As in all courses, the projected competencies necessary for successful employment and growth in responsibility should be used as a basis for educational objectives, instruction, and evaluation.

---

[2]Treece, *op. cit.*, p. 130.

Suggested course objectives. The following list of objectives is planned for a basic, comprehensive course in business communication taught at the collegiate level. A few of these objectives can be safely omitted for some courses: for example, those that are limited to written communication because of other instruction in speech, or courses that exclude report writing because it is to be taught later. Regardless of the type and purpose of the class, however, objectives should reflect a comprehensive, unified approach, not a narrow, specialized one. (These goals are expressed in terms of the student's viewpoint.)

1. To understand the theory and concepts of the communication process, especially as they apply to business situations and behavior
2. To strengthen ability in listening, reading, thinking, and speaking
3. To develop a logical, ethical approach to solving business problems through communication
4. To increase the ability to inform and convince through communication
5. To learn the forms and purposes of the more commonly used business reports, letters, and other kinds of business writing
6. To improve the ability to make decisions involving the selection and organization of content and the choice of media and format
7. To learn to communicate information and ideas in written form by:
   a. Developing a clear, concise, convincing, and correct writing style that is adapted to the readers of the message
   b. Learning and applying high standards of physical presentation in preparing business messages
8. To learn the basic techniques of report preparation, including how to collect, evaluate, analyze, organize, interpret, and present data in written and oral messages
9. To strengthen the ability to analyze written and oral communication
10. To develop an understanding of nonverbal communication.

These preceding objectives conform to those recommended by the American Business Communication Association for a required, 3-credit course in business/organizational communication, as described in a report approved by the Board of Directors as an official statement on December 27, 1973. These objectives, stated from the teacher's viewpoint, are:

1. To make the student knowledgeable about effective communication behavior
2. To teach the student to communicate more effectively through practice and evaluation of his skills improvement
3. To sharpen the student's analytical ability.[3]

Areas of subject matter recommended by the American Business Communication Association in the official statement are as follows:

1. Communication theory, media, and means
2. The scientific method of inquiry
3. Applied logic (through problem solving, evaluation, justification, data presentation and interpretation, decision making, and so on)

---

[3]"Standards for Business Communication Courses." *ABCA Bulletin.* March 1974. p. 18.

4. Expository techniques and strategies
5. Psychology in communication behavior (such as motivation, reinforcement, perception, and the like).[4]

To summarize these goals and areas of content, instruction in business communication should improve the students' ability to read, write, listen, speak, and think—an ambitious and difficult task. These goals are applicable and attainable, however, even if the main emphasis in a particular course is upon written communication. The need for these abilities has not changed, except to increase, because of modern technology.

Communication theory, techniques, and applications. Communication theory is often thought of only in terms of detailed models of the communication process, or of research reports of findings that had already been determined by generations of common-sense observers. (Some "research" in all fields results in such findings.) Communication theory (or principles) includes such topics as perception, communication barriers, and interpersonal relationships as they affect communication. Theory also includes such pragmatic bits of instruction as the advice that the direct order of arrangement increases readability and that positive, pleasant words are more persuasive than negative words. The structure and "rules" of the English language also comprise a part of communication theory.

The principles of communication must be applied to the solving of business problems through written and spoken words. Listening to, reading about, and discussing communication principles—although these necessary activities are in themselves forms of communication—are less beneficial than applying these principles to realistic, challenging business situations and problems.

In all courses, teachers are likely to emphasize portions of the content that they particularly like or those in which they have the most expert knowledge. For example, some teachers seem more intent on teaching students how to obtain employment through written and oral communication than to communicate effectively once they begin work. Some teachers think that report writing is dull (it can be) and hasten through the report writing section, even though report writing is a stated portion of the course content. Former English teachers may emphasize grammar and punctuation; former typewriting teachers are likely to be overly concerned, to the extent of disregarding other important factors, about letter form and arrangement. Marketing-oriented instructors may spend more time than they can afford on sales writing.

None of the above-mentioned areas are unimportant. Written communication should be grammatically correct and effectively punctuated; letters should be attractively typewritten; students should acquire experience in resumé preparation; and so on. The point is that courses in business communication, even if built around business writing, should contain many aspects of instruction. Emphasis should be upon basic principles and applied techniques, not upon narrow specializations. Students find instruction in

---

[4]*Ibid.*

business communication interesting and challenging when they are encouraged to communicate in the classroom, to participate in decision-making processes, and to strengthen creativity.

INSTRUCTION CAN BE RELEVANT TO CHANGING RESPONSIBILITIES

To summarize, instruction in written communication should be relevant to the changing office environment, but instructional goals and methods should not be changed with every new development. To do so is impossible; to attempt to do so is unnecessary and undesirable. A foundation of basic knowledges and skills, including a study of human behavior and an expert use of the English language, will enable students to adapt to ever-changing conditions and responsibilities. Most important of all, students should be taught to expect change and to exert the necessary effort to meet new challenges with confidence in their ability to excel.

CHAPTER 8

Reprographics

DENNIS E. BAUER
Bowling Green State University, Bowling Green, Ohio

The world of the printed copy, "office reprographics," has been changing at a phenomenal speed for the last decade. Today the office copier is as common as the electric typewriter, and the offset press is as easy to operate as the duplicating machine.

The change which has had the greatest impact on office reprographics has been the transition from the task of typesetting to that of "cold-type composition." Cold-type composition and the automation of the offset press have enabled more and more businesses to develop their own in-plant printing centers, thereby enabling each business to produce quality copies of reports, newsletters, bulletins, programs, and business forms at less cost than ever before. Once, every business had to send out work that required the experience of professional printers. Now professional work can be completed by the in-plant printing and duplicating centers.

Today, the typist may be required to prepare copy for the duplicating center and must, therefore, possess the knowledge and skill necessary in the area of copy preparation, paste-up, layout, and design. Definitions related to duplicating are as follows:

Office reprographics. A part of the graphic arts that is concerned with reproduction in the office. Emphasis is placed on direct image masters and copy layout.

Cold-type composition. Composition by machines such as typewriters or other photocomposing machines. Copy is composed at the typewriter instead of using molten metal. The term "cold composition" is the opposite of "hot composition" which uses hot metal type such as the Linotype.

Layout. The arrangement of written material, pictures, illustrations, and other art work on a page.

Paste-up. The process used in securing copy, pictures, etc. to layout sheet. This would include trimming and positioning the copy and illustrations, then affixing by means of rubber cement, tape, or wax.

Fluid process. The copy is typed directly on a master with a second sheet behind containing aniline dye which in turn makes a reverse image on the back of the master. Copies are then made by a spirit duplicating machine which deposits a small amount of this "carbon" from the master onto each sheet of paper.

Mimeograph process. The mimeograph process uses a wax coated tissue which is "stencilized" by the typewriter to allow ink to pass through the stencil and leave an ink image on the paper.

Offset process. The method by which the master picks up ink and "offsets" the image on a second roller called a blanket cylinder. The blanket cylinder contacts the paper and produces the printed copy.

In a study conducted by Motley and Bauer, it was found that of 135 businesses located in five major industrial areas in Illinois, 38 fluid duplicators were being used, 22 stencil duplicators, 133 offset presses, and 392 copiers.[1] This study did not reflect the reprographics equipment used by small business, educational institutions, public libraries, hospitals, and religious institutions, which are also high users of the "office reprographic type" of equipment. According to this recent study the demand for various reprographic processes has changed from the "industrial printing center" to "office in-house printing centers." This means careers are now opening for secretarial and office personnel to handle such jobs as those of offset press operator, layout and design, and composition typist.

FLUID DUPLICATING PROCESS

The fluid duplicating process is the easiest and least expensive of all reprographic processes. Not only is the equipment inexpensive but the materials used can be purchased at less cost than the supplies which are used for other reprographic processes. The fluid process will be used on the job by secretaries who seek employment in educational institutions and related areas. Students should be introduced to this duplicating process; however, a limit of two or three jobs is usually sufficient for mastery of the fluid duplicating process. Teacher education institutions may want to spend some additional time on fluid process, explaining color reproduction, preparation of masters from transparencies, and preparation of thermal masters.

The learning activities for this process should include the following:

1. Preparation of memorandums from a rough draft
2. Layout and organization of tests
3. Layout of single-fold progams
4. Preparation of bulletins and notices including the use of illustrations and multiple color.

Advantages and disadvantages of the fluid duplicating process are summarized below:[2]

Advantages

1. Finished copy can be produced quickly.
2. The glossy paper needed for fluid duplicating is less expensive than many papers intended for other forms of duplicating.

---

[1]Motley, Robert J., and Bauer, Dennis E. "Illinois Businesses Surveyed for Business Machines Usage." *IBEA Reports,* February 1978.

[2]Bauer, Dennis E., and Strahl, John W. *Office Reproduction Processes.* First edition. San Francisco: Canfield Press, 1975. p. 14.

3. The processes relating to preparing materials for the fluid duplicator are not too time consuming to learn.
4. The cost of purchasing a fluid duplicator is generally less than costs for other kinds of duplicating equipment.
5. The machine is rather simple in its mechanics, and maintenance costs are low.

Disadvantages
1. Only 500 copies can be produced from the finest quality mastersets.
2. Direct sunlight will fade finished copy.
3. Carbon deposits can be easily smeared when corrections of errors are made.
4. The appearance of the finished copy is not as professional as found with other duplicating processes.

INK MIMEOGRAPH

The mimeograph duplicating process has been taking on a new image in recent years. A surprising revival is occurring in mimeograph usage due basically to the improvements made in the electronic scanners. The electronic scanners are capable of producing a stencil from a paste-up copy in less than three minutes. Scanners also come equipped with color separation capabilities enabling the reproduction of color photos and pictures. The simplicity of the equipment's usage, the low cost, and increased quality have enabled the mimeograph process to become competitive with the offset press. The electronic scanner is made by most companies that manufacture a mimeograph, and their mimeograph sales have tripled in the last five years due to the advances in the electronic scanner.

The learning activities for this process should include the following:

1. Preparation and layout of tables
2. Proper format and duplication of minutes
3. Preparation of memorandums, especially from a rough copy
4. Preparation of design of business forms
5. Postal card memorandums and notices
6. Single-fold bulletins and programs
7. Layout and preparation of notices and flyers
8. Layout and preparation of 2-column and 3-column newsletters and newspapers.

Advantages and disadvantages of duplication by mimeograph follow:[3]

Advantages
1. Equipment costs range from $400 to $1,500.
2. Copies are of a good quality and legible in a variety of colors of ink.
3. The equipment is clean and relatively easy to operate.
4. Stencils can be stored and reused at a later time.
5. Copies are relatively inexpensive.
6. Electronic scanners allow paste-up copy and pictures to be used.

---

[3]*Ibid.,* p. 51.

Disadvantages

1. The final copy is not as professional in appearance as the offset.
2. Stencils have only a limited production life of up to 3,000 copies.

Several special features of mimeograph duplicating should be noted.

Thermal stencils. Stencils can be prepared in five seconds or less by using a thermal stencil which is imaged by placing a typed copy beneath the stencil and then running them through a thermographic copier. The major advantage of this process is speed, but the mediocre quality of the copy will limit the use of thermal stencils.

Electronic scanners. Scanners are rapidly replacing the scope for picture and illustration reproduction, simplifying color reproduction and reproducing existing original printed materials, diagrams, and photographs.

The electronic scanner uses a photocell which scans the printed copy and activates a stylus which burns into a vinyl stencil an image identical to the original copy. Pictures and illustrations can also be reproduced onto an electronic stencil and then inset on a regular mimeograph stencil. Any paste-up copy can be used with the scanner to produce a quality newsletter. The development of the scanner, however, has introduced a new job skill to office reprographics, that of paste-up, layout, and design.

Color reproduction. Color work may be done by using a second ink pad placed over the cover sheet; 50 to 100 copies can be produced before re-inking is necessary. The most practical method, however, would be to have additional ink drums or additional silkscreen parts to change the color of ink. The color change takes no more than 30 seconds, while at the same time enhancing the quality of the job. Also, some electronic scanners can be purchased that have color separation capabilities. The scanner merely separates the three primary colors, red, yellow, and blue, onto three stencils. They are then run on three different ink drums, each containing one of the primary colors. As the paper is run through each color, the combination of the primary colors creates the other colors of the spectrum. Color reproduction can be fun, and the results of such an effort can be fantastic.

OFFSET PRESS

The offset press process is frequently preferred over other duplicating processes because of the high-quality appearance of its finished copy, capability of running up to 10,000 copies from one plate, low cost per copy, and versatility in color and picture reproduction. The tabletop offset press has simplified the set-up/clean-up procedures to the point that it has become as simple to operate as the ink mimeograph. Many offset presses manufactured today are as automatic as a photocopier and in some cases just as fast. The major limitation is generally the cost of equipment. Because of the high cost of offset presses, they cannot be justified unless a large volume of reproduction work is done on a regular basis.

The need for secretarial students to have experience running the offset press is questioned when their primary task will be in the preparation of copy to be sent to the printing center. However, a basic understanding of the operation of the offset press enhances a secretary's capabilities to produce excellent copy for reproduction. Too, many typists are using their skills as composition typists on typesetting equipment.

The learning activities for the offset process should include the following:

1. Preparation of direct image masters
2. Essentials of paste-up, layout, and design
3. Preparation of paper and metal plates
4. Use of stroke-on composition typewriters
5. Operation of the offset press including machine preparation and clean-up
6. Experience with a variety of jobs.

The offset process, too, has advantages as well as disadvantages:[4]

Advantages

1. The offset process is recommended because of the high-quality appearance of finished copy.
2. Offset reproduction is good for jobs requiring runs as high as 10,000 copies.
3. Variety of copy work is almost unlimited when doing paste-up work.
4. Cost per copy is relatively low.
5. Color reproduction is a simple process.
6. Photoreproduction can be handled with various copiers.
7. An offset press can print more than 150 copies each minute of operation.

Disadvantages

1. Initial cost of equipment is higher than many other reproduction methods.
2. An operator needs specific training on operation of equipment.
3. The set-up and clean-up time can slow down production.

OFFICE COPIERS

The use of the office copier is growing at a phenomenal rate. Technological improvements of copier equipment are also being made at an accelerated rate. Since the office copier is relatively simple in its operation, a school cannot justify the purchase of several copiers for the sole purpose of instruction. Students instead should be introduced to (1) basic differences in the electrostatic, thermographic, and diazo copiers, (2) advantages and disadvantages of the wet and dry process copiers, (3) preparation of copy for thermal stencils, (5) the preparation of overhead transparencies, and (6) the legal aspects of using the office copier. The following guidelines might be implemented when using office copiers:

1. If more than 10 copies are needed, other duplicating processes that might be less expensive per copy should be investigated.
2. Inexpensive copiers will do a satisfactory job for intraoffice needs.
3. When quality is important in final copy, the electrostatic copiers should be considered since many brands reproduce on bond paper.

---

[4]*Ibid.*, p. 99.

4. Total copying needs should be considered when purchasing copiers. Some copiers will transfer originals to offset masters, transparency film, colored paper, mimeograph stencils, fluid masters, gummed labels, and letterhead stationery; they will also reproduce in color and print on both sides of the paper.

PROGRAM DEVELOPMENT

Planning considerations: As the classroom is being planned for office reprographics, consideration should be given to the following:

1. Conduct a community survey to determine the types of equipment used by local business and industry.
2. Review follow-up studies of former students to determine what they are doing on the job and what skills they lacked in office reprographics.
3. Plan to use meaningful jobs; include activities similar to on-the-job stations within the community.
4. Evaluate the purchase of equipment carefully; equipment and maintenance costs can be prohibitive.
5. Develop a workable room layout and rotation plan.

Equipment needed. Remember that today's office employees may be found working in schools, business offices, department stores, churches, hospitals, industry, public libraries, public utilities, city and county offices, and governmental offices. This variety of employers will require a wide variation of preparation by the office reprographics instructor. Familiarity should be provided for the following equipment and processes:

1. Adding and calculating machines
2. Word processing equipment—automatic typewriters and dictation equipment
3. Fluid duplicators
4. Ink mimeograph—silkscreen or ink drum
5. Electronic stencil makers
6. Offset press—tabletop or floor models
7. Offset platemaker—paper and metal plate capability
8. Headlining equipment
9. Hot waxer
10. Copier—thermographic
11. Proportional spacing typewriters
12. Microelite and primary typewriters
13. Light tables and T squares
14. Composer or typesetting typewriters.

As equipment costs go up and the need to replace outdated equipment becomes frequent, the classroom teacher must turn to additional sources to obtain equipment and resources so that the office reprographics program provides all the necessary learning experiences. Most of the equipment needed for a comprehensive office reprographics program can be found somewhere in the school system or community. Equipment may be borrowed from other departments within the school. If a rotation plan is used, some equipment will be used for short periods of time, perhaps not long enough to justify the duplication of equipment purchases within the same school system. Most public libraries, hospitals, and churches today are using electronic scanners and are usually willing to allow the school to use their equipment if supplies are furnished by the school. Some equipment may be rented for one or two weeks, which would allow enough time for students to become acquainted with its basic operation.

Service contracts. Many office equipment dealers provide a service contract option for the equipment they sell. However, service contracts for a single office reprographics laboratory could cost as much as $5,000 per year. Therefore, the instructor must use discretion before putting all equipment under service contract. It is helpful to keep a log of all equipment repairs for a period of one year, including frequency of breakdown and estimated cost of repair if the equipment was not under a service contract. An analysis of this log after one year will determine whether or not the service contract was more costly than a periodic service call throughout the year. The instructor can also learn to do minor repair work such as the changing of ink pads, feed rollers, and cleaning of machines. Since most repair work is charged by the hour, waiting until more than one machine needs attention before calling in the repairman can hold costs down. Developing a rapport with the maintenance men is advantageous; they are willing many times to provide a hint that might prevent another service call. When placing service calls, it is advisable to report the mechanical failure over the phone so that service personnel will bring the necessary parts and tools. Sometimes a service call can be avoided when only a small adjustment is needed and can be conveyed to the instructor over the telephone.

SPECIAL INSTRUCTIONAL CONCERNS

Paste-up, layout, and design. As the duties of the office employee change from machine operation to paste-up and copy preparation, it becomes necessary to spend more instructional time on the correct methods and proper tools to be used in the preparation of a final copy to be sent for duplication. The skills of paste-up, layout, and design become valuable to office workers where printing centers use either ink mimeograph or offset press.

The paste-up unit might include the proper usage of grid paper, rubber cement, hot waxer, border tapes, clip art, pressure sensitive letters, and T square. The copy must first be prepared on a typesetting typewriter; next, pictures, typed copy, and headlines are affixed to a sheet of paper, and the paste-up is proofread before being sent to the printing center. The paste-up is then transferred to an electronic stencil, paper offset master, or metal plate. Paste-up artists are difficult to find and business firms frequently revert to training their own artists in order to fill the demand for these employees.

The following requirements of a paste-up artist should be emphasized in the classroom:[5]

1. The ability to apply the learning on one kind of job to that of another.
2. Typing—error-free along with reasonable speed.
3. Manual dexterity to handle tools of the trade.
4. Attainment of the rules of grammar and the ability to learn to spell or look up words not known.
5. Good retention—to remember what is verbally discussed regarding the desires of a customer who wants something set up.
6. The ability to visualize what is desired on a printed page—to have some idea of what the finished product will look like before using trial and error methods which can be costly.
7. An interest in seeing output of the job—enough interest to analyze and evaluate the job after it has been printed. This self-analysis should point out how the job could have been improved.

An office reprographics instructor can learn these skills to pass on to the students by attending one-day workshops which are presented throughout the United States by various graphic supply companies.

Decision making. Decision making becomes a very important factor in a duplication center. Decisions must be made concerning the total cost of the job, the best printed quality copy, the deadline date, number of copies, quality of paper, and duplicating method to be used. A case method may be used so that students can apply their skill and knowledge when making decisions involving the various reprographic jobs.

ROTATION PLAN

Because the cost of office equipment limits the number of work stations, the best method for instruction is usually the rotation plan. Each student spends a specified number of class periods working on each reprographic unit. This plan allows the teacher to individualize by permitting some students to omit entirely the difficult units, while the better students may work on additional units. Figure I shows a typical rotation schedule that might be used.

The instructor will add additional equipment as it applies to each unit. For example:

Mimeograph unit. Include instruction in paste-up, light table, electronic scanner.

Offset unit. Include instruction on the headliner, typesetting, hot waxer, paste-up using clip art, and border tapes.

Typing unit. Include instruction on the proportional spacing typewriters, microelite, primary, and automatic typewriters.

The requirements of each unit may not be the same for all students. Individual needs may be met by adding to or deleting the number of exercises to be completed.

---

[5]Graham, Walter B. *Complete Guide to Paste-up.* Philadelphia: North American Publishing Co., 1976. p. 3.

FIGURE I. Rotation Schedule for Office Reprographics

Student's Name _____

	Unit I	Unit II	Unit III	Unit IV	Unit V
Begin Unit					
Due to be graded					
STUDENT NAME 1. _____ 2. _____ 3. _____ 4. _____ 5. _____ 6. _____	MIMEO	MIMEO	DITTO	TYPING	OFFSET
1. _____ 2. _____ 3. _____ 4. _____ 5. _____ 6. _____	OFFSET	MIMEO	MIMEO	DITTO	TYPING
1. _____ 2. _____ 3. _____ 4. _____ 5. _____ 6. _____	TYPING	OFFSET	MIMEO	MIMEO	DITTO
1. _____ 2. _____ 3. _____ 4. _____ 5. _____ 6. _____	DITTO	TYPING	OFFSET	MIMEO	MIMEO
1. _____ 2. _____ 3. _____ 4. _____ 5. _____ 6. _____	MIMEO	DITTO	TYPING	OFFSET	MIMEO

EVALUATION

The evaluation process in office reprographics can be the most difficult segment in the teaching of the entire course. Two basic requirements are necessary in order to have a satisfactory evaluation of each student: (1) student's self-evaluation and (2) teacher's evaluation. Students should be allowed an opportunity to evaluate their own performance based on predetermined criteria. Enough extra time should be allowed so that a student may redo a job if he/she feels that it does not meet minimum performance standards. The teacher's job of evaluation becomes a little more complex as all work should be evaluated according to neatness, ability to follow directions, uncorrected errors, creativeness, and effort put into each job. It becomes difficult to evaluate each of these variables, and a simplified evaluation tool becomes imperative. A maximum number of points should be assigned to each job and a number of points allowing the job to be acceptable at minimum performance standards. Earning less than minimum performance points might mean redoing a job.

The best aid for helping students to determine minimum performance is to have many examples of previous students' work posted at each work station. This picture can provide a yardstick for students to measure against.

Some objective testing is advisable as it forces the student to learn the names of the machine parts and their functions for each machine. Also, the name of each part usually identifies the job performed, which helps to ensure a student's maximum understanding of the operation of the machine.

SUMMARY

It is estimated that more than 50,000 "in-plant shops" are presently being used in this country. This means that high school graduates of office reprographics training programs will generally be employed by companies having in-plant shops as opposed to employment in the commercial printing shops. Nearly 50 percent of the total employment in in-plant positions are filled by women, thus indicating a new avenue for employment of women having a background in clerical skills. Students should be allowed maximum freedom in determining how their jobs are to be duplicated, how they are to be designed, and in applying techniques that will enhance the quality of the job. The technological changes are numerous each year. The teacher's challenge is to keep abreast of latest developments, maintain an up-to-date office reprographics laboratory, and enable students to meet current job performance requirements.

CHAPTER 9

Mailroom Procedures

JOSEPH J. COATAR

Health Care Services Corporation, Chicago, Illinois

It has been the custom of many top management people to view the mailroom operation as an optional department with their organization. However, in recent years increases in the postal rates and postal budgets have forced top management to take a closer look at the mailroom. Despite this trend, the mailroom still, in many companies, remains the type of operation that most people think they can manage better than the person in charge.

IMAGE

It is the responsibility of the mailroom manager to persuade top management that the mailroom operation makes a major contribution to the overall productivity. The location of the mail operation is most important. It must have accessibility for incoming and outgoing work and must be cheerful and pleasant enough for good working conditions. It should not be located in some excess place that has no other use, such as in the basement. The employees should be qualified people with intelligence and dexterity to perform the functions of processing mail. Mailroom personnel must feel the importance of their place within the organization and realize that high-quality work and good performance on the job are appreciated. It is necessary that this attitude permeate from the manager to line supervision through action and attitude. Individuals should be commended both orally and in writing for good performance, just as they are criticized for subpar work.

TRAINING

It is desirable, where volume will permit, to have a department trainer to train new employees. The person should be knowledgeable in all mail operations and be in a higher grade level, but usually just below supervision grade.

An effective tool for a trainer to use is a flexibility chart. This is merely a form with the employee's name on the left side and the various functions to be performed listed from left to right across the top of the form. The department trainer, supervisor, or whoever maintains the records of training hours should use this flexibility chart as a reference. It is not necessary to file or retain a copy. The latest chart should be a compilation of aggregate training hours.

INTERNAL HANDLING

It is necessary for the mailroom supervisor or manager to be familiar with the U.S. Postal Service to know delivery times and times mail can be picked up. He/she decides whether or not spending extra dollars on outside carriers for pickups will help get the mail to user departments sooner. The work day may be extended as much as possible by overlapping employee starting times. The manager should be aware of the *mix of mail;* know the volume of *correspondence, flat mail,* or particular type of mail that is paramount to the business; and know volume by frequency—daily, weekly, hourly. He/she should know the peaks and valleys in the mailroom operation for proper staffing—gathering this data is time and money well spent. The manager is also responsible for prioritizing the sequence of working mail, dependent on the urgency within user departments. Mail, after being prioritized, should be distributed to people at work stations.

The manager must have the ability to measure the work as it is given to the employee. To do this, some sort of reasonable expectancy (RE) for each type of work handled may be developed. One simple way to determine these expectancies is, for a short period of time, to issue activity sheets to the employees and have them record the times they spend on each activity and the volume that they handle during those particular times. This activity sheet should be designed to show the increments of time in 30-minute segments. By utilizing this particular activity sheet over a period, say two to three weeks, the manager can analyze the various volumes and times for each individual and take a cross section of the entire group area, thereby reaching a medium of good expectancy from the highs and lows. This method has proved very effective and very useful because the individuals themselves have really determined what the work expectancy should be. When the manager has a good idea of how much time the work should take to be completed, the work should be dispatched to the individuals from a central control point, based on an hour or 2-hour increment. This is sometimes called a *short interval scheduling method.* This procedure has to be designed to fit the individual operation, if it is to be effective. The manager should use his/her own initiative to develop the work load within the department.

Information gathered in developing work expectancies can be used to properly staff the mailroom—matching the volume of mail to the expectancies. These figures should be reviewed periodically because expectancies can vary by individuals. Such records are also an effective tool for use in convincing management when additional personnel are needed.

INCOMING MAIL

The incoming mail, when received from the post office, should be dumped onto a large table or other area where various sorts can be made. Lock box mail, flat letter mail, correspondence mail, etc. should be segregated and distributed.

Lock box mail. One point to consider in the handling of incoming mail is the private mail, or the *not-to-be-opened* mail, that prevails in all organizations. This is mail that is marked to the attention of an individual or a particular department. It is very time consuming in handling because of the need to search the entire batch of correspondence mail in order to get it in the hands of the proper people. The most efficient way to handle this type of mail is to obtain a lock box from the post office. To implement this procedure, it is necessary to convince management to have all incoming mail for an individual, or a particular department, that is not to be opened received under a lock box number. Thus, this mail can be processed very rapidly because the post office will be doing the sorting. Management should know that time used searching can be spent in processing the regular business mail.

Misroute mail. It is beneficial to instruct all departments within the company to send any mail that is misrouted back to the originating area for redistribution. An effective procedure may be one of utilizing the in-house envelope covered with a large, bright-colored sticker designated as Misroute Mail, Please Return Immediately to Mailroom, something that will highlight the enclosed material. Generally, individuals who receive misrouted mail are no more knowledgeable than the person who sent it. Rather than taking a chance on sending the mail elsewhere, they should return it to the mailroom. The mailroom manager should train some personnel to have complete knowledge of the entire operation so that they can make a final judgment. Misroute mail many times can cause a delay in payment of invoices, payment of claims, or other important functions of the organization. It is beneficial to try to record the amount of misroute mail handled within a month and include it in a monthly report to management, along with quality control figures, to make them aware of the misroute mail problem within the mail department.

Dating the incoming mail. Most companies use a date stamp within the particular user department. A date stamp, even though it may be a little more time consuming, contributes to efficient mail processing. A suggested type of date stamp is a 4-roller stamp, three of the rollers being numerical and the fourth alpha. The three numerical rollers can be used to stamp the date. The fourth roller (alpha) can be assigned to an individual mail handler. This type of stamp is flexible and can be used for quality control purposes. It makes people aware of the fact that there is a manner in which they can be checked, and thus the use of the stamp itself brings better quality. Date stamping the mail, as it enters the mailroom or any central point, can be designated as the start of cycle time for material that has to be processed throughout the organization. Again, this should be the determination of a manager of the mailroom and of the management itself.

Delivery of in-house mail. It is necessary to have proper equipment in the mailroom for sorting mail by individual floor or by various delivery stops within the company. If the firm is located in a multiple floor building and uses a lift elevator arrangement, it is suggested that the tubs used to transfer mail be properly marked to assure their return to the mailroom. People are frequently reluctant to return these tubs because they are so convenient for use within their own department. The mailroom manager should analyze the various delivery times on the floors themselves. A good rule of thumb is to have four deliveries a day for each floor: two in the morning and two in the afternoon, generally starting about 8:15 a.m. and closing out about 4:15 p.m. People who have mail to be sent after the 4:15 pickup should be notified through a memo that such mail, if carried to the mailroom, will go out that day with the rest of the mail. Again, the frequency of mail deliveries per floor should be based on the needs of management. Fewer deliveries, in many cases, could be satisfactory and less costly; certainly fewer people would be required, and the dollar savings would be substantial.

One of the newest pieces of equipment on the market for delivering interoffice mail is the Mailmobile, which is battery-operated and electronically controlled and can be programmed to suit most department needs. If analyzed properly, it can be sold to the particular management on an improved service and cost reduction basis. It is very helpful to instruct the management in the use of this equipment through group meetings, before the installation, to gain better results from the equipment itself. However, the organization must have the type of floor plans needed for utilization of the Mailmobile.

Addressing interoffice envelopes. Another point to consider is the *proper addressing of interoffice mail.* It is suggested that a memo be issued to all management with instructions on the manner in which interoffice mail should be addressed. A time period for implementation should be established. Then, any mail improperly addressed should be returned to the sender. Management must know this procedure is utilized to assure fast and prompt delivery.

DEPARTMENT BUDGET

The budget of a mailroom, particularly within recent years, has increased substantially, primarily because of the escalation of postal rates. The way postage rates have risen within the last decade should make management more cognizant of the need to control these dollars. The mailroom manager must establish a close budget and utilize all types of mail, rather than concentrating on first class. (This procedure will be described in more detail later in the chapter.) It is necessary to scrutinize volume by category and determine exactly what type of mail should be used. One should certainly consider the use of United Parcel Service because of the cost. It has some limitations, however, and one has to be aware of the postal regulations. Periodically, the mailroom supervisor or manager should bring to management's attention what the daily mailings consist of, because sometimes mailings are continued through habit without management's fully realizing that some mail may no longer be necessary or that some material could be revised so it could be handled through a less expensive class of mail.

USE OF CUSTOMER SERVICE REPRESENTATIVE
FROM THE POSTAL SERVICE

All management of the mailroom should be well acquainted with the customer service representative from the USPS. Usually, these individuals are very knowledgeable and can make the manager's job in the mailroom less aggravating through better communications with the USPS. It is the responsibility of the customer service representative to keep customers supplied with the latest data or material published by the USPS. However, representatives will not necessarily volunteer the information a particular business needs because they cover many scopes and types of businesses. One must ask specifically for his/her individual needs! It is well to have supervisory personnel acquainted with the actual handling of the firm's mail at the postal facilities. The post office conducts tours and their personnel will acquaint all users with the method by which they process mail. This coordination benefits both parties and also makes the users aware of the problems that the post office encounters in processing the mail.

On-site meter setting. The USPS has individuals, who for a fee, come to a facility and fill postage meters right on the premises. Again, it should be determined whether or not it is profitable for the individual firm. This procedure may be beneficial if personnel cannot be spared to go to the post office. Also, one should consider the security of having these meters filled under the observance of the mailroom manager's supervision to prevent any possible collusion for theft between company people and representatives of the USPS.

Postal council. The Postal Service in many areas has a local postal council which is made up of representatives from all types of mailers. This is basically an arrangement that permits mailers to get together to discuss their problems and obtain satisfactory help from the Postal Service in solving these problems. Postal councils can be formed regardless of the size of the community and are respected by the Postal Service as a necessary means for satisfying their customers. Again, one should contact representatives to obtain more information regarding the local postal council.

SPECIAL MAIL JOBS

It is very important for the manager of mail services to have complete control of all special mail projects going through the department. It is helpful to have the requesting department fill out a *user request* describing the mailing in its entirety—quantity, type of postage, required delivery dates, and so forth. Many companies develop a special mailing committee which consists of representatives of the mail department, forms control, purchasing, printing department, and user department. The main reason for establishing this committee is to coordinate efforts in order to realize the economical delivery of special mailings. A job number should be established for use by all personnel involved to coordinate the mailing if it originates from outside the company. It is important to prepare a report for management on individual special mailings, designating the actual costs as related to postage and labor dollars, to assist management to determine whether or not these types of special mailings are necessary or productive.

POSTAGE CHARGE BACKS

Many companies have designed a method to charge back each department for postage. There are various thoughts on this particular subject. It does take a good deal of monitoring to control the charge-back costs, such as separation of mail, recording of dollars spent on postage meters, and so forth. One of the main reasons for charging back postage is to make the users aware of and responsible for the actual dollars spent within their department. This method should be analyzed, however, to see if it is really necessary; it is questionable whether the cost of monitoring is worth the effort. Other controls should be considered that possibly achieve the same results.

MAIL TESTS

Outgoing mail. It is a good policy to design a form to time outgoing mail periodically. The form should include the meter date and the time that the mail left the premises, as well as a place for the receivers to insert the time and date it was received at their office. It is also advisable to include a stamped, addressed return envelope. The documentation based upon the periodic test can be helpful in determining if outgoing mail is being delivered promptly.

Interoffice mail. It is well to design a method to test delivery of interoffice envelopes also. A test sheet may be attached to an envelope at the originating point, with departure time inserted as the item leaves the mailroom. The person making delivery should insert the arrival time, remove the sheet, and return it to the originator. This procedure could be applied to all employees, or on a spot basis if desired. A sampling of 10 percent of the total mail delivered in a day should be conclusive.

OUTGOING MAIL

Zip codes. The need for zip codes on as much mail as possible should be stressed in order to take advantage of automated equipment for expediting delivery. It is interesting to see the volume of mail sorted mechanically with zip codes compared to the delays involved in the manual operation needed for processing mail without a zip code. Personnel throughout the organization need to be trained to put correct zip codes on all mail.

Presort mail. A discount of 2 cents per piece is available on letter type mailings of 500 or more pieces of presorted first-class mail. With any kind of volume, substantial savings can be realized (10-13 percent). The individual company is really absorbing the work that would ordinarily be performed by the post office, thus the discount. Basically, the requirements to conform to presort discount are as follows:

1. Each envelope must carry the words "Presorted First-Class" printed or stamped as part of, or adjacent to, the meter or permit imprint.
2. Mail must be sorted by zip code—ten or more pieces in the same 5-digit zip code must be grouped together, with fifty or more pieces to the same 3-digit zip code grouped together.
3. Any mail that does not fall in these two categories is called *residue* mail and should carry the full 15-cent rate. It can be counted, however, towards the 500 minimum volume.

4. Tray this mail (metered) in the method required by the post office, and the post office will dispatch it immediately.

5. Materials to complete presort should be furnished without charge from the post office: rubber bands, trays and sacks, color coded dots, tags, labels, etc.

Again, it is suggested that the mailroom manager utilize the customer service representative to the fullest! To expedite regular mail, batches should be marked for *local* or *out-of-town* delivery.

Some suggestions that most companies can use to expedite their outgoing mail are as follows:

1. Check with post office officials to determine any method mail can be sacked by various distribution centers, labeled properly, and perhaps delivered to the airport.

2. Categorize and sort if possible into trays.

Express mail. Express mail, a new major class of mail offered by the U.S. Postal Service, is guaranteed to expedite postal delivery service for high-priority shipments. Express mail service offers same day or overnight service within the United States, and high-speed delivery to certain foreign countries. If the customer's shipment is not available for pickup, or is not delivered, at the stated time, postage is refunded (unless the delay was caused by a strike or work stoppage). With next-day service inside the United States, items deposited by the customer at the post office of origin by 5:00 p.m. are available for pickup at the post office of destination as early as 10:00 a.m. the next post office working day. For a small additional charge, the customer can request delivery to the addressee's premises, which will be made by 3:00 p.m. of the day after mailing any day of the week.

Express mail, which began as an experimental overnight delivery service in 1970 between Washington, D.C., and New York City, is now offered from most metropolitan areas in the country. Its delivery record during the years of testing shows more than 95 percent of all shipments were delivered on time, with over 99 percent within 24 hours. Service is now offered from more than 900 cities. For information and details on the availability of express mail service, interested persons may contact their local post office.

MAILROOM TIPS

Following are a mailroom checklist and 54 mailroom tips adapted from materials developed by Herbert W. Akers, customer programs specialist with the U.S. Postal Service.

Mailroom Checklist

Location of Mailroom:

( ) Convenient to USPS delivery
( ) Central location
( ) Convenient to rest of organization
( ) Near elevators

Size:

    ( ) Adequate for volume of mail
    ( ) Room not cut-up or crowded
    ( ) Good mail flow established
    ( ) Good quality lighting

Environment:

    ( ) Clean
    ( ) Well painted
    ( ) No junk or old furniture
    ( ) Personal lockers available
    ( ) Adequate staff for peak volumes
    ( ) Training available for staff
    ( ) Library of postal information available

Equipment:

    ( ) Properly equipped for kind of mail and volume
    ( ) Mail opened mechanically
    ( ) Equipment properly maintained
    ( ) Adequate work spaces
    ( ) Proper scales for each type of mail
    ( ) Adequate sorting bins
    ( ) Clean color-coded labels

54 Mailroom Tips

1. Check your scales—five quarters weigh a little less than one ounce.
2. Scales that are not level do not weigh accurately.
3. Warm water will help seal problem envelopes better.
4. Complete unused meter stamps are redeemable at 90 percent of face value.
5. Use Address Correction Requested on all mail—a bargain for 25 cents.
6. Stock different sizes of envelopes—the right size for everything.
7. Always use green diamond envelopes for the best first-class mail service.
8. Dirty scales waste postage—they should be cleaned and checked annually.
9. Automatic sealing tape dispensers save money and do a better job.
10. Post cards mailed for 9 cents must not be larger than 4¼″ by 6″.
11. Keep all personal mail out of company mailrooms.
12. Mail early and mail often for the best possible service.
13. Get to know your customer service representative or postmaster.
14. Always provide a library of Postal Service publications for the mailroom.
15. Constantly test mail service so that delivery times are well known.
16. Explore business-reply-mail costs very carefully.
17. Address Correction Requested is FREE—until your customer moves.
18. Explore the guaranteed overnight delivery of express mail.
19. Investigate meter settings by Postal Service in your own office.
20. Explore the costs and convenience of metered reply mail.
21. Exchange your old Zip Code Directory for a new one—FREE at your post office.
22. Subscribe to the *Postal Bulletin*—save costs by staying up to date.
23. Learn the cut-off and dispatch times of your postal facility.
24. For better mail service keep your mailroom clean, well lighted, and neat.
25. Learn how the USPS tray program will help in your mailroom.

26. Support your local Postal Customers Council programs.
27. Watch mailing machine maintenance—illegible stamps may delay mail.
28. Learn the difference between *regular* and *programmed* express mail.
29. Use clean, color-coded, embossed plastic for labels on sorting bins.
30. Don't waste valuable time opening mail by hand.
31. Study large mailings closely—1/4" trimmed off may save many dollars.
32. Remember invoices may be enclosed with third- and fourth-class packages—FREE.
33. Always purge your mail list annually.
34. Establish an internal mail schedule, publish it, and stick to it.
35. Establish a smooth flow for both incoming and outgoing mail.
36. Ask your CSR or postmaster why your mail will move faster in trays.
37. Check your parcels carefully—Do you really know your damage rate?
38. Always subscribe to *Chapter 1, Postal Service Manual* to stay well informed.
39. Investigate the fast service of special handling.
40. Understand the difference between registered and certified mail.
41. Learn how to utilize firm mailing books.
42. Understand that priority mail isn't an ultra fast delivery service.
43. Special delivery mail rarely works well for business addresses.
44. Explore third-class bulk mail—the regulations are simple.
45. Always bundle metered mail (it's a regulation) and your mail moves faster.
46. Use reinforced filament tape for maximum parcel protection.
47. Always use precision scales for international mail.
48. Explore all types of insulated, bubble, and reinforced envelopes.
49. Investigate nylon pouches for postage savings to branches and customers.
50. Subscribe to FREE "Memo to Mailers" and retain in ring book as library.
51. Try mailroom memos to entire organization for more postal awareness.
52. Always use advertising stuffers for maximum return on postage costs.
53. Investigate polyester film tape for maximum label protection.
54. Explore all of the uses and advantages of mailgram.

IMPLICATIONS FOR BUSINESS EDUCATION

Obviously, the mailroom is a crucial factor influencing the efficiency with which information is transmitted into and out of an organization. With soaring mail costs, business is taking a close look at mailroom operations. Despite the advent of electronic mail, predictions point to the need for an increasing number of employees knowledgeable in mailroom functions and capable of managing mail services. Students in business education who are preparing for entry-level positions in the office, and advancement in those positions, should have a sound background in mail processing.

CHAPTER 10
Records Management

JAMES C. BENNETT
California State University, Northridge

Problems in the handling of recorded information are not new. They have been a part of the business environment for thousands of years. Historical data indicates that recordkeeping existed in the early Assyrian, Chaldean-Babylonian, and Sumerian civilizations. For example, in a Ph.D. thesis at the University of Illinois in 1964 entitled "Business Record Keeping in Ancient Mesopotamia," Orville Russell concluded that business recordkeeping may have made substantial advancements during the period of 4500 to 500 B.C. He felt that the system was a simple recordkeeping one based mostly upon receipts, expenditures, listings, and contracts. Most of the records were only original evidences of transactions, so the system was a recordkeeping one rather than a bookkeeping or an accounting system.

As a managerial function in business, however, records management is new. In most major corporations, records management programs have evolved during the past two decades. A study of the records management profession by Wilmer Maedke, reported in the July 1976 issue of the *Records Management Quarterly*, revealed that over half of the 867 private businesses and governmental agencies that responded had organized their records management programs between 1965 and 1975.

Contemporary records management actually started with the establishment of the two Hoover Commissions in 1947 and 1953. Two Task Forces on Paperwork Management were significant elements of those commissions. Both of these task forces were headed by Emmett J. Leahy, considered by many people as the father of modern records management.

The recommendations of the two Hoover Commissions resulted in significant legislation in records management as well as a wide variety of other advancements in records management policies and procedures at the federal level. In fact, the recommendations from these studies resulted in the elevation of records management from a clerical to a managerial function.

Thus, the pioneering work in records management was done at the federal government level. State governments moved into the picture, and then private industry saw the advantages and began developing programs. An editorial in the October 1978 issue of *The Office* emphasized the importance of records management in business by the fact that such programs now have the support of top management. Also, according to a recent survey, three-fourths of the top executives in major U. S. corporations were aware that poor records management could result in significant operational problems.

PROBLEM AREAS

Studies of office operations reveal that various problems do exist in companies that do not have records management programs. Some of these problems are:

The human nature to hoard is carried over into records operations.

High retention costs of useless records are not understood.

Governmental requirements concerning records retention are not known.

No distinction is made between active and inactive records.

Recognition is not given to vital records and no protection is provided against fire, theft, or other hazards.

The most effective classification systems are not being used to ensure easy storage and rapid retrieval of information.

There is no standardization of filing equipment, and equipment being used is not adequate for a company's needs.

A careful analysis of micrographics systems is not always made before a new system is installed.

Records are not being used in helping to plan the future developments of a company.

Records management has not been recognized and accepted as a significant management function in a company's operations.

COST FACTORS

The costs of creating and maintaining records have become astronomical. An article in *Fortune* magazine in November 1976 gave many examples of such costs. For instance, General Motors estimated that it spent $190 million on government paperwork and related administrative costs in 1974. Eli Lilly & Co. reported that the costs of its government paperwork were about $15 million a year and that more hours were devoted to paperwork than to research on drugs for cancer and heart disease.

The *Report on the Commission on Federal Paperwork* published in 1977 estimated the costs of federal paperwork at $100 billion a year, or about $500 for each person in the country. Estimates of costs to some of the major segments of society were:

The federal government	$43 billion a year
Private industry	$25 to $32 billion a year
State and local government	$5 to $9 billion a year
Individuals	$8.7 billion a year
Farmers	$350 million a year
Labor organizations	$75 million a year

These are costs associated only with federal requirements. When one adds local and state requirements plus all of the costs involved with nongovernmental records needed within a business organization, the costs become a significant part of the total operating expenses. Most statistics reveal that at least ten percent of a company's total expenses are devoted to information processing.

There is no end in sight to the need for information or the costs incurred in providing that information. There is help, however, through a scientific approach to controlling that information—records management.

A VIEW OF THE FUTURE

Therefore, because of a recognition of the serious problems and costs in the processing of information, the field of records management has emerged as a significant area in the changing office environment. It has evolved rapidly during the decade of the seventies and will continue to do so into the 1980's. Many futurists in the office technology field believe that there will be a merging within the next decade of records management, information systems, word processing, telecommunications, reprographics, micrographics, and data processing into a total *information management* concept. And, many people feel that the records manager may be the most qualified person to deal with this concept.

Regardless of the advances in technology, however, the continuing importance of *people* cannot be minimized. John J. Connell, executive director of the Office Technology Research Group, believes "The executive in charge of tomorrow's business operations faces the awesome task of managing technology, information communication—and people." In his January 1979 article in *Administrative Management*, "How Your Job Will Change in the Next 10 Years," he emphasizes that the office of the future will be a people place. He suggests, "How readily office employees will accept new technologies will depend on how responsive the new technologies are to people's needs."

Without question, this is true in records management—because records are created, used, and maintained by people for people to help in making decisions. To be successful, the records manager must have a clear understanding of the people in the office environment as well as a comprehensive knowledge of all of the complex technologies of information management.

BASIC CONCEPTS

Whatever the future may bring, the basic concepts of records management will remain constant. These concepts must be clearly understood for one to achieve the basic goal and objective of effective records management: to provide information when and where it is needed—and at the lowest possible cost.

The basic concept of records management involves the control of recorded information from the original creation to the ultimate disposition—which may be either permanent retention or destruction. The records cycle beginning with the creation of records involves use, maintenance, preservation, protection, and finally disposition.

Contemporary records management is not just paperwork management. A record can be found in any format capable of storing data—paper, microform, videotape, computer storage, and other such media. Although paper is still the most prevalent medium, many people believe that this may not be true in the future. William Benedon, records manager for Lockheed Aircraft Corporation, in a presentation at a 1977 national conference of the Association of Records Managers and Administrators indicated his belief that there will never be a completely "paperless society" but that there will be a society of "less paper."

MAJOR FUNCTIONAL AREAS

There is not unanimous agreement on what areas of the office environment should be a part of the records management function. A publication of the Association of Records Managers and Administrators, *Why Records Management?*, indicates that the major areas of records management are:

> Records retention schedules
> Inactive records storage
> Information retrieval
> Files management
> Microfilm information systems
> Vital records protection
> Forms and reports management
> Correspondence management
> Historical documentation.

These nine areas can be synthesized into the logical sequence through which recorded information must progress: from creation through maintenance to disposition.

CREATION OF RECORDS

The primary concern at this initial stage is to create information that is needed for decision making—but to create no more than is necessary and to create it at the lowest possible cost. Major costs are currently incurred in the areas of forms, correspondence, and reports. The records manager can fill a significant role by helping to control the creation of these documents.

In all of these areas, the major costs are associated with the personnel processing the information. The cost of the average business letter, for example, has risen to about $5. The major part of this cost is related to dictator and stenographer time. The same is true for forms, reports, and other source data.

The areas of word processing, business communications, and telecommunications play major roles in this phase of records management. A more effective utilization of people, procedures, and equipment can significantly reduce the cost of creation and improve the quality of what is created.

MAINTENANCE OF RECORDS

The maintenance of records covers many functions. Records must first be kept active for immediate and frequent use and then transferred to inactive storage for use on a less frequent basis. The decision to move from active to inactive storage should be controlled by a retention schedule—a key element in any effective records management program.

A retention schedule is a document developed by first taking an inventory of all records held in a company and then analyzing those records for their retention values. The schedule indicates the length of time a record should remain in the active file area, the time for it to remain in an inactive storage area, and the destruction date or a notation for permanent retention. If retention schedules are followed, significant savings can be realized and improved service can be given to users of records. Because of space costs, a cubic foot of records may cost $10 a year for housing in an active office area but only $1 a year for housing in an inactive storage area. This storage area may be company owned or leased or may be rented from a commercial records storage business.

For active records, an effective filing system is a prime requisite for a successful operation. Many records managers believe that an active record should be available for a user within one minute. Filing systems are alphabetic, numeric, or alphanumeric. The alphabetic system is still the most frequently used. A good system will not be too complex, and appropriate procedures will be developed for rapid retrieval and easy filing and refiling. Adequate controls must also be used to ensure that records are not lost in the system.

Filing systems may be manual, mechanized, or automated. With an increasing need for rapid retrieval of information, the computer is playing a more significant role in retrieval systems. With an integration of micrographics and the computer, active records can be retrieved from storage almost instantly.

Inactive records are traditionally housed in corrugated cardboard boxes on steel or wooden shelving units in a low cost storage area. These records must be available when needed; they are not necessarily *dead records*.

While an active record should be available within a minute, an inactive record normally has a 4- to 24-hour availability time. This time is dependent on the location of the records center as well as the service and transportation facilities. Computers are also being used for helping to control the inactive records, and they are particularly helpful in identifying records that are to be destroyed. Although a majority of inactive records can be destroyed at some point in time, some records must be kept on a permanent basis for a variety of reasons. Many are kept as archival records for historical purposes. The archival function of a company is frequently given to the records manager as one of his or her responsibilities, and this can be a very important role for the records manager. Archival business records can be very valuable in the areas of marketing, public relations, planning and development, and litigation. The historical implications of a business organization should not be forgotten.

VITAL RECORDS PROTECTION

A critical facet of records management is the protection of vital records. This protection should be provided for active as well as inactive and archival records. Most companies categorize their records as vital, important, useful, or nonessential. Vital records, which account for about five percent of the total holdings of a company, are those records which could not be replaced or duplicated if they were destroyed in a disaster. They include such records as accounts receivable, engineering drawings, product specifications, research data, personnel data, articles of incorporation, contracts, deeds, patents, etc. A business may not be able to continue operating if its vital records are destroyed.

Vital records may be given special protection through a hard facility concept of vaulting. A vault may exist within the company or it may be leased through commercial protection facilities. These commercial facilities are frequently underground, such as the ones in a salt mine in Kansas and in a mountain in New York. Or, a company may use a soft facility concept for protecting vital records. This approach involves dispersing a duplicate copy of a record to another location. Regardless of which system is used, vital records must be protected from fire, theft, and a variety of natural as well as human hazards. Computer records are becoming especially vulnerable and must be given extra care.

MICROGRAPHICS

The increased significance of micrographics is one of the most important impacts of contemporary records management. The use of microfilm dates back to early experiments in the 1850's. In 1870, for example, microfilm was used for espionage purposes during a Prussian siege of Paris.

Space savings was the initial primary purpose for the development of microfilm, and this is still a major advantage since space requirements can be reduced as much as 98 percent. More significant uses now, however, relate to the use of micrographic copy in automated retrieval systems and for vital records protection.

The format of the microform has changed and now includes, in addition to roll film, microfiche, microcard, aperture card, and ultrafiche. Ultrafiche provides for a much greater reduction ratio; an entire book can be stored on a sheet of film an inch square in size. Research is being done with holographic and laser technology whereby one million pages of documentation can be stored in an area the size of a sugar cube.

The most significant contemporary development in micrographics is COM—Computer Output Microfilm. In this process, data is fed into the computer and processed directly onto a film medium. This provides for much easier applications of electronic storage and retrieval of computer printout data.

With the increased importance and use of micrographics, the records manager must be aware of the vast number of products on the market. Wise choices must be made in selecting cameras, processors, readers, and printers. Again, the prime considerations are service and cost.

EDUCATION AND TRAINING

As records management programs have increased in industry, a critical need has emerged for additional training and education in records management technology at all levels —university, community college, and high school.

One of the early studies in collegiate education for records management was done by Mary Griffin at Ohio State University in 1961. She surveyed records managers as well as educators and concluded that records administrators should possess knowledge of basic business economics, business organization and management, as well as an understanding of the functions of finance, personnel management, sales, procurement, production, and research and development. If a person is to help manage the records of all aspects of a company's operations, the need is clear for a broad background in business. This is in agreement with the curricular pattern in most collegiate schools of business. A student interested in records management is also given specialized training in all of the information management areas.

In 1961 there were very few courses in records management. Of the schools that responded to a national survey in 1961, only 16 percent offered a course in records management. This compared to 40 percent of the schools that responded to a national survey in 1972 and reported in the July 1973 *Records Management Quarterly.* Many schools are now expanding their curriculum in records management, and some even offer a specialization in this field. There is an equal need for education at the community college and the high school levels as there are many jobs within the records management field that do not require a university degree.

Job descriptions in records management were developed for the first time to be included in the *1976 Dictionary of Occupational Titles.* The jobs were categorized relative to type of educational background needed. The jobs that would require a university background are:

> Records management director
> Records management analyst
> Records management coordinator
> Reports manager
> Forms manager.

Jobs that would require a community or junior college background are:

> Records center supervisor
> Reports analyst
> Forms analyst.

Jobs that would require only a high school background are:

Records technician
Micrographics services supervisor
Micrographics technician
Records center clerk
Records clerk/file clerk.

In order to give assistance to educators in developing courses to help in preparing students for the jobs that are available to them, the 1977 Education Committee of the Association of Records Managers and Administrators, under Chairperson Helene Zimmerman of Central Michigan University, developed three course outlines for various levels of records management education. These suggested course outlines—for a one-semester survey course in records management at the university level, for a junior or community college course, and for a high school program—follow. (They are subject to change, pending approval.)

Association of Records Managers and Administrators, Inc.
Course Syllabus for
"Introduction to Records Management"
A Three-Credit, One-Semester Course for
Four-Year Colleges and Universities

1. Introduction to the Records Management Course
2. Importance of Records Management
   A. History
   B. Scope
   C. Purposes
   D. Legislation such as right to privacy laws
3. Developing, Organizing, and "Selling" Records Management Programs
4. Records Creation
   A. Meaning and importance of controlling the creation of records
   B. Routing and management of incoming and outgoing mail
   C. Correspondence control
      1. Letter writing
         a. Increasing letter production efficiency
         b. Effective writing techniques—improving comprehension
   D. Forms control
      1. Analysis of existing business forms
      2. An organizational approach to business forms management
      3. Techniques of designing new forms
      4. Forms printing, purchasing, and inventory control
   E. Reports and directives control
      1. Analysis and evaluation of existing reports and directives
      2. Techniques for improving reports and directives
5. Records Maintenance
   A. Awareness of the status of "hard copy" and "automated" records
   B. Principles of records maintenance and retrieval systems

C. Methods of surveying and inventorying records
   1. Utilization of professional records management consulting firms
   2. In-house inventorying
   3. Questionnaire vs. physical inventory
D. Methods of sorting records
E. Records classification systems and rules governing these systems
   1. Alphabetic
   2. Subject
   3. Numeric
   4. Geographic
   5. Other classification systems
F. Technical records systems
   1. Medical
   2. Engineering
   3. Legal
   4. Industrial
   5. Other
G. Equipment and supplies for maintaining records
H. Centralized vs. decentralized records maintenance systems
I. Basic steps of records maintenance
J. Development and implementation of records retention schedules
   1. Appraisal of records
   2. Research of retention requirements
   3. Writing retention schedules
   4. Approval and implementation of schedules
K. Records centers and methods of records transfer
   1. Transfer procedures
   2. Inventory and indexing procedures
   3. Designing and equipping records centers
   4. Records center operations
L. Vital records storage
   1. Selecting vital records
   2. Vital records protection
   3. Vital records preservation
   4. Archival storage
M. Records disposition
   1. Means of disposing of records
   2. Procedures for disposing of records
N. Cost analysis of records maintenance
   1. Physical layout and space utilization
   2. Analysis of equipment and supplies
   3. Analysis of labor and overhead costs
6. Micrographics and Its Applications to Records Management
   A. Microforms
   B. Determining the feasibility of microfilm applications and systems
   C. Microfilm equipment and supplies
   D. Cost analysis of microfilm applications, equipment, and supplies
   E. Computer Output Microfilm
7. Records Management in the Data Processing Center
   A. Objectives of records management in the data processing center
   B. Disaster plan

C. Media of machine-readable records
D. Model systems analysis
E. EDP retention schedule approvals
F. Magnetic tape to microfilm
G. Recreating tape from microfilm

8. MIS—Management Information Systems
   A. Implications of management information systems and corporate memory
   B. Nature and function of an MIS
   C. Design and development of an MIS
   D. MIS—man vs. system
   E. Cost considerations
   F. Advanced computer analysis techniques for management
   G. The future of MIS

9. Records Management Manuals
   A. Development of a manual
   B. Use of a manual in the office
   C. Analyzing and updating the manual

10. Evaluation of Records Management Programs
    A. Importance of periodic program evaluation
    B. Methods of program and performance evaluations
    C. Methods and procedures for evaluating programs and procedures
    D. Evaluation of procedures and programs by outside consultants

11. Organizing and Implementing "In-Service Records Management Training Programs"

12. Word Processing
    A. Organization
    B. Equipment and layout
    C. Cost considerations
    D. How word processing affects the records management program

13. Reprographics
    A. Processes
    B. Operating standards
    C. Characteristics of copy

14. Mail Operations
    A. Organization
    B. Equipment and layout of office
    C. Procedures
    D. Cost considerations

15. Career Opportunities in Records Management
    A. Job titles, duties, and responsibilities
    B. Qualifications required for records management positions
    C. In-service education and advancement

Association of Records Managers and Administrators, Inc.
Course Syllabus for
"Introduction to Records Management"
A Three-Credit, One-Semester Course for
Community Colleges, Vocational-Technical Schools, and Junior Colleges

1. Introduction to the Records Management Course

2. Importance of Records Management
   A. History
   B. Scope
   C. Purposes
   D. Legislation such as right to privacy laws
3. Developing, Organizing, and "Selling" Records Management Programs
4. Records Creation
   A. Meaning and importance of controlling the creation of records
   B. Routing and management of incoming and outgoing mail
   C. Correspondence control
      1. Letter writing
         a. Increasing letter production efficiency
         b. Effective writing techniques—improving comprehension
      2. Management of original records and copies
   D. Forms control
      1. Analysis of existing business forms
      2. An organizational approach to business forms management
      3. Techniques of designing new forms
      4. Forms printing, purchasing, and inventory control
   E. Reports and directives control
      1. Analysis and evaluation of existing reports and directives
      2. Techniques for improving reports and directives
5. Records Maintenance
   A. Awareness of the status of "hard copy" and "automated" records
   B. Principles of records maintenance and retrieval systems
   C. Methods of surveying and inventorying records
      1. Utilization of professional records management consulting firms
      2. In-house inventorying
   D. Methods of sorting records
   E. Records classification systems and rules governing these systems
      1. Alphabetic
      2. Subject
      3. Numeric
      4. Geographic
      5. Other classification systems
   F. Technical records systems
      1. Medical
      2. Engineering
      3. Legal
      4. Industrial
      5. Other
   G. Equipment and supplies for maintaining records
   H. Centralized vs. decentralized records maintenance systems
   I. Basic steps of records maintenance
   J. Development and implementation of records retention schedules
      1. Appraisal of records
      2. Research of retention requirements
      3. Writing retention schedules
      4. Approval and implementation of schedules
   K. Records centers and methods of records transfer
      1. Transfer procedures

        2. Inventory and indexing procedures
        3. Designing and equipping records centers
        4. Records center operations
    L. Vital records storage
        1. Selecting vital records
        2. Vital records protection
        3. Vital records preservation
        4. Archival storage
    M. Records disposition
    N. Cost analysis of records maintenance
        1. Physical layout and space utilization
        2. Analysis of equipment and supplies
        3. Analysis of labor and overhead costs
6. Micrographics and Its Applications to Records Management
    A. Microforms
    B. Determining the feasibility of microfilm applications and systems
    C. Microfilm equipment and supplies
    D. Cost analysis of microfilm applications, equipment, and supplies
    E. Computer output microfilm
7. Career Opportunities in Records Management
    A. Job titles, duties, and responsibilities
    B. Qualifications required for records management positions
    C. In-service education and advancement

Association of Records Managers and Administrators, Inc.
Course Syllabus for
Records Management in High School

    I. Introduction to Records Management
        A. Why a business maintains files
            1. Need for storage of records
            2. Need to retrieve information
        B. The role of records management in today's world
            1. Importance
            2. Scope
            3. Purposes
    II. Nature of Business Records
        A. Correspondence
        B. Reports
        C. Forms
        D. Directives
        E. Microforms
        F. Computer output
    III. Records Inventorying Methods
        A. In-house vs. professional consulting firms
        B. Questionnaire vs. physical inventory
    IV. Basic Rules for Various Records Classification Systems
        A. Terms Used
        B. Rules for
            1. Alphabetic

    2. Geographic

    3. Subject

    4. Numeric (straight number, chronological, terminal digit, middle digit)

    5. Phonetic systems such as Soundex

    6. Cross referencing

    7. Follow-up

V. Records Storage and Retrieval Procedures

  A. Procedures for maintaining a records system

    1. Guides

    2. Folders

    3. Placement of materials in folders

    4. Active and inactive materials

  B. Handling of material

    1. Notations for signaling materials ready for filing

    2. Procedures for preparing materials for file

      a. Inspecting

      b. Indexing

      c. Coding

      d. Sorting

      e. Labeling folder

      f. Inserting material into folder

    3. Retrieval procedures

    4. Steps for locating a missing record

  C. Special types of materials

    1. Computer tape files

    2. Microforms

VI. Hardware and Software

  A. Hardware

    1. Drawer files

    2. Open-shelf files

    3. Desk files

    4. Card files

    5. Rotary files

    6. Visible files

    7. Vertical files

    8. Power files

    9. Automated retrieval systems

    10. Mechanical systems

  B. Software that accompanies each type of hardware

VII. Using a Records Manual

  A. Organization chart

  B. Company policies

  C. Records inventory

  D. Retention schedule

  E. Rules for records classification systems

VIII. Retention and Disposition of Records

  A. Permanent record identification

  B. Retention period for various records

  C. Identification of active and inactive records

  D. Implementation of retention schedule

  E. Purging files according to company policy

F. Transfer and storage of records
G. Disposition of records

IX. The Records Center
  A. Reasons for having a records center
  B. Facility requirements
  C. Equipment
  D. Layout
  E. Commercial records centers
  F. Managing the records center
    1. Acquisitions
    2. Search and charge-out procedures
  G. Emergency planning

X. Fundamentals of Micrographics
  A. Basic elements
    1. Film
    2. Cameras
    3. Lens
    4. Resolution
    5. Reduction ratio
    6. Lighting and density
  B. Microforms
    1. Roll film
    2. Aperture cards
    3. Jackets
    4. Microfiche
  C. Film duplication
  D. COM (computer output microfilm)
  E. Advantages of microfilming

XI. Reprographics
  A. Processes
  B. Operating standards
  C. Characteristics of copy

XII. Mail Operations
  A. Organization and procedures
  B. Equipment
  C. Layout
  D. Cost considerations

XIII. Career Opportunities

At any of these levels, one survey course would not be sufficient training for any person going into records management. The courses outlined should be supplemented with such courses as office management, office systems, data processing, word processing, and business communications. Also appropriate would be additional specialized courses in micrographics, reprographics, and management information systems.

PROFESSIONAL DEVELOPMENT

Another significant development in the advancement of the profession of records management was the establishment of the Institute of Certified

Records Managers in 1975. The Institute is administered by a Board of Regents which is structured to include members from the private business sector, the federal government, state governments, city governments, and the academic community. The Institute has three sponsors: the Association of Records Managers and Administrators; the Society of American Archivists; and the National Association of State Archivists and Records Administrators.

In order to become a Certified Records Manager (CRM) a person must successfully complete a six-part examination, subscribe to the Institute's Code of Ethics, possess three years of experience in different elements of records management, and hold a baccalaureate degree from an accredited college level institution. At the discretion of the Board of Regents, experience may be substituted for education on the basis of two years of experience for one year of education. The following outline describes the six parts to the examination:

Part 1—Records Management Principles and Program Organization. This part of the exam is general in nature and applies to management principles and techniques as well as specific records management applications.

Part 2—Records Generation and Control. This part involves creation of documents: correspondence management, forms control and design, control of reports and directives, and reprographics.

Part 3—Active Records Retrieval, Systems, and Equipment. This part primarily covers filing principles, techniques, systems, and equipment.

Part 4—Records Retention Scheduling, Protection, and Records Centers. The emphasis in this part includes records disposition, inactive maintenance, and protection. Also covered are the records inventory, retention schedule, vital records, and archives.

Part 5—Technology of Records Management. The technological tools available to the records manager are covered in this part of the exam. These include microform, data processing, data communication, transmission systems, word processing, and systems analysis.

Part 6—Case Study. In this part, the applicant applies the subject matter contained in the other five parts. Case studies and practical exercises are given.

CONCLUSION

The future of records management is bright in the changing office environment. Technologies will change but the principles and objectives will remain the same: to provide information when and where it is needed at the lowest possible cost.

Without question, the future will involve using a wide variety of media —some not yet developed—for creating, storing, and retrieving the exploding wealth of information. Exciting new careers will emerge for our students of tomorrow. The contemporary records manager, with a depth of knowledge and experience in all facets of information technology, will be able to cope with and accept the challenges of the office of the future.

Part III
HUMAN RESOURCES

CHAPTER 11

Human Resources Development and Utilization

ZANE K. QUIBLE

Michigan State University, East Lansing

An organization's human resources are often its most precious commodity. Many organizations have found no better investment can be made than the development of its human resources.

Many people still have the mistaken notion that when given the opportunity, employees are quite capable of assuming most, if not all, of the responsibility for developing themselves. An abundance of evidence exists to indicate the erroneous nature of this attitude.

The results of ineffective human resources development and/or the poor utilization of human resources are reflected in many different ways. Employees tend to have high turnover rates. Their work is produced at slow rates and is of poor quality. Employees tend to have a poor attitude about their jobs and their employers. They derive little or no satisfaction from their jobs. The list is almost infinite. Each of these situations can cost even the smallest organization thousands of dollars annually.

The actual cost of human resources developmental activities is considerably less than the value gained from the expenditure. Unfortunately, it is sometimes difficult to calculate in terms of dollars and cents the actual return on the investment. Human resources development often results in residual benefits that cannot be easily calculated in monetary terms.

HUMAN NEEDS IN THE WORK ENVIRONMENT

Man, by nature, has insatiable needs. A good number of these needs can be fulfilled by work and the environment in which work takes place. Money, which is a basic reason most people work, is needed to fulfill certain types of needs. Other types of needs cannot be satisfied with money.

Maslow's Hierarchy of Needs[1] is often used by behavioral scientists as a basis when studying human needs. According to Maslow, five different levels of human needs exist:

Physiological needs
Safety needs

[1]Data based on Hierarchy of Needs in "A Theory of Human Motivation" in *Motivation and Personality*, Second edition, by Abraham H. Maslow. Copyright © 1970 by Abraham H. Maslow. By permission of Harper & Row, Publishers, Inc.

110

Belonging and love needs

Esteem needs

Self-actualization needs

These five levels of needs are arranged in a hierarchical order. The higher-level needs (esteem and self-actualization) are not important until lower-level needs (physiological and safety) have been fulfilled. Thus, one will not be concerned about the nonfulfillment of esteem needs until safety needs have been fulfilled, for example.

Physiological needs include such factors as food, water, oxygen, rest, muscular activity, and freedom from extreme temperatures. In an industrial society, the wages and salaries derived from one's work are used to satisfy several of the physiological needs. Prolonged deprivation of most of the physiological needs jeopardizes the life of the human body.

Safety needs have two dimensions: physical and psychological. The physical dimension involves clothing, shelter, and freedom from danger. Money is typically necessary to obtain clothing and shelter.

The psychological dimension of safety needs includes job security and most fringe benefits. The environment of the work place is likely to have a direct impact on the amount of job security an employee feels is present. An environment which produces a feeling of job security among employees is much healthier psychologically than one which does not produce such a feeling.

Belonging and love needs become important once physiological and safety needs have been satisfied. This category includes the need for belonging to a group, the need for companionship, the need for love or affection, and the need for socialization.

The environment in which employees work is especially important for satisfying the need for belonging to a group and the need for socializing. The effective manager or supervisor realizes the important role played by the work environment in fulfilling belonging and love needs.

Esteem needs are also affected by the environment in which employees work. Esteem needs, like safety needs, have two dimensions: self-esteem and the esteem of others.

The self-esteem needs include one's desire for achievement, self-respect, confidence, and mastery. The esteem of others includes recognition, attention, prestige, and status. While self-esteem needs are internal, esteem needs tend to be external.

If the work environment thwarts one's esteem needs, employees tend to feel dejected, useless, and incompetent. If an employee experiences these feelings for a long period of time, behavior of a hostile or neurotic nature may result.

Self-actualization needs, the highest of the five levels of human needs, are the most difficult for employees to satisfy. Self-actualization refers to a person's ability to become the individual one is capable of becoming. In essence, it is one's ability to achieve maximum potential.

Several factors inherent in the work environment may be responsible for one's inability to fulfill the self-actualization needs. One common factor is the job itself. The jobs of some employees make it impossible to achieve maximum potential. Another factor is the absence of development activities designed to help employees reach their maximum. A third factor inherent in the work environment that sometimes thwarts the fulfillment of employees' self-actualization needs is the seniority system. Such systems typically promote people on the basis of their longevity with the organization rather than on the basis of their work performance. A final reason some employees are unable to fulfill their self-actualization needs occurs when their goals and ambitions are set at a level higher than their abilities will permit them to achieve.

Managers and supervisors who are responsible for directing others should have a clear understanding of human needs. The more clearly managers and supervisors understand human needs, the more effective they are likely to be in their relations with others.

The fact that human needs vary considerably from one person to another makes it especially important for managers and supervisors to be astute in recognizing individual needs. To do so will result in a much more effective utilization of human resources.

EMPLOYEE COMPENSATION

The effective utilization of human resources presupposes that employees receive wages and salaries consistent with the demands of the jobs they perform. To pay employees less than the worth of the job is a managerial practice that cannot be condoned. Employee morale and the satisfaction they derive from their jobs are likely to suffer, resulting in poor quality work and low production rates.

The practice of paying wages and salaries consistent with job demands has several positive outcomes. Employee turnover is reduced. Employees are motivated to perform at higher levels. Employees are more satisfied with their jobs and the work they perform.

The basis of employee compensation is job evaluation. Before an equitable compensation system can be developed, the relative worth of the job has to be determined, which is the primary purpose of job evaluation. The greater the job's contribution to the organization, the greater is the job's evaluated worth. While job evaluation determines the basis of the compensation, a salary administration process determines the rate of compensation. Several job evaluation techniques exist, including ranking, job grading, factor comparison, and the point method.

When determining compensation rates for specific jobs, several factors must be considered, including the following: relative worth of the job, competitive wage rates for comparable jobs, cost of living index, wage and salary legislation, and collective bargaining.

Relative worth of the job. Determining the relative worth of a job is basically a job evaluation process. Employees deserve and have the right to expect that their salaries are properly related to the demands of their jobs and to the salaries paid to employees performing other jobs in the organization. Salary inequities, either real or imagined, result in lower employee morale.

Competitive wage rates for comparable jobs. To be able to hire competent employees, competitive wage rates for comparable jobs in the community must be considered. Depending on the community, a variety of prepared salary surveys can be utilized. In communities for which prepared surveys do not exist, an organization may have to conduct its own survey.

Some of the prepared surveys useful for determining competitive wage rates for office positions include the following:

National Survey of Professional, Administrative, Technical, and Clerical Pay conducted annually by the Bureau of Labor Statistics. Included are salary data for 81 different positions as well as brief descriptions and information about fringe benefits.

Compensation Comparisons—Industrial and Financial Management compiled by Edward N. Hay and Associates. This data, which is also updated annually, summarizes trends in the employment practices of exempt (from minimum wage and overtime pay requirements of the Fair Labor Standards Act) executive, management, and technical employees.

Directory of Office Salaries prepared by the Administrative Management Society includes salary data on 20 commonly found office and data processing positions. The directory, which is updated annually, provides the weekly salaries for each of the 20 positions in the cities in which an AMS chapter is found. The directory also provides regional average salaries and nationwide averages for each of the 20 positions, as well as information on fringe benefits.

AMS Guide to Management Compensation, another survey compiled by the Administrative Management Society, provides salary data on 20 key exempt middle management positions. This survey also provides information on fringe benefits and on trends in company policies regarding hours of work, paid vacations, holidays, and pension plans.

Cost of living index. A basic factor used by many organizations in making compensation decisions, the cost of living index is more frequently used for determining salary increases than for determining base salaries. Its use is even more frequent during times of inflation since an adjustment of employees' salaries by the amount of the index enables them to maintain their purchasing power.

With increasing frequency, wage negotiation between labor and management involves an escalator clause. The use of an escalator clause means that the salaries are mathematically tied to the cost of living index. Such clauses frequently stipulate that when the cost of living index increases by a given percentage, employees' wages will automatically increase by a specified amount, which is generally the amount of the increase in the index.

Wage and salary legislation. From time to time, federal legislation impacting on employee compensation is passed. Included are such acts as the Fair Labor Standards Act (which requires the payment of minimum wages and overtime pay) and the Equal Pay Act (which forbids paying members of one sex less than the members of the other sex when the tasks performed by both sexes are equal).

The first significant legislation affecting compensation was passed in the 1930's. Since that time, Congress has on three occasions enacted legislation that froze salaries and controlled the amount of salary increases.

Collective bargaining. Employee compensation practices in organizations in which collective bargaining is found are different from those practices found in nonunionized organizations. Base salaries and the amounts of salary increases in unionized organizations are agreed upon by labor and management, which involves the process of negotiation.

Historically, organizations with unionized employees are often thought to be responsible for setting salary trends. These trends have to be followed by the nonunionized organizations if a competitive position is to be maintained.

Once the relative worth of each job is determined, a chart is prepared that depicts the monetary worth of jobs on the vertical axis and the relative worth of jobs on the horizontal axis. Marks are placed on the chart at the point where the monetary worth and the relative worth of each job intersect one another. Drawing a straight line on the chart at the point where an equal number of marks are above and below the line identifies the organization's average compensation line. An identical chart is prepared for comparable jobs in other organizations in the community. The compensation line for the organization and the compensation line for the community are subsequently compared. An analysis of the two compensation lines identifies how much more or less the organization pays than the average salaries for comparable jobs in other companies in the community. The organization then determines the need for an adjustment in base salaries as well as the amount of the adjustment.

After the official compensation line has been decided upon, a salary range for each job is determined. The range is usually fixed at a certain percentage above (range maximum) and below (range minimum) the average salary for each job. The use of overlapping salary ranges for similar jobs accommodates the promotion of employees into high-level jobs that pay higher salaries.

EMPLOYEE APPRAISAL AND EVALUATION

The appraisal of employee performance is another important dimension of human resources development. Making employees aware of their weaknesses is likely to motivate them to improve and subsequently overcome their weaknesses. And when employees are made aware of their strengths, reinforcement occurs. Another reason for using employee appraisal is that human nature causes people to want to know how they are performing in their jobs; the absence of such information results in insecurity.

Throughout the years, many techniques have been developed for use in formally appraising employee performance. Some of these are graphic rating scales, peer ratings, results-oriented appraisals, and field review appraisals.

Graphic rating scales. The graphic rating scale is the most widely used technique of employee appraisal. As its name implies, a rating scale is used on which performance traits or characteristics and qualitative values (superior, above-average, etc.) are identified. The rater, most often the employee's supervisor, determines the degree to which the employee possesses each trait or characteristic present on the scale.

The graphic rating scale is not without limitations. It is often difficult, if not impossible, to assign a weight to each trait or characteristic. Consequently, each is treated equally, when in reality it is doubtful that each trait or characteristic is equally important to one's job.

Another difficulty inherent in graphic rating scales is that raters often have different perceptions of the qualitative elements. What is "excellent" performance to one rater may be "average" or only "slightly above average" to another. A fairly realistic way of overcoming this deficiency is the use of descriptive phrases (for example, "consistently completes assigned tasks at a fast pace") rather than the descriptive words.

The objectivity of graphic rating scales can be enhanced by randomizing the qualitative values on the rating scale. To place the same qualitative values in a straight vertical or horizontal line makes it too easy for the rater to assign the individual being rated the same qualitative value for each trait or characteristic when differences, in fact, do exist. Such rating practices inject bias into the rating process.

Peer rating. One of the newer appraisal techniques, peer rating utilizes co-workers to evaluate one's performance. A distinguishing characteristic of this technique is that co-workers often see a different type of behavior/performance pattern than do supervisors. This technique is perhaps most effectively used when a new group leader has to be chosen from the members of a work group.

Results-oriented appraisal technique. The results-oriented appraisal technique is perhaps the most psychologically sound of all the techniques. With this technique, the supervisor and employee mutually set goals or objectives designed to help the employee improve his/her performance. A certain amount of time is allotted for fulfilling each goal. The goals mutually agreed upon by the employee and the supervisor must be measurable.

At periodic intervals, perhaps every six months, the supervisor assesses the degree to which the employee's goals have been achieved. Those goals which have been satisfied are no longer viable goals. The goals which have not been satisfied continue as goals for the next evaluation period. In some instances, unmet goals are restructured. If employees desire a more frequent feedback interval or if the situation warrants more frequent feedback, informal evaluation of goal achievement may take place every month or every three months.

As an evaluation technique, results-oriented appraisal is psychologically sound. Whereas other techniques concentrate on the past, the results-oriented technique concentrates on the future. Therefore, employees know they start anew each evaluation period.

Field review technique. The field review technique is one of the newer techniques discussed in this chapter. This technique uses an objective outsider, usually someone from the personnel department, to conduct the appraisal. The employee whose performance is being evaluated and the employee's supervisor are questioned orally about the level of performance.

The field review technique provides assurance that quality evaluation procedures are utilized since the evaluators are skilled in the appraisal process. It also results in fairly uniform, consistent ratings. No longer is there a concern about the validity of ratings provided by overly lenient or overly strict supervisors.

Once the appraisal process has been completed, an appraisal interview should be conducted. The purpose of the interview is to develop and facilitate two-way communication between the supervisor and his/her subordinates. It also enables the employee being rated to learn about the results of the appraisal. Sometimes appropriate courses of action designed to help the employee overcome weaknesses or shortcomings are also discussed. Consequently, the appraisal process takes on a new dimension in human resources development.

TECHNIQUES OF HUMAN RESOURCES DEVELOPMENT

Human resources development has several components. We have seen that human needs in the work environment play a significant role in the development process. Employee compensation, another aspect of human resources development, also has a significant impact. Employee appraisal helps employees develop their performance efficiency. Each of these three components has an indirect impact on human resources development.

The training and development programs provided for employees is another vital component of human resources development, the result of which has a direct impact on improving employee performance. Other components having a direct impact on human resources development are employee orientation and employee counseling. Each of these three topics is discussed in the following sections.

Employee orientation. The purpose of employee orientation is to help individuals adjust more readily to their new jobs and to the organization in which they work. Well-designed orientation activities result in a reduction of the number of errors employees make as well as increase the amount of job satisfaction and security employees derive from their positions.

Employee orientation programs are comprised of a number of topics, including the following:

1. History of the organization
2. Purpose and functions of the departments which comprise the organization
3. Important policies of the organization
4. Goals of the organization and the departments
5. New and future developments in the organization's products/services
6. Compensation and fringe benefits
7. Promotion opportunities and procedures.

Many organizations have instituted a "buddy" plan for their new employees. The plan involves the assigning of an experienced employee to each

116

new employee. The "buddy" is used to answer any question the new employee has but is reluctant to ask the supervisor.

Employee counseling. Another activity impacting directly on human resources development is employee counseling. The areas in which supervisors provide counseling must be judiciously screened. The lack of supervisory experience and training has produced some rather negative results in employee counseling. To overcome this deficiency, many supervisors, as part of their development process, receive instruction in employee counseling.

Training techniques. Over the years, a variety of techniques have been developed for training employees. The following provides a discussion of several of these techniques.

THE LECTURE METHOD involves unilateral communication between the lecturer and the audience. Used properly, the lecture method can be a very useful training technique. In terms of cost, it is very economical. Other advantages are the large amount of information that can be presented in a short period of time, and that learners can be exposed to outstanding practitioners or experts.

The lecture method is not without weaknesses or criticism. Rarely does this method provide for individual learner differences nor are there many provisions for learner feedback, reinforcement, or practice. The success of the lecture method is determined by the ability of the lecturer. Generally, the lecture method can be enhanced by utilizing audience participation and visual devices.

PROGRAMMED INSTRUCTION, as a training technique, is especially useful for training employees in certain phases of office work. Nowadays, two formats of programmed instruction exist: textbook material and teaching machines. In either case, the learner responds to a question after which the correct response is made available to the learner. If the response is correct, the learner proceeds to the next sequence. If not, the learner is asked to either (1) review the material about which the incorrect response was given or (2) read additional material in the programmed unit.

Psychologically, programmed instruction is very sound. Learners receive immediate feedback, they can proceed through the material at their own pace, and they take an active role in the learning process. Disadvantages result from a lack of programmed materials. Developing such materials is an expensive, time-consuming, and laborious process.

CLOSED-CIRCUIT TELEVISION is becoming increasingly popular as a training technique. The organization either prepares its own tapes or purchases prepared tapes. The tapes can be used for training office employees in nearly any phase of office work.

As a training technique, closed-circuit television is especially useful for showing close-up shots of work processes and for showing human interaction. A primary advantage of the technique is its one-time preparation cost and its availability for almost continuous use.

COLLEGE-LEVEL REFRESHER COURSES are becoming a more important training technique. In some instances, the course may be taught within the organization, while in other instances, the course might be taught at an educational institution. Such courses cover a variety of topics. One of the unique characteristics of such courses is the extreme flexibility in their design. The fact that such courses are generally taught by educational personnel adds to their effectiveness.

ROLE PLAYING, because of its play-acting nature, is especially useful in teaching employees how to handle a variety of human relations problems. When this technique is used for training, some of the learners assume the role of the individuals involved in a given situation. Other learners not involved in the role-playing situation have an opportunity to assess the suitability of the actions of the learners involved in the role-playing skit.

Perhaps the greatest advantage of role playing is the immediate personal interest it generates. Its limitations include its time-consuming nature and the fact that only a few learners can be actively involved at one time.

THE CASE METHOD involves giving the learners a description of certain conditions about either a hypothetical organization or a real organization. The learners are asked to analyze the situation, to identify problems, to develop solutions, and to make recommendations. The fact that each learner is involved results in an active learning situation.

The primary advantages of the case method are the provisions for fairly immediate feedback and the frequent transfer of learning from the training situation to the real situation. The technique can be criticized because it generally does not allow teaching of principles nor does it typically provide learners with all the information they need for realistic problem solving.

THE INCIDENT METHOD is closely related to the case method. When the incident method is used, the learners are given a minimum of information concerning the situation being considered. The learners have to ask the trainer questions in order to obtain the information they need to solve the problem. When the learners feel they have sufficient information, they concentrate their efforts on solving the problem. The crux of this technique is the ability of the learners to ask the *right* questions. At the conclusion of the problem-solving phase, the trainer discusses with the learners other pieces of information they needed to solve the problem but failed to obtain.

BUSINESS GAMES are especially useful for training learners about the economic processes of an industry, an organization, or a subunit of an organization. The technique utilizes a set of rules developed from economic theory or from the financial operations of an industry or an organization. The set of rules determines how various input variables (raw materials, capital, equipment, personnel, etc.), along with certain mediating variables (wages, finished product prices, and advertising expenses), affect the output variables (quantity sold, amount of profit, and net worth.) The learners determine the product prices, the budgeted amount for advertising, the amount of new equipment to purchase, the number of new employees to hire, and so forth. To add realism to the situation, many business games utilize a computer.

A definite advantage of business games is their very realistic nature. On the disadvantages side are the gadgetry image and their tendency to be time consuming.

118

THE IN-BASKET has been found especially useful for training office employees in the areas of problem solving and decision making. The information used in the in-basket is representative of the materials that would accumulate in one's desk in-basket over a two- or three-week period. The information is likely to consist of a variety of internal and external communications, reports, and other documents. The learner is asked to decide on the priority of each situation in the in-basket as well as recommend how each situation should be expedited.

The technique is especially advantageous because of its realistic nature in developing decision-making skills. A primary disadvantage of the technique results from the fact that it is not especially useful for teaching general principles.

THE EDUCATION-EMPLOYER COOPERATIVE TRAINING TECHNIQUE combines formal classes with on-the-job experience. Cooperative training, which is typically found at high school and college levels, enables students to be enrolled in school and at the same time have part-time employment. The school experiences teach the learners how various tasks are carried out. The on-the-job experience gives the students an opportunity to put their knowledge into practice. The learners receive direction from both the employers and the coordinators.

The most distinctive advantage of this technique is the realism which it provides. On the negative side is the feeling some employers have about investing in learners who may not continue to work for them once the cooperative experience ends.

ON-THE-JOB COACHING is a commonly used method for training office employees. When this technique is used, the learner's supervisor is also the trainer. No other technique is likely to be as realistic as this technique. Because the success of the technique is greatly dependent upon the supervisor who assumes the training role, many supervisory training experiences include sessions on how to become more effective trainers.

CERTIFICATION PROGRAMS OF RELATED PROFESSIONAL ORGANIZATIONS

A variety of associations and organizations sponsor professional certification programs. These programs enhance the professionalism of employees by providing evidence that certificate holders have met certain professional qualifications and criteria. Each program requires the passage of an exam, and most also have education and work experience requirements. These programs have had a positive effect on the development of human resources.

The following is a list of several certifying programs as well as the names and addresses of the sponsoring associations or organizations.

Certified Professional Secretary, sponsored by the Institute for Certifying Secretaries, a department of The National Secretaries Association (International), Crown Center G10, 2440 Pershing Road, Kansas City, MO 64108

Professional Standards Program, sponsored by the National Association of Educational Secretaries, 1801 North Moore Street, Arlington, VA 22209

Professional Legal Secretary, sponsored by The National Association of Legal Secretaries (International), 3005 East Skelly Drive, Suite 120, Tulsa, OK 74105

Certified Legal Assistant, sponsored by the National Association of Legal Assistants, Inc., 3005 East Skelly Drive, Tulsa, OK 74105

Certified Medical Assistant, sponsored by The American Association of Medical Assistants, Inc., One Wacker Drive, Suite 2110, Chicago, IL 60601

Certified Administrative Manager, sponsored by the Administrative Management Society, Willow Grove, PA 19090

Certified Records Manager, sponsored by the Institute of Certified Records Managers, P. O. Box 89, Washington, DC 20044

Certified Public Accountant, sponsored by the American Institute of Certified Public Accountants, 1211 Avenue of the Americas, New York, NY 10036

Certificate in Management Accounting, sponsored by the Institute of Management Accounting of the National Association of Accountants, 570 City Center Building, Ann Arbor, MI 48104

Certified Internal Auditor, sponsored by The Institute of Internal Auditors, Inc., 249 Maitland Avenue, Altamonte Springs, FL 32701

Chartered Property Casualty Underwriter, sponsored by the American Institute for Property and Liability Underwriters and the Insurance Institute of America, Providence & Sugartown Roads, Malvern, PA 19355

Chartered Life Underwriter, sponsored by the American College of Life Underwriters, Bryn Mawr, PA 19010

Certificate in Computer Programming, sponsored by the Institute for Certification of Computer Professionals, 35 East Wacker Drive, Chicago, IL 60601

Certificate in Data Processing, sponsored by the Institute for Certification of Computer Professionals, 35 East Wacker Drive, Chicago, IL 60601

SUMMARY

Effective development and utilization of human resources is crucial in any organization. Failure to effectively develop and utilize employees causes many problems of a significant magnitude. The overall effect of these problems is likely to be felt throughout the organization for a period of time after the problems have been resolved.

A distinguishing characteristic of effective supervisors or managers is their ability to develop and utilize their subordinates. This characteristic is often one of the most—if not the most—important characteristic looked for when judging the effectiveness of individuals as supervisors or managers.

The role of human resources is basic to the office operation. Students in office management programs, as well as business teacher education programs, need to understand the need for and the techniques of human resources development and utilization.

CHAPTER 12

Physical Environment in the Office

DAVID J. HYSLOP

Bowling Green State University, Bowling Green, Ohio

Although changes have occurred rapidly in many areas of office procedures and administration, perhaps no area has seen more changes than that of the physical environment of today's offices. A vast array of new office furniture and equipment, accentuated through the use of pleasing and colorful layouts, has made the office a dynamic and functional place to work or visit. Some of these changes may seem subtle to the casual observer; but others, such as open landscaping, may seem quite revolutionary when compared with the environment of older offices.

Changes have occurred (and are still occurring!) in nearly every phase of the physical environment of the office—from office design to the use of lighting, air and sound conditioning, and security systems, to name a few. The use of modern equipment, such as text-editing, telecommunications, reprographic and micrographic equipment, has had a major impact on the office through changes in work procedures and office design. The concern for the physical factors in an office has also fostered greater study and interest in the effect of the physical environment on the worker—a field of study termed ergonomics. In its simple meaning, ergonomics is defined as the application and integration of all the necessary factors that contribute to a productive and satisfying work environment. Ergonomics, therefore, attempts to examine *all* physical elements in the office environment to help increase human capability and performance, thus making the office a more efficient and effective place of work.

The intent of this chapter is to examine key components in the physical environment of the office and to highlight changes that have occurred during the past few years.

PHYSICAL LAYOUT OF THE OFFICE

The design of any office is, or should be, shaped largely by the work performed and the needs and desires of the people who will work or visit there. Planning and organizing an efficient, economical office layout is an important task and requires careful and continuous study. No one physical layout would be appropriate for all offices: what may work well for one office could be inappropriate for another. What may be effective for an office today may not be the best layout at some time in the future.

There are several factors to consider when selecting the right design for an office. These include:

The space requirements and available space. The office layout must provide adequate space for each employee in order to facilitate the employee's work requirements. The actual space provided will vary, of course, according to the space available, the furniture and equipment used, the type(s) of work space needed, and the nature of the work to be performed. The space requirement usually begins at a minimum of 100 square feet for each person and may go as high as 400 to 500 square feet for the office of a major executive. (It is important to note that office space frequently relates to the hierarchical levels of the office: that is, the higher the individual is on the organization chart, the larger the office will be.)

When determining space requirements, it is helpful to look at communication patterns and work flow within the office. Work flow is the movement of information between people, including the routing of paperwork and work processes that occur. The communication patterns include the necessity and frequency of communications that occur when completing a given task. These patterns can include all types of communication: phone messages, personal contacts, or written messages. A logical office arrangement is one where employees who have need for frequent communication are located in close proximity to one another so that work flow activities require a minimum of travel steps.

The number and types of employees to be accommodated. All present employees must have sufficient space in which to work efficiently. A good office layout may also reflect future manpower needs, especially if a great deal of expansion (or contraction) is anticipated. Allowances for each employee, based on the employee's position in the office organization, are normally made and considered a part of the fringe benefits or prestige that accompany the position.

The work areas needed within the office. The modern office usually has a variety of work areas ranging from individual work stations to reception areas, conference rooms, mail rooms, equipment rooms, and the like. Each work area will require an appropriate layout and should be individually planned. Some offices also have divided work areas or even more specialized areas. For example, one corporate president requested that his new work area accommodate three distinct meeting situations: one for discussions from his desk, another for more relaxed discussions across a coffee table, and a third in an adjoining formal miniconference room.

The importance of appearance and prestige. If an office is to be thought of as a pleasing and efficient place to work or visit, the layout must be constructed to achieve this effect. Many office designers realize that the appearance the office projects can favorably or unfavorably affect both the office employees and clients. People normally have pride in an office that is neat, clean, and attractive; clients normally associate an attractive office with one that is efficient, up to date, and reputable.

122

OPEN OFFICE LANDSCAPING

The open landscaping (or open concept) is a result of the concern for making the office an attractive and functional place to work. This layout originated approximately 19 years ago and calls for the elimination of most fixed walls—creating a large open area which is divided into work stations by acoustical partitions. Whereas the traditional office design focused on the desk and the enclosed office, this design highlights the concept of work stations and the need to have work areas follow natural lines of work flow and communications.

The use of open office landscaping has been growing at an impressive rate. Many existing offices are being converted to this concept while new offices are being planned using the concept. As of 1980, close to half of all office construction in the United States is being designed along the open landscape model, substituting work station modules for conventional rectangular desks and immovable walls and fixtures.

The central part of the open landscape is the work center. It is in the work center that each employee accomplishes his/her work. Unlike the traditional desk, the work center is a combination communications, equipment, and records center in which the employee has, within arm's reach, the tools needed to complete whatever work is assigned. Of course, the work center will still have an area comparable to the traditional desk, but it will *also* have whatever other equipment and furniture are needed. The work center can be thought of as a self-contained area, in contrast to the traditional arrangement in which a worker may have to travel away from the desk area to use equipment, files, etc.

With the expanded use of text-editing equipment, word processing concepts, telecommunication technology, and the computer, the work center can be a highly efficient area where the employee can function far better than at the traditional work desk. Designers of work-center furniture have been careful to study the optimum arrangement of people, furniture, and equipment so that each center requires a minimal number of worker motions and amount of time to complete a task.

Along with the work center, other office furniture is also an integral part of the open office. Manufacturers of modular furniture are designing more functional and flexible furniture to meet the ever-changing needs of the office. With many major firms producing this new furniture, a variety of styles, designs, and colors are available. Instead of providing employees with several different desks, tables, or files, modular furniture attaches additional work areas to the central area or within close proximity. Some work centers take on the final design of a U-shaped configuration, in which the employee has the center area for the major part of his/her work and both sides available for expanded work activities or the installation of equipment and/or files.

Partitions are also an important part of the open office concept. Partitions are used to enclose a work area and simultaneously provide acoustical control, privacy, and line-of-sight geography. Line-of-sight geography features the capability of visually observing the various work centers from a distant site and may be very important for the office with a myriad of work centers or one which clients have to frequent.

Perhaps the greatest advantage of using partitions is that privacy is provided as well as openness. The acoustical quality of the partitions mutes ordinary conversations or equipment noise so that distractions to other employees are minimized.

Partitions are available in many different textures, colors, patterns, and prices. Firms can select from partitions which are curved or straight, flush to the floor, or raised off the floor with legs. They are available in various heights and sizes, and may be free standing, ceiling suspended, spring loaded, or interconnecting at various angles. Partitions are usually flame retardant and have various noise reduction coefficients.

EVALUATION OF OPEN OFFICE LANDSCAPING

Advantages. Most people agree that when properly planned and executed, open office landscaping allows organizations to change office layout faster and less expensively than when there are walls to be moved. This high degree of flexibility may be extremely important to growing organizations which experience continual staffing changes and reorganization. The cost of rearrangement in the open office landscaping is considerably less expensive than the cost of remodeling or rearranging fixed office spaces. Less rearrangement or down time is experienced when reconfiguring an open office as compared to the conventional office, thus producing a savings.

For new office construction, the open concept can also be cheaper. Not only are the building costs cheaper (as much as $10 per square foot), but the open concept also frees more floor space.

Another advantage cited by many users of open office landscaping is improved worker efficiency. This benefit may result from improved communication processes and more efficient work routing and work flow. Supporters of this concept contend that it results in increased communication within the office, especially between supervisor and subordinate. Furthermore, work and information can flow faster because workers and work stations can be grouped to achieve maximum efficiency.

A last advantage claimed by proponents of this concept is the greater emphasis on making the office a pleasant and attractive place to work. Many firms add color and variety to the office environment by using plants, small shrubs, paintings, pictures, and other decorations along with the open concept.

Disadvantages. Not all people are thoroughly convinced of the merits of open landscaping. Some feel that not enough privacy is afforded to employees, which can make personal conversations difficult. Although the acoustical partitions provide some privacy, they may not allow enough. Consequently, employees may be unwilling to communicate naturally or may go elsewhere to conduct personal or private business.

A second concern of office personnel is the lack of a private office—long regarded as a status symbol attached to a particular position. For business people used to having their own offices, the fear of losing this status symbol could serve as a demotivator.

Another frequently mentioned concern with open landscaping is the necessity for closeness or togetherness in the physical arrangement. Apart from privacy, some employees feel they can function better when working alone or in an enclosed environment. They resent the notion of working within sight and sound of a supervisor and feel this arrangement may contribute to tenseness or a feeling of being analyzed or observed. This feeling can greatly affect office productivity and harmony.

OFFICE LIGHTING

Information processing in any office requires a sufficient quantity and quality of light. It is widely known that lighting can have both a physical and psychological effect on employees. The values or benefits to be gained by proper lighting can include (1) greater productivity (2) better work quality, (3) reduced fatigue and eye strain, and (4) increased morale.

The quantity of light in an office, as measured by *foot candles*, is extremely important in allowing employees to see clearly, quickly, and easily. Sufficient lighting, however, should always be related to the task being performed. Tasks involving a high degree of detail or study (such as bookkeeping or accounting) will require more illumination than tasks not associated with detailed work. The individual differences, if any, among employees should not be overlooked when considering a lighting system. Some employees may need—or prefer—more illumination in their work areas.

A more recent approach to office lighting is to use *task lighting*. Rather than having *all* areas of an office with identical illumination, only work (or task) areas requiring high light quantity are so illuminated. Other areas (such as passages, aisle ways, storage) do not receive as great a quantity of light—on the theory that less light is actually needed. Some newer office buildings are including task lighting as part of construction specifications, using the apparent energy savings from reduced lighting as justification. Existing offices, however, may not realize any economic advantage because of the cost incurred in changing to task lighting.

An equally important aspect of lighting is that of quality. Lighting possesses good quality when it is relatively free from glare and is diffused evenly throughout the work area. The brightness of the light should be fairly uniform throughout the work area or else excessive eye strain, caused by frequent dilation and contraction of the pupils, may result.

A number of lighting plans may be chosen for an office. Lighting may be direct or semidirect, with all or most of the light coming directly from the source to the working area. Or light may be indirect or semi-indirect, with all or most of the light reflected from the ceiling downward to work areas. A last possibility is that of general diffuse lighting where the light is diffused both to the work areas and to the ceiling. Thus general diffuse lighting combines both the features of the direct and indirect lighting and is used widely in offices today.

Fluorescent lighting provides evenly diffused lighting, reduces glare, and is economical. Fluorescent tubes last longer than filament bulbs, generate less heat, and use less electrical current.

SOUND CONDITIONING

Another important environmental factor in the office is sound conditioning which includes procedures to reduce or eliminate excessive noise. Controlling the noise in an office can be attained by different means: reducing or eliminating the source of the noise, using sound-absorbing materials, or using a masking system to make the noise less noticeable. (The best way to eliminate noise is not to create it in the first place. This can, in part, be accomplished by having an appropriate office layout.)

What is excessive noise? Normally, any noise can be termed excessive if it exceeds a specified decibel level or if it causes distractions which interfere with employee work capabilities. Sudden, short-lived noise can be just as harmful from a production point of view as longer, more intense noise. The most desirable range of noise is from 40 to 50 decibels. At this level the noise is not greatly noticeable and should not interfere with employees' work. Higher noise levels, associated with office equipment or machines, may result in reduced efficiency caused by a lack of concentration and greater fatigue.

Reducing or eliminating the source of the noise, although not always possible, may be accomplished by isolating noisy equipment or initially selecting machines and equipment that are free of noise. If this approach is not feasible, a second alternative is to soundproof the work area so that the noise does not travel excessively. This soundproofing can be accomplished by using specially constructed materials for walls, ceilings, or floor areas.

A third possible way to reduce noise level is to mask out extraneous or unwanted noise. Masking involves the use of a constant, but muted, sound which is evenly distributed throughout the office area. Usually a speaker system can be used to distribute the masked sound, which is also called white noise.

MUSIC IN THE OFFICE

Music can serve as an environmental aid because it has the ability to soothe emotions and give a physical and psychological lift to employees. The use of music has increased over the years and has also been expanded for use on telephone systems in some offices.

Basically, music is designed to reduce fatigue caused by strain, job monotony, or general tiredness from long periods of work. By relieving fatigue and job monotony, the hoped-for result is one of increased productivity and job satisfaction. Some firms specializing in the installation of music systems give glowing reports on successes achieved by firms using music. These successes have included increased job satisfaction, lower absenteeism, fewer clerical errors, and increased productivity. Although it may be impossible to predict that these results will occur in every office, it does appear that using music may, at least, provide some advantages for the office that uses it.

A variety of music systems are available for use in the modern office. Some new offices use their own source of music (tapes, stereo systems) piped throughout the office using a public address system. Others purchase their music from a specialized firm, such as Muzak, and a small office may rely on a conventional radio for its musical selections.

A major part of the success of music lies in its programming and use. Music should be related to the desires of employees and should reflect the mood and temperament at any given time. Normally, music is programmed to match the body cues of individuals; it may be cheerful and bright in early morning, to encourage swift movements, and become more subdued by midmorning, a time generally associated as a peak in the worker's performance cycle. Later in the day, similar changes in programming are made to ward off employee fatigue and boredom.

The music a firm uses is normally orchestrated arrangements with limited vocal selections. The music is intended to soothe, so it should not be loud or distracting. Employees should not consciously be listening to the music or else their attention to a task will be lessened. A novel approach to creating music for everybody was taken by one firm that issued stereo earphones to employees so they could listen to the music of their choice without distracting others in the office!

COLOR CONSIDERATIONS

Color is an important variable in an office design, particularly because of its relationship to other environmental factors such as lighting, furniture, layout, etc. Color is important, also, because it creates an aesthetic as well as functional effect for workers or visitors in an office.

Office colors must be chosen carefully for walls, floor coverings, drapes or curtains, and furniture. Although a variety of individual color plans can be wisely used, some general guidelines in color selection should be followed. Walls, ceilings, and other reflective surfaces should primarily use light, soft colors, such as light yellow or light green. Floors or carpet, since they have no reflective value, may be darker. To create a particular mood, certain colors can be selected. For example, the use of blue, green, or violet, associated with serenity or coolness, can help to create a calm, relaxed mood; warm colors such as red, orange, or yellow can suggest a cheerful, friendly atmosphere.

A noticeable trend in offices today is toward more color diversity, yet still retaining a coordinated color scheme. Color should be selected as carefully for an office as in decorating a new home. Fortunately, office design and furniture manufacturers have a wide choice of color schemes in their furnishings which will add life and interest to the physical environment.

CURRENT CONCERNS

Although many modifications have already been made in existing offices, the office is still in a state of transition. Some external and internal factors causing this continued transition include (1) the need to conserve energy, (2) the necessity to have flexibility in the work environment, (3) the desire for and stress on increased productivity, (4) necessary security precautions, and (5) the need to accommodate changing technology, especially equipment and communication innovations.

The need to conserve energy. Energy conservation has emerged as one of society's major goals and is perhaps overdue in the attention and concern that should have been given earlier to it. Our society has witnessed the effect of energy shortages and has seen how vulnerable we are to a shortage of natural resources. The national goal of increased awareness and policy formation to reduce energy consumption has affected how new offices and buildings are constructed and how they will operate. Designers and contractors are energy conscious in the materials they use, the physical design of the building, and the various systems (heating, lighting, ventilation) required to operate the building. Newer types of building materials are being identified which are capable of reducing energy consumption, thus resulting in conservation of our limited resources while still reducing office operating costs.

Controlling temperature, humidity, and ventilation are common considerations when attempting to reduce energy use. More energy-efficient heating, cooling, and ventilation systems are available today and should be investigated as possible energy savers. Computer-assisted systems can also help control energy use by instantaneously sensing the need for and reacting to changes in the environment. Some of the most common techniques for reducing energy today involve maintaining lower temperature settings during the work day, reducing the heat or air flow to rarely used or unoccupied work areas, and cutting back on utility requirements during nonworking hours, including weekends.

Another measure to save energy today is to reduce lighting. Many offices have eliminated all lighting (except that needed for security purposes) during nonworking hours. Other offices have reduced their lighting use by limiting the quantity of light at any given location. A major reason for adopting task lighting is to reduce energy costs. Also, some offices are relying more on natural light to illuminate work areas and provide part of the heat needed.

A major change in energy conservation for an office is still on the horizon: solar heat. Although experiments and limited use of solar heat are under way today, it is estimated that widespread use of this heating system is still years away. Certainly, if solar heat does win wide adoption, new changes will be evident in the physical environment of the office.

Flexibility in the office environment. As stated earlier in this chapter, an office should be both a pleasing and functional place to work. Thus, if an office is to be functional, it will always be faced with changes associated with new office procedures and methods, caused by a variety of factors.

128

New methods and procedures may be generated by the need to provide better service, comply with external regulations, or to meet the needs of a changing work force. Many office managers view change and the need for flexibility in planning, organizing, and controlling office operations as paramount concerns facing offices today.

The need for increased productivity. A number of studies have shown that office productivity has not risen to balance increased operating costs; in fact, some research studies indicate that productivity has increased little, if at all, during the past ten years. With the growing need for efficient and well-managed offices, more attention is being given to assessing the productivity levels of employees in the office as a whole. Work measurement studies are providing more reliable and useful data upon which to determine operating standards and, consequently, evaluate the progress in achieving new standards.

As people, equipment, and work processes are integrated in the office, productivity data will be used to measure the success or failure of the office. The impact of the arrangement and integration of the physical environment on the worker will also become part of the analytical process for which productivity norms will be established. Innovations or changes in the physical environment will be studied before determining what action will be taken.

The need for security. Increased attention to office security has resulted in stringent methods of controlling access to information and facilities. The fear of illegal entry, destruction of important records or equipment, disclosure of information, or just malicious vandalism has prompted offices to reexamine their security needs and precautions. Some office buildings have limited access by using identification cards or security forces to permit entry; other offices have elaborate entry-sensing devices to tell when an unauthorized person has entered the premises.

Security must be a physical environmental concern both inside and outside the office. The office that has either confidential information (banks, government offices) or expensive equipment (computers, communication equipment) must be especially careful of violations in security. The same concern for security should be followed by limiting the use and availability of records to employees; locking file cabinets, keeping records under the watchful eye of office supervisors, and properly destroying unneeded records (by shredding, burning, etc.) are ways to maintain desired security.

Offices that have various forms of electronic data processing must use security precautions to eliminate possible wrongful use. Many firms have designed elaborate coding systems which allow only authorized personnel to have access to EDP equipment or programs. One office, for example, has four security barriers that must be properly bypassed before the user can have access to the equipment.

Accommodating technological advances. Few people would dispute that we are in the midst of a technological era in which electronic equipment has changed our work and personal lives. The office has greatly benefited from the use of equipment such as:

Facsimile telecommunication
Automated text editing
Reprographics
Micrographics
Dictation/transcription
Electronic data processing

However, any equipment's success depends on how employees use it and how well the equipment aids in achieving work goals. As more and more investments are made in equipment, the office manager must know if the equipment is worth the cost and if it will increase operating efficiency. Also, the manager must study the ways in which the equipment will change present work methods and procedures. In many offices it is not really a question of whether or not to purchase or lease new equipment; the question is usually one of determining the best way to integrate the equipment into the office environment.

FUTURE OFFICE DESIGNS

Visionaries claim the office of tomorrow will be a paperless office in which all information processing will be done electronically using highly sophisticated computerized equipment. They see the office as a place where the entire work activities of an employee can be completed through entering or retrieving data from computerized processing or storage systems at a single physical work location.

Although the paperless office may be years away—if it ever comes—certainly the office of tomorrow will be well equipped with electronic communication devices. The capabilities of this equipment will allow information processing to occur outside of the typical office setting—in another part of the building, at home, in a car, or even on the beach! The physical environment of the office will be drastically extended: communication components may be located in several remote locations but still connected through a variety of easy-to-use communication channels. There will be no closing time for the office; the work could be completed whenever or wherever the employee chooses. Coordination of information will be possible through remote locations, using telephone/computer lines.

This new office will become more *equipment-intensive*, with larger sums of money spent to obtain the use of the equipment desired. More and more, employees will rely on equipment to extend human capabilities. Results will be faster and easier to obtain; efficiency and effectiveness will be increased manyfold.

The physical environment in this office may resemble an aircraft cockpit, with the worker surrounded by all the controls necessary to accomplish the assigned work. Many of the routine, boring tasks will be done automatically, freeing the employee to assume more meaningful or creative assignments. The office should continue to be a desirable place to work and one full of interesting and rewarding challenges!

CHAPTER 13

Alternative Work Schedules

MARGARET P. HARDY

Hueytown High School, Hueytown, Alabama

How can the manager of the office reduce absenteeism by 50 percent, make tardiness a thing of the past, cut overtime expenses, and improve employee morale? The answer may be a *Gleitzeit*. That's the European term for flexible working hours. The American counterpart is flexitime. Testimonials from satisfied users include statements such as, "Employees don't feel watched all the time." "It's hard to justify tardiness when you have a 2-hour leeway." "It is better because of less afternoon fatigue."

The idea of flexible working hours originated in Germany in 1967 with a German aerospace firm. Because of inadequate roads leading to the plant, the firm was plagued by employees' tardiness at its research and development center at Ottobrunn. In an effort to combat this, management introduced a system known as Gleitende Arbeitzeit or gliding working hours. This system allowed the employee to arrive at work and leave at times of his own choosing within certain specified hours. In ten years the idea has spread to other European countries, as well as to Japan, Australia, New Zealand, the United States, and Canada.

Flexitime is one of several alternative work schedules which break with the traditional five-day, 40-hour work week. These alternative schedules include all types of variations of the standard work schedule. Those systems experiencing the most widespread usage are flexible working hours (flexitime) and permanent part-time employment. In fact, President Carter recently signed bills permitting a three-year study of flexitime schedules for employees in federal agencies and requiring agencies to expand part-time jobs.

FLEXITIME

The usual flexitime schedule consists of a core period (mandatory hours) during which all employees must be present and flexitime (discretionary hours). The core period extends from 9:00 a.m. until 4:00 p.m. On either side is a flexible time band which is sometimes referred to as *quiet times*. These bands extend from 7:00 to 9:00 a.m. and from 4:00 to 6:00 p.m. The bandwidth for a bank, for example, could run from 7:30 a.m. to 6:00 p.m. Employees are expected to work the contracted number of hours per day, per week, and per month.

Some flexitime models provide that hours cannot be carried forward to the next daily work schedule. Other models provide for "banking" hours. Workers can accumulate daily or weekly debit and credit hours should they work more or less than their contract hours. The total hours which may be banked are usually limited to 10 or 15 hours. Some companies require workers to begin at approximately the same time each day for a week in order to aid management in assuring coverage at all times during the regular hours of business. Other systems allow workers to change their arrival and departure time provided they have the approval of their supervisors. Still other systems allow workers complete flexibility to come and go as they choose.

Timekeeping systems for recording the time and attendance vary from company to company. Basically four methods are used: the honor system in which employees keep up with their hours and turn them in at the end of the week; time accumulators, which are special electronic devices that display an employee's time worked over a given period, but do not show times of arrival and departure; computer-based systems activated by plastic cards which have the capability of keeping payroll records; and traditional manual recording systems utilizing time sheets or sign-in/sign-out sheets. New time-recording hardware, whether leased or purchased, can run as much as $60 per employee. However, the payoff can cover these costs with the first year. For example, Pacific Gas and Electric spent $40,000 to install and administer a flexitime system for a department of 575 draftsmen. In the first year alone the company realized more than $300,000 in savings from increased production and from reduction in overtime, sick leave, and absenteeism. One problem which must be anticipated—many workers react negatively to the installation of time-recording systems. They consider it a professional insult.

History and trends. Flexitime has spread rapidly since it was first initiated in Germany in 1967. It is now reported that over 50 percent of Germany's white-collar workers are on flexible time systems. The idea spread to other European countries including Switzerland, where an estimated 40 percent of the labor force uses this system. The United States has been slow to undertake this new work schedule. It was first introduced here by international corporations and banks and is spreading faster than any management innovation in memory. It has been estimated that about 300,000 employees use some form of flexi-scheduling in nearly 1,000 U.S. companies, organizations, and government agencies. State governments are considering flexitime, and a number of counties and municipal governments have experimented with it. It has been particularly popular in civil service. In industries, those operations which are relatively independent as distinguished from assembly line operations are more favorable to flexi-scheduling. Even though it is not ideally suited to assembly line operations, a number of manufacturing plants have also experimented with flexitime, including Motorola, General Electric, and Olivetti. Its use does not appear to be limited to any particular types of organizations. Flexitime has been utilized in food, cosmetics, light equipment, pharmaceutical, manufacturing, and banking, to mention a few users.

By 1973 there were approximately 30 large U.S. firms and 200 smaller organizations permitting appropriate employees to select their working hours within established limits. The first U.S. company to adopt flexitime was the Control Data Corporation in 1972. It was introduced first on a pilot basis in its Minnesota plants and expanded to include the entire corporation in 1973. A 1975 survey showed that three-fourths of its 25,000 employees in the United States were on one or more types of flexitime schedules. Hewlett-Packard Company switched to flexitime in June of 1972. The firm now has approximately 90 percent of its employees participating in a flexible work schedule in 22 of its worldwide manufacturing facilities. In May 1974 the company conducted a survey of all their U.S. companies using a flexible working schedule. Of the participants in the survey, more than 90 percent indicated that flexible working hours had had a positive or negligible effect—but not a negative effect. A follow-up survey was conducted in May 1975 at its Colorado Springs Division. The purpose of this survey was to validate the findings of the 1974 survey. It was determined that the 1974 survey results fairly accurately reflected the 1975 survey of the Colorado Springs Hewlett-Packard Company.

Banks were among the first to try flexitime. The First National Bank of Boston and the State Street Bank and Trust were forerunners. Other banks which have adopted the system are the Bank of California, San Francisco, and Industrial National Bank, Providence, Rhode Island. Insurance companies have installed flexischedules also. Metropolitan Life Insurance of New York has over 15,000 employees on flexitime at its home office. Flexible work hours schedules have been instituted at other companies including Mutual Life Insurance of New York, Massachusetts Mutual, Occidental Life of California in Los Angeles, and John Hancock. American Airlines is the first to use flexitime in the airline industry. Flexitime was introduced to the utilities by Pacific Gas and Electric Company. Two large industrial companies that have begun using flexitime are the Firestone Tire and Rubber Company and the Sun Oil Company of Philadelphia.

In 1974 a federal agency, the General Accounting Office, submitted a report to Congress explaining the benefits of flexible hours. It was recommended that the Civil Service Commission reexamine and possibly seek legislation to permit testing of flexitime. In the election year of 1976 the Senate failed to act on a bill passed by the House of Representatives recommending a federal experiment under the Civil Service Commission (now called the Office of Personnel Management) to study the application of flexitime. However, in late 1978 the Federal Employees Flexible and Compressed Work Schedule Acts were passed, authorizing a three-year study of flexible working hours experiments in government. Already, some 200,000 people in more than a dozen agencies are working under some form of flexitime. These include workers in the Library of Congress, Geological Survey, Environmental Protection Agency, Treasury Department, Office of Personnel Management, Defense Mapping Agency, and the Department of Agriculture. The biggest switch from a 40-hour, 5-day week work schedule will be in the Defense Department with its 80,000 civilian employees. The Army, Navy, and Air Force offices have been given permission to experiment with flexible hours. Most agencies are expected to use the 11-hour day being tried by the Social Security Administration in Baltimore. Workers will be permitted to set their own hours within that time period, provided they put in eight hours.

Flexible scheduling has spread to county and municipal governments also. Alexandria, Virginia, has an experimental program providing for six city departments to be open as early as 7:00 a.m. and as late as 7:00 p.m. All employees must be on duty during the departments' busiest hours. The District of Columbia has used flexible scheduling for some time. In 1973 Inglewood, California, expanded the hours in which municipal offices are open. Residents can take care of business between 7:30 a.m. and 6:00 p.m. The city manager reports the public likes it, the employees like it, and it's saving money for the city.

Advantages of flexitime. The use of flexitime affects three areas: the employees, management, and society. The reactions to this new work schedule have been spontaneous, favorable, and widespread.

ADVANTAGES TO EMPLOYEES. The major advantage to employees is that employees have more time with their families. This is particularly important to mothers with young and school-age children. Some mothers leave their offices at 3:00 p.m. every day to be at home when their children return from school. Others report to work at 10:00 a.m., having delivered their children to school on the way. When both parents are on flexitime, a little juggling of schedules makes it possible for mother or father to be home when the children are home. One manager stated that one of the important advantages to him was that employees no longer needed to lie or give some vague reason for absences when time was needed to take care of personal affairs or medical appointments. Flexitime permits individuals the freedom to work when they are better prepared physically and psychologically. As one early-riser put it, "I get more done when I'm alone—no one to bother me." Employees also enjoy a reduction in travel time and personal frustration when they are able to adjust their schedules to avoid peak traffic hours. The increase in leisure time is twofold. The employee enjoys more rest and relaxation, and recreational facilities and services will realize increased income.

One of the advantages often overlooked is the opportunity for greater participation in civic, cultural, and educational activities. Flexitime could have a direct effect on community colleges and universities in providing programs, both on and off campus, to teach workers living skills, with emphasis on community services, in addition to working skills.

ADVANTAGES TO MANAGEMENT. One of the first results apparent after flexitime is installed is the reduction in absences and the rapid decline in late arrivals. One worker summed it up this way: "It's hard to justify tardiness when you have a 2-hour leeway." Contrary to the thinking of nonusers of flexitime, employees do not take advantage of the system.

More workers tend to come to work earlier. Some report at the same hour, and some arrive later. One manager reports that they also tend to settle down to work sooner in order not to disturb those who arrived earlier and are already working. When employees can adjust their schedules to correspond with fluctuating work loads, the results are less idle time and greater productivity. In 1972 Mutual Life Insurance Company of New York installed flexitime with 22 billing clerks in an effort to salvage production time lost to habitual tardiness. An evaluation of the effectiveness of flexitime after six months' use showed that lateness had vanished; daily billing per clerk had increased 20 percent while complaints about errors had diminished. By 1974 flexitime scheduling had been adopted by 40 percent of the employees at the company's headquarters.

ADVANTAGES TO SOCIETY. The first major societal benefit of flexible work schedules is a vast reduction in traffic and commuter problems. New York City approached this problem first in 1970 with staggered work hours. The concentration of air pollution resulting from congestion of automobiles at peak periods of the day is diminished. Transportation companies are able to provide better service to their customers without having to buy additional equipment.

Flexibility in scheduling extends management's ability to select from a larger labor resources pool made available for employment. This will be significant in the 1980's when labor projections indicate there will be a decrease in first-time entrants into the labor market.

Perhaps the most important advantage from the individual member of society's point of view is that services provided by institutions like banks and insurance companies can be extended for longer periods of the day.

Limitations and disadvantages. Flexitime is not the answer for every company. All companies and all employees do not like flexitime. Companies with poor personnel relations and strict management controls would find it very difficult to make the changeover to flexitime. The failure rate is low, however. In a survey of 196 firms by the American Management Association only about 8 percent had discontinued their flexible scheduling. Over half of these companies who discontinued flexitime had used it for less than six months. About 80 percent who dropped flexitime did it before two years had elapsed.

DISADVANTAGES TO COMPANIES. Two of the problem areas most often reported are in management and work supervision problems. These two areas together account for over half of the problems encountered. Other problems which occur occasionally are abuse of flexitime by employees, timekeeping problems, and a poorly designed model.

A key to preventing problems is to anticipate them and to plan to prevent their occurrence. Problems such as coverage are usually worked out by the employees themselves by voluntarily rotating schedules and covering for each other. Solutions to supervisory problems, such as overcoming resistance to flexitime, require educating the supervisors to the new concept. This begins during the planning and developing stages before flexitime is presented to the employees. Most surveys indicate there is less resis-

135

tance when supervisors are included in the early stages of planning. Employee abuses are solved by relying on peer pressure to curb offenses or by removing guilty employees from the flexitime system.

There appeared to be no major differences in characteristics between users and discontinuers. No single dimension leads to failure, although supervision problems were most frequently mentioned. Some supervisors felt that demands on their time and their work load increased disproportionately because of the planning, controlling, and scheduling required. Others felt it was too difficult to implement company-wide. This complaint does not seem a valid one since some organizations use flexitime successfully throughout their company while others restrict its use to certain departments. Support workers, such as telephone operators, cafeteria workers, and custodial and security personnel usually are not placed under flexible schedules. One of the major disadvantages of flexitime from management's point of view is the potential for increased electricity and administrative costs because of increased use of facilities. Another disadvantage is related to the difficulties in coping with unexpected contingencies. Elimination of this disadvantage requires precise scheduling and planning.

DISADVANTAGES TO THE INDIVIDUAL. There are two major disadvantages to the individual. Some workers who increase their earnings through overtime work may experience a reduction in earnings because overtime tends to decrease under flexitime. Also, many workers resent having their arrival and departure times strictly recorded even though they enjoy the freedom of being able to arrive at and leave work at the times they choose. Possible solutions to this problem would be to allow each employee to maintain his own personal time record and to include top managers in the timekeeping system, thereby rendering it more democratic. Although workers may very much support these solutions, management may not.

It becomes apparent that the successful use of the flexitime system depends on what steps are followed in the implementation of the system and the early involvement of supervisors and employees in the planning process.

PART-TIME WORKERS

Today an important new group of workers are those who work part time. This is not seasonal employment; nor is it shorter hours resulting from economic recession. Permanent part-time employment is regular employment during working hours that are shorter than full-time employment. It is usually defined as fewer than 35 hours per week. This group of workers has been steadily increasing since 1954. It now comprises about eight percent of the labor force.

Part-time workers and minishifts. Permanent part-time employment may be used in a variety of ways. Normally, part-day employment is most common. Full day, but part week or part month, may also be used.

The minishift and job sharing are alternatives which are often overlooked. With the minishift the part-time worker works a short shift before, after, or during the regular daily schedule. The shift usually consists of 4 hours and is used in conjunction with jobs requiring more than 8 but less than 16 hours to complete. The use of part-time minishifts allows increased utilization of office space and equipment and avoids the need for scheduling overtime for full-time day workers. This use of part-time workers prevents backlogs of work in certain departments, thus averting bottlenecks. Part-time evening minishifts are frequently used by banks which lease computer time and also by other data processing organizations, such as insurance companies. Faced with no room to add additional employees and a work load in its claims processing and keypunching departments which could not be completed in an 8-hour day, a West Coast insurance firm began using an evening part-time minishift because the output from these departments was essential to the functioning of other departments on the following day.

Job sharing is part-time employment in which two workers share one full-time job. A number of combinations are possible. One person may work mornings and the other person may work afternoons. One may work the first three days and the other may work the last two days. The two workers may alternate weeks. The two employees sharing the job must work well together and coordinate their activities. This requires careful evaluation and selection of the workers involved. The employer realizes several benefits. One worker's strengths will offset the other worker's weaknesses, and continuity is assured. In the event of one worker's absence, the co-worker is available to fill in. There is less confusion and disruption when one worker resigns since one remains to train the replacement. When job sharing first appeared on the employment scene, it was considered primarily the utilization of two part-time workers during a regular work-day schedule. Little mention was made of its effect upon unemployment. Labor leaders have turned their attention to job sharing as a means of combating unemployment.

Neither the minishift nor job sharing are used extensively. However, they are used enough to be considered worthwhile part-time options. The use of part-time employees can be found in most industries. It has been less common in government; however, there are signs of interest in pilot projects to determine the practicality of the part-time worker in the government. Legislation has been enacted to increase part-time career opportunities within the Civil Service at all grade levels, including professional and managerial positions.

Labor supply. There has been a steady increase in part-time workers in the past decade. During the period of May 1959 to May 1977 there was an increase of ten million part-time employees. Two-thirds of this increase was accounted for by women, as they are far more likely than men to work part time. Many youths begin their working lives as part-time workers while still enrolled in high school. The normal tendency of young people to work part time while continuing their education has been influenced by federal/ state employment programs for high school and college students, student loan programs, and the Veterans Readjustment Act of 1966. During the period of May 1954 to May 1977 workers under 25 years of age accounted for about 45 percent of the growth in part-time employment. The trend toward earlier retirement, coupled with a higher social security earnings ceiling, is expected to contribute to further increases in part-time workers. Among some older groups there has been a significant increase in the proportion of part-time employees. This is probably accounted for by persons who remain in the labor force to supplement retirement benefits or to maintain personal contacts. Whatever their motives, the supply is still growing rapidly.

Occupations and industries. One of the most important factors in making part-time jobs available has been the growth of the service-producing industries. These industries normally employ a higher proportion of voluntary part-time workers than do the goods-producing industries. In 1977 about 30 percent of all service employees worked part time voluntarily. Sales persons and clerical workers are the most likely to work part time within the white-collar occupations. Those jobs requiring higher skills and a greater degree of supervisory responsibilities are less likely to be filled with a part-time employee.

The use of part-time employment varies widely by industries. The highest number of part-timers are in services, finance, insurance, real estate, and the wholesale and retail trade. Those organizations which use part-time workers are much more likely to have recurring demands for their efforts, such as daily, weekly, or monthly peaks. Banks, for example, experience heavy traffic on Monday mornings, Friday afternoons, or at midday. During these peak periods, part-time tellers ease the workload. Another example is that of organizations which have extended hours of operation, such as retail stores with evening and weekend hours.

Part-time workers and unions. Another factor associated with use of part-time employment is union membership. Part-time employees are less likely to be union members because of the membership dues and their feelings of independence. However, this too depends on the industry. In areas such as finance and insurance, there is little union membership. On the other hand, in the wholesale/retail trade and transportation/communication/utilities industries, there is often substantial union membership among part-time workers.

The AFL-CIO takes a dim view of the trend of hiring part-time workers. They contend that people out of work need full-time employment, and in view of this attitude, unions have made little effort to recruit members among the part-time workers. However, one union, the Retail Clerks International Association, has been recruiting and reports that one-half of its 700,000 membership is made up of part-timers. It would not be surprising to see other unions follow the path of the RCIA.

The use of part-time employees represents a wealth of potential for improving manpower utilization. There has been a reluctance on the part of managers to hire these workers because of the many myths about their availability, reliability, and ability. Retired workers, homemakers, and unemployed 16-21-year-olds represent 30 million potential employees. There are 27 million housewives and retirees alone who could be tapped for a part-time force. Most wives are accustomed to responsibilities and would bring to part-time employment skills learned before marriage. Although some wives may be lacking in specific job skills, they are as readily trainable as full-time workers, and employers can easily recruit college-trained women. Some retired workers have had work histories which established their reliability and acceptance of responsibilities. The list of skills available among retired workers is unlimited, and each has an employment record which can be readily verified. Students, though lacking in experience, bring with them academic and vocational abilities learned in school, such as drafting, bookkeeping, typing, and shorthand.

Advantages and disadvantages of using part-time employees. The advantages derived through the use of part-time employees outweigh the disadvantages. Flexibility in scheduling is most often cited as the biggest advantage resulting from use of these workers. Management can alleviate some of the stress during peak hours by using part-time workers. Part-timers are especially useful in meeting staffing demands which arise from vacations, sick leave, and terminations.

Absenteeism is one of industry's major problems. On any given day, it is estimated three to seven percent of the work force may not show up. Estimates of losses in annual wages paid to absent workers are in excess of $15 million, but this cost is not associated with the part-time worker who has a special interest in reporting to work—no work, no pay.

Another factor which concerns management is tardiness. However, this problem is also reduced since part-time workers are paid only for the hours worked.

Turnover costs are reduced with a program for part-time employment. Often the reasons for an employee's resignation are of a temporary nature. The retiring worker also could elect to move to a part-time schedule rather than quit. Ordinarily when full-time workers retire, they take with them valuable experience and training. The experience and knowledge of both of these workers could be available to their organizations through a part-time work program.

Lower labor costs often result from the use of these workers since they usually are paid a lower wage than the full-time worker. This saving varies from organization to organization. Aside from the lower hourly wage rate, the organization benefits by having to provide fewer fringe benefits. Fringe benefits constitute the fastest growing component in labor costs today, but those benefits made available to the part-time worker vary widely. They are normally extended on a very limited basis. Most organizations providing a vacation do so on a prorated basis. Approximately 75 percent of employers provide this benefit to part-time employees, while sick leave and pensions are provided by slightly less than one-half of the employers. A few organizations provide life insurance, but less than 20 percent provide for health insurance and profit sharing.

The use of part-time workers can substantially pare overtime payments while increasing output as proven through the use of minishifts after the regular day schedule. One company's comparison between full-time workers and part-time workers on a trial run showed the same. However, the results of performance over a longer period showed the part-time workers turned in a better performance. The only explanation for the increased output was that the part-timers experienced less fatigue and did not have to pace their work as did the full-time workers.

Foremost among the disadvantages are those pertaining to personnel activities. The use of part-time workers does mean more administrative detail. For instance, the use of two or more part-time workers doubles the interviewing, testing, recordkeeping, and training required for one full-time worker.

If all part-time employees work the same time, the span of supervision is greatly increased. Should these employees work a minishift after the regular 8-hour day, communication and continuity of effort between the regular workers and part-time workers become a real problem.

Reactions of union leaders toward the hiring of part-time workers varies from company to company. Unions have tended to look on the part-timer as a threat to the full-time worker, but opposition will probably become less as part-timers are now eligible for union membership under the National Labor Relations Act.

The question of providing pensions for part-time workers is a highly controversial one. To many employers, a pension is paid to a worker for long and faithful service to the organization. The part-time worker does not fit this definition although the worker may have served faithfully over an extended period on a part-time basis. Another problem confronting the employer who grants pension rights to the part-time employee is concerned with the standards required under ERISA, the Employee Retirement Income Security Act of 1974. ERISA guards against pension-plan abuse and provides pension portability to workers who change employers. Many employers are unwilling to assume either the administrative or financial responsibility entailed by including large numbers of part-time employees.

FUTURE CONSIDERATIONS

Twenty years ago a proposal that employees be allowed to decide when they wanted to arrive at work or to leave work would have evoked much laughter. Yet today a significant number of workers participate in flexitime work schedules.

Two alternative plans have already been reported; others will emerge in years ahead. One alternative proposal would adapt the 40-hour week over a two-week period and is known as flexiweek. Flexiweek is a working schedule that alternates four-day and six-day weeks to average 40 hours per week. Flexiweek, if adopted, would turn Saturday into a regular business day. Discussion has begun in Sweden, France, and Germany about a working year contract—or flexiyear. The number of hours worked within a year would be determined—within a certain range—by the employer and employee through collective bargaining. There is still discussion about the advantages and disadvantages of this system in Sweden and France, while it already has been implemented in Germany on a limited basis. At least 12 firms with a total of 1,000 employees are using the working year plan.

In determining the work schedule most beneficial for its operations, an organization must consider its own needs, those of its workers, and those of the community. Those organizations which use flexitime are most likely to use part-time workers and job sharing. Management realizes greater flexibility in planning and scheduling through the use of a combination of these alternatives and reaps the benefits of both types of work schedules.

Alternative work schedules may provide a spin-off heretofore overlooked. With the capability of managing their own time, employees will be able to take advantage of previously unattainable educational opportunities, thereby participating in a lifelong learning experience. This may be the most important benefit of all to the individual, to management, and to society.

CHAPTER 14

Time Management

DENNIS L. MOTT

Oklahoma State University, Stillwater

Nobody can stop, save, stockpile, or set the pace for time. People can, however, manage time, by controlling the way they view time and the way they see themselves in the time picture.

Some people withdraw from the present and live in the security of the past. The familiarity of daily situations and a complacent sense of accomplishment can cause modern day leaders to become obsolete in their own age.

People also may live with past failure or shortcomings and see future success as limited by actions they should or should not have taken. These individuals find the present dominated by a cruel past that limits their productivity and virtually eliminates creativity.

Pressure to succeed or pressure to not fail may also force people to live in fear of the future. When success is emphasized too much, the worker feels more and more reluctant to venture out and chance ruining everything.

Time management is present-oriented, future-planned, and tempered by the lessons of the past. With time planning everyone can live in the present and plan for the future. The past should only offer guidance for the future and help people to capitalize on the lessons learned from experience.

Business resources are usually considered to include money, machines, labor, land, and technology. However, the time resource also must be managed or all the other managerial efforts will be minimized. Time is the most scarce resource—unless it is managed effectively nothing else can be managed.

Business teachers prepare workers and managers for a complex business world. They teach about management, law, accounting, taxes, office management, administrative assistance, and supervision. But seldom do they teach about the effective use of time.

Time management is using time to get what is wanted from life. This demands a clearly established value system about work, family, social activities, and possessions. A final payoff of time management is not only increased productivity but also control of career and life activities.

TIME PLANNING

A daily plan for activities and actions is essential for personal success in complex modern businesses. It appears, however, that a high percentage of people lead a grab-bag life. They take on whatever appears on their desk with little attention paid to importance, priority, or long-range effects.

A daily plan should start with a quiet hour or whatever time frame is needed to plan for success. This time is used to establish a working schedule for the day. It will assist in separating the important, urgent, and meaningless tasks. The net result is an organized day where priority items receive priority time allotments.

TIME LOG

Time control must begin with time awareness. A basic question to ask is, Where does time go? Nearly everyone assumes they know where their time goes, but they are often in error. Extensive research and study reveals a basic conclusion about time control: A time log is needed to discover how time is *really* being used.

Time logs may be completed on a form such as Figure I or on a note pad, but several important guidelines should be considered.

1. Time should be logged every 15 minutes for a two-week period.
2. Daily goals established during the time planning period should be kept clearly in mind.
3. Time use must be evaluated at the end of each day to determine whether it was used in the proper manner.

Analysis of time logs usually reveals several interesting time problems. Foremost is proof that people waste time in the same manner each day. They may not waste time at the exact same time each day, but they often talk to the same people about the same things! To further confuse the matter, they often talk about subjects which are unimportant to the job or beyond their ability to change or control. For instance, time logs have shown excessive time spent talking about sports, politics, religion, administration, and weather conditions. Each person must decide whether his/her time is used effectively—or simply used!

A second time problem usually involves ineffective prioritizing of activities. Urgent matters always seem to receive more attention than important matters; thus the time-tension cycle is never broken. Perhaps a more serious problem is being involved in routine details which are not important, or necessary.

Time logs will also emphasize the fact that most people do not have much spare time. Unless their time is used effectively, they will quickly run out of time before important tasks are completed.

TIME MANAGEMENT

A time log is essential, but time management is not that simple. Time logs will identify several time wasters, but each person must carefully evaluate to see if an analysis supports the identification.

A time waster is any task or activity that takes more time than it should for successful completion. For example, some socializing is not only

FIGURE I. Time Log

NAME _____ DATE _____

GOALS_____;_____;_____

	ACTIVITY	PRIORITY 1–Urgent 2–Important 3–Routine 4–Discretionary 5–Wasted	EVALUATION Could you have used your time more efficiently? (Example: delegate to _____; organize, plan, train someone else to handle it; combine, eliminate, etc.
8:00			
8:30			
9:00			
9:30			
10:00			
10:30			
3:30			
4:00			
4:30			
5:00			
5:30			

important to departmental or company morale but also an essential aspect of most people's lives. Each person must separate essential socializing from excessive socializing. The major problem is an attitude or habit adjustment, which by anyone's measure is not an easy task.

COMMON TIME WASTERS

Nearly every organization believes its time problems are unique and unsolvable, but quite the opposite is often true. Time studies completed by management consulting firms indicate that people in different positions and careers have basically the same time problems. For example, a profile of time wasters from different groups of workers (including office managers, administrative assistants, city managers, school administrators, executive secretaries, university administrators, engineers, students, data processing

144

managers, and funeral directors) shows common time wasters. Although they may differ in priority importance, they are still considered to be time wasters. Common time wasters, combined to form a cross-section profile, are shown in Table 1.

TABLE 1. Common Time Wasters for General Work Group

Time Waster	Weighted Score	Ranked Importance
Telephone	1016	1
Drop-in visitors	984	2
Meetings	937	3
Socializing	754	4
Failure to delegate	700	5
Lack daily plan	650	6
Inability to say "no"	587	7
Incomplete information	510	8
Crisis management	415	9
Personal disorganization	360	10

Information shown in Table 1 hints at curriculum content which should be included in office management courses. Action to eliminate time wasters would enhance the incidence and speed of career growth and advancement.

TIME PROBLEMS OF OFFICE WORKERS

General information about time problems shows a direction, but specific time problems of office workers are needed to provide the impetus for change.

Time studies dealing with office workers (including secretaries, office assistants, executive secretaries, clerical workers, word processing personnel, and administrative assistants) reveal the status and order of time problems for office workers. Table 2 shows a time-wasting profile for office workers.

Once again the definition of a time waster must be emphasized. A time waster is an action or activity that takes more time to accomplish than it should. The telephone, for instance, is the most effective time saver we have, but in its use it can also become a time waster.

TABLE 2. Common Time Wasters for Office Workers

Time Waster	Weighted Score	Ranked Importance
Drop-in visitors	642	1
Errands	581	2
Telephone	579	3
Socializing	500	4
Routine details	450	5
Lack daily plan	400	6
Procrastination	390	7
Illegible handwriting	310	8
Crisis management	300	9
More than one boss	215	10

SOCIETAL AND ORGANIZATIONAL CONSTRAINTS

Identification and awareness of time problems is a very small part of a solution. People develop strong and quite often protective habits about their lives and particularly their time. To solve time problems some personal habits may need to be changed.

Some societal clichés or beliefs can be quite detrimental to time management. It is a near universal belief, for example, that the busiest person should be contacted when important tasks need attention. This can create two major and serious problems for business. First, the busy person, no matter how capable, will soon be forced into a position of mediocrity if an unending flow of heavy responsibility keeps coming his/her way. Second, the growth and well-being of an organization will soon rest too heavily on one person. Therefore, the death, transfer, or retirement of this person would render a serious blow to the whole organization.

Human frailties such as excessive pride in accomplishment can also create problems. Some people carry duties and responsibilities with them when promoted to other positions. Human nature tends to create a protective atmosphere about performance and responsibility. Once a person has been commended on a job well done, the fences go up and a life-long commitment to that activity is often intact.

Our society has created the idea that long hours and perspiration are directly correlated with success. But business is results-oriented—young workers must learn to work smarter, not harder.

Habits are difficult to modify—much less change—so successful time management has to be an evolutionary, not a revolutionary, process. To break away from damaging, success-limiting personal habits the following guidelines may be helpful.

1. Start the change with incremental steps. Crash diets are not as successful as planned persistent weight-losing programs. The same is true for time management techniques.
2. Set deadlines for change and improvement. Be realistic, yet persistent. A goal and plan may need to be modified several times, but the result is greater control of time, career, and life.
3. Evaluate progress continuously. Keep goals and objectives in mind and develop a system.

Poor time management habits are as difficult to change as any other personal or professional habits. It is important to realize that modifying habits at a young age is normally easier and more successful than at a later age.

PRINCIPLES OF TIME MANAGEMENT

According to Webster, a principle is a fundamental truth, a basic doctrine, or a governing law of conduct. The principles of time management which follow are commonly accepted.

1. *Time analysis.* Keep a daily log of activities for at least one week. Taken in

15-minute increments, it is essential as a basis for effective time analysis. Repeat semiannually to avoid reverting to poor time management practices.

2. *Anticipation.* Anticipatory action is generally more effective than remedial action. Avoid surprise by expecting the unexpected.

3. *Planning.* A majority of problems seem to stem from action without thought. An hour spent in effective planning will save three to four hours in execution. Failing to plan is often planning to fail.

4. *Deadlines.* Impose deadlines and exercise self-discipline. Adhering to deadlines reduces indecision and procrastination.

5. *Flexibility.* Flexibility is necessary to serve forces beyond one's control. Time should not be over- or underscheduled.

6. *Indecision.* Critical points of decision cause many people to hesitate or refuse to decide. Indecision is a decision *not* to decide and many times can be very costly.

7. *Procrastination.* Deferring, postponing, or putting off decisions or actions can become a habit. It causes lost opportunities, increases deadline pressures, and often generates crises. Decisions should be made at the earliest appropriate time.

8. *Consolidation.* Grouping similar tasks within divisions of the work day will help eliminate repetitive action. This will economize the use of resources including time and effort.

9. *Implementation and follow-up.* Implementation of time planning and follow-up is essential for effective time management. Follow-up should be a daily routine.

10. *Success imperative.* Time is the most critical of all resources. As Ben Franklin put it: "When your time is up, you're done." The ability to organize and utilize time effectively is the success imperative. Without it nothing else can be managed.

CLOSING ESCAPE HATCHES

Even though office employees feel a need to adjust their time use to ensure more effective performance, they tend to neutralize their efforts with halfhearted commitment. Many excuses are used to explain away a failure to change, but the fact remains—they are just excuses. For example, office and management personnel tend to exclaim that they do not have time for time management, when in fact they do not have time to ignore time use and improvement. Others claim they plan to do it next week, next month, or after they get important matters under control. But tomorrow never comes. Somewhere it is written that things that do not change remain the same, and it is true about time management. A halfhearted effort will dictate failure from the very beginning.

Other employees contend they cannot change because co-workers will not change. This perpetuates a vicious cycle of time wasting which will never be improved unless a plan for action is initiated.

Time management requires continuous and gradual progress. If it were easy, nobody would have the time problems which seem to plague office workers, managers, and executives.

WHAT TO DO AND TEACH

Some basic and tested techniques for improved time use can be incorporated into classroom teaching and learning. Time management is the sum total of many timesaving actions rather than one or two technique changes.

For teaching about effective time use, emphasis should be placed according to normal management function areas. These include planning, organizing, directing, and controlling. Several other divisions could be included, but essential areas should be covered first. Techniques to include are as follows:

Planning
- Write a daily plan.
- Keep a time log and analyze the results.
- Anticipate the unexpected.
- Impose deadlines.
- Allow ample time (leave 15–20 percent unscheduled).

Organizing
- Study routine activities.
- Plan to complete tasks during work hours.
- Examine delegation possibilities.
- Understand job description.
- Streamline paperwork.
- Plan to manage change.

Directing
- Delegate.
- Control urge for perfectionism.
- Take initiative for action.
- Require response deadline (avoid as soon as possible, etc.).
- Resist upward delegation.

Controlling
- Set deadlines and announce them.
- Do not leave tasks unfinished (complete at one sitting if possible).
- Use travel and waiting time to advantage.
- Use a time for planning each day.
- Make decisions when essential facts are known (for most decisions 20 percent of the facts are criteria for 80 percent of the outcomes).

A mastery of these 21 techniques can contribute to the effectiveness and productivity of office employees. The worker who realistically uses this most scarce resource, time, also prepares for job advancement opportunities.

ANALYZING AND SOLVING TIME PROBLEMS

Identifying a time-wasting activity is only the first step toward a solution. Each activity listed as a leading time waster must be studied to determine a systematic plan for its elimination or modification.

When attempting to solve a time problem the majority of effort (80 percent) should be placed on identification of the cause. Once identified, the solution normally takes a minimal amount of time but requires a great amount of will power.

Drop-in visitors was the leading time waster for office workers (see Table 2), but could become a minor disturbance if handled correctly. For drop-in visitors the root of the problem may be either internal or external or a very serious combination of both. Table 3 depicts an analysis and recommended solution for a typical drop-in visitor problem.

TABLE 3. Drop-In Visitors—Time Waster Analysis and Solution

Internal Causes	Solutions
1. Not aware of seriousness	1. Complete time log of both personal and business visitors. Then evaluate in terms of both extent and cause.
2. Want to socialize	2. Plan to socialize at other times and places such as coffee breaks or lunch.
3. Do not want to offend	3. Work must be completed; thus a less sensitive attitude must be developed.
4. Feel need to be available	4. Separate being available for business and socializing.
5. Make decisions that others can and should be making	5. Practice effective delegation. It does not happen overnight, but progress can be incremental.
6. Have no plan for handling the drop-in visitor	6. Develop techniques for terminating conversation and also discouraging personal visits. Standing up on entry of visitor may help keep the time down. Be honest; if work must be continued, tell the visitor.

External Causes	Solutions
7. Open door policy	7. Schedule closed door periods where *most* calls and visitors are not accepted. This allows time for concentrating on important activities. Open door should not be construed to mean physically open, but instead should refer to *open for those who need assistance.*
8. Interdepartment movement	8. When people observe others walking around (to place letters in out-basket, sharpen one pencil, make one copy of a letter or form, etc.), it becomes an open invitation to follow them to their office and *drop in!*
9. Desire to be involved	9. Knowing all the answers to big and small problems tends to create a constant flow of people to the *source!* When people begin to abuse personal time it might be the result of being too helpful. Take a log and determine whether people become bothersome about things they should already know!

149

For each time waster an analysis and solution worksheet should be completed. Hardly anyone wastes an hour at a time, but wasting 10 minutes 10 times a day is the difference between performance with stress and control with quality.

CONCLUSIONS

Each year thousands of employees from hundreds of businesses look to consultants for advice on how to manage their time. Experience adds emphasis to the need for more effective time use, but the fact remains that time management can and should be learned and applied at the earliest possible age. Time-wasting profiles from business employees emphasize the need for including time management in business education classes. The need is apparent, and the application is possible in many different business education classes with limited changes in current course structure.

Part IV

OFFICE COMPETENCIES, OCCUPATIONS, AND CAREER OPPORTUNITIES

CHAPTER 15

Basic Communication Competencies
Section A: Writing

JACK E. HULBERT
North Carolina A&T State University, Greensboro

Exactly how much American business spends on written communication each year is incalculable, but the amount is enormous. Thousands of hours are devoted daily to planning and writing letters, memorandums, reports, employee manuals, advertisements, news releases, and bulletins. It has been estimated that if all the letters written in the United States in one day were laid end to end, they would circle the country nine times. In fact, the cost of producing individually dictated and typewritten business letters alone has been conservatively estimated at $75.7 billion annually.

In today's offices which perform the vital centralized, coordinating, administrative functions of modern business, accuracy and clarity of what is written are crucial to intelligent business decisions, productive actions, and successful organizational operations. Lack of writing skills is not only disastrous in its effect upon efficient office operations, but also devastating in its impact upon the career potential of young workers.

What are the basic writing competencies needed by today's office workers? In addition to the obvious necessity for high-level competencies in fundamentals such as spelling, punctuation, grammar, vocabulary, sentence and paragraph structure, English usage, and proofreading, office workers must possess abilities to (1) think logically, (2) analyze the audience, (3) organize ideas, (4) write clearly, (5) write concisely, and (6) write tactfully and courteously.

ABILITY TO THINK LOGICALLY

Logical thinking is the foundation upon which all effective writing is based. Since the need for most business communications arises from problem situations, it is mandatory that office personnel be able to analyze clearly the problem at hand before attempting to communicate about it. Thoroughly understanding the problem and logically reasoning to determine necessary action are prerequisites of successful writing. Business writing—or any type of writing for that matter—cannot be convincing and forceful unless it is based upon sound logic.

If the ideas the writer is attempting to communicate are not clear in his mind, they definitely cannot be clearly communicated to or interpreted by the reader. Effective business writing must be a product of logical thinking *guaranteeing* that the reader *will understand* its meaning, not an act of faith that the reader will somehow be able to decipher the message. If a reader responds properly to a message which has not been thoroughly thought through prior to writing, the result has more to do with luck than logic.

ABILITY TO ANALYZE THE AUDIENCE

Office workers must possess ability to analyze accurately their audience. Audience analysis provides insights into readers' interests, needs, goals, feelings, and personalities. If business messages are to succeed, writers must keep their readers' characteristics clearly in mind.

A primary objective of business communication is to gain sympathetic understanding of one's message in order to evoke desired responses from readers, and writers greatly increase their chances of achieving this objective by carefully considering audience characteristics. It is well known that readers react most strongly to messages which affect them directly or with which they can empathize. It is only human nature for readers to be more concerned about themselves than about writers or the companies they represent, and they are more likely to read a message when they see the pronoun "you" rather than the pronouns "I," "we," or "us."

Audience analysis helps the writer focus on the reader and, whenever possible, show the reader how he or she will benefit from doing as the message asks. By practicing audience analysis, writers find it easier to perceive situations from the reader's viewpoint and to demonstrate that they are aware of and interested in doing something about the reader's needs and interests. Even the simplest request obtains a better response when the reader is shown the personal benefits to be derived from compliance.

ABILITY TO ORGANIZE IDEAS

Ability to organize one's ideas is of paramount importance to successful business writing because of the way in which the human mind absorbs and processes information. The mind is like an information storage-retrieval system. For readers' minds to comprehend and store information effectively, it must be classified according to some logical plan. This systematic classification and storage of information, then, facilitates accurate and efficient retrieval of the information for later use.

The process of organizing for writing involves (1) dividing the subject into its component parts, (2) arranging these parts in a systematic order, (3) developing each part in turn, and (4) providing the connective tissue to draw all the parts and details into a logical whole.

Even if the message is a short memorandum containing few ideas, good writers will make at least a mental outline. A simple list arranged in the most meaningful order is of great help in ensuring organized thoughts, logical presentation, and clear meaning.

Able writers organize their ideas prior to writing so that they can focus their reader's attention on salient points. When they begin to write, they already know what must be said, in what order it will be said, how it will be said, and what reaction to expect. In organizing for writing, as in most human endeavors, it is advisable to remember the Seven P's of Planning—Proper Prior Planning Prevents Pathetically Poor Performance.

ABILITY TO WRITE CLEARLY

Business executives stress clarity as a supreme goal for any writer. However, achieving this goal is no small task because individuals—from various backgrounds and with unique experiences—frequently attach different meanings to the same words. In fact, few things are more complex than writing a simple message intelligible to all readers. Office workers must exercise care to write clearly and simply not so that their readers *may* understand, but so that they *will* understand.

If a message is to be clear, it must contain correct and complete information expressed concisely. It must be free of ambiguities. The chances that a message will be clear are greatly improved if the writer uses short, simple, familiar words; constructs correct and logical sentences and paragraphs; maintains a level of readability appropriate to the audience; and uses examples, analogies, and visual aids to illustrate points. Jargon should be avoided unless the writer is certain that the reader understands it. If technical words that the reader may not understand must be used, the writer should define them clearly and briefly.

If a message lacks clarity, it is useless because it cannot be properly interpreted and, therefore, will not obtain the desired response. It has wasted the writer's time, the reader's time, and the organization's money. It may even be harmful if it causes frustration, irritation, or confusion resulting in unproductive or detrimental action.

It is much more important that a business writer attempt to *express* ideas clearly and simply than that he attempt to *impress* readers with length and complexity. Office workers must remember that communication—not sophistication—is the name of the game. Good business writers have one thing in common—they prefer being understood to being admired for their literary flair.

ABILITY TO WRITE CONCISELY

Office workers must be able to write concisely without sacrificing clarity, completeness, or courtesy. A business message should be concise in words but comprehensive in thought and meaning. The idea is to use words that cover more ground than they occupy, giving the reader the most meaning in the fewest words.

Conciseness is one of the most important characteristics of business writing because a concise message saves time and money in dictating, typing, and reading. How long should a business message be? It should be just long enough to contain the information necessary to accomplish its purpose effectively—no longer.

Unnecessary information can distract the reader and cloud the purpose of the message. It is time consuming and annoying to have to extract relevant facts from a tangle of extraneous information. It also can be insulting to include information of which the reader is patently aware. Repetition is sometimes necessary for emphasis; but if information is repeated two or three times without reason, the message becomes wordy. Irrelevancies and redundancies should be eliminated.

Good business writers know that a message must be clear so that it will have meaning; accurate so that it will be enlightening; interesting so that it will be remembered; but, above all, *brief* so that it will be read.

ABILITY TO WRITE TACTFULLY AND COURTEOUSLY

Tact and courtesy are sincere expressions of consideration for the feelings of others that place those with whom one communicates at ease. Because these qualities contribute to a writer's ability to avoid offending others—especially in delicate situations—office workers must be able to write tactfully and courteously.

True, business messages should be concise, but not abrupt to the point of being insulting. There is always room for common courtesy and thoughtfulness, although in a business message these qualities should be skillfully and unpretentiously interwoven with the substance of the message and not belabored to the point of insincerity.

In business writing, tact and courtesy pay big dividends by disposing others to similar behavior. Courtesy helps to strengthen pleasant and profitable relationships—as well as to create new ones—just as surely as lack of courtesy destroys them. All the time and money spent in developing the good will of customers, clients, or employees through sincere interpersonal relations can be squandered by one thoughtlessly worded written message.

Tact and courtesy are even more important in written communication than in oral communication because the latter provides spontaneous feedback which can signal a need for rephrasing, reemphasizing, correcting, or outright retracting. In written communication, writers have no such opportunity to restate messages diplomatically. One's courtesy—or discourtesy—are indelibly etched in black and white. One can write hundreds of tactful messages, and it may seem that no one notices; but if he or she writes a tactless sentence, it is certain that nobody will forget it.

No office worker can write successfully without mastering the arts of tact and courtesy. They are fundamental attributes of business writing—the absence of which is fatal to the best of talents.

SUMMARY

Office managers readily acknowledge the importance of writing skills to efficient office operations. They realize that poorly written communications can destroy customer and client good will and patronage; result in confusion, illogical decisions, and unprofitable operations; and create employee ill will. Also, lack of writing skills can have negative impact upon the career development of young workers slated for positions of responsibility—a personal as well as an organizational loss.

Sums spent by American business on written communication are staggering. Some business experts estimate that corporations spend approximately $75.7 billion annually on correspondence alone, with the average letter or memorandum costing between $3 and $6. Moreover, each piece of correspondence that does not communicate as intended is worthless—probably worse than worthless if one considers its detrimental effect on good will and resultant loss of patronage.

To communicate effectively in writing, office workers obviously must possess high-level competencies in fundamentals such as spelling, punctuation, grammar, vocabulary, sentence and paragraph structure, English usage, and proofreading. They also must possess abilities to (1) think logically, (2) analyze the audience, (3) organize ideas, (4) write clearly, (5) write concisely, and (6) write tactfully and courteously. These competencies can make or break efficient office operations as well as the career potential of young office workers.

Section B: Reading

JAMES CALVERT SCOTT

Western New Mexico University, Silver City

Reading is so important, so essential for survival, that years ago it became known as the first of the three R's. While the importance of reading is widely recognized, relatively little is known about it in the office environment. A few doctoral studies have identified major weaknesses that affect the performances of office workers, and most of these weaknesses are in reading-related areas: language and vocabulary skills, following directions, use of reference materials, reading and transcribing shorthand notes, and proofreading. But what is reading?

In the context of the office environment, reading may be conceptualized as a highly complicated, purposeful thinking process which is used to acquire information, to develop new ideas, and to solve problems via the interpretation of printed symbols. Perhaps the three main outcomes of the reading process—acquiring information, developing ideas, and solving problems—can be construed as elements of an ongoing circular reading-thinking construct (see Figure I). It is virtually impossible to separate the intertwining reading and thinking processes. After acquiring information, office workers read and interpret the information in order to develop new ideas. The new ideas are evaluated and a decision is made to utilize the best idea to solve a problem. Once the problem is solved, the solution is recorded and stored for future use.

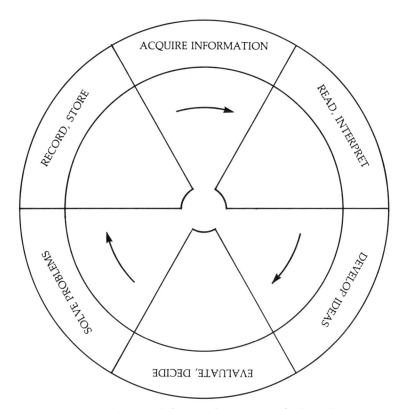

FIGURE I. Key Elements of the Circular Reading-Thinking Construct
in the Changing Office Environment

Before workers can read effectively and succeed in the office environment, however, they must possess certain characteristics. Office workers must have good visual acuity in order to interpret printed symbols. They must be able to concentrate fully on the task at hand and to remember it accurately. Office workers must have adequate knowledge of the working environment and its systems as well as appropriate technical and nontechnical vocabulary. Since reading authorities estimate that at least 60 percent of comprehension is attributable to vocabulary, office workers must acquire appropriate job-related vocabularies. They must also have strong language arts skills to function competently in the office environment. These essential characteristics coupled with adequate basic reading skills allow office workers to develop the specialized reading skills necessary for success.

Flexibility, the ability to adjust the reading rate to fit the purpose for reading and the materials, is an important reading-related skill that eludes many office workers. Too often they plod through all reading tasks at the same rate. When office workers read for pleasure and are not interested primarily in comprehension of details, they often read in excess of 400 or 500 words per minute. When office workers are reading and studying information which they will later use and when comprehension of details is important, they drop their reading rates significantly, typically to between 100 and 250 words per minute. For specialized purposes, such as skimming for a general idea or an overview, office workers can read successfully at high rates of speed. When scanning for specific bits of information, they can read effectively at even higher rates of speed. Office workers can enhance their overall efficiency by reading at flexible rates which consider purposes and materials.

The ability to follow directions is essential for success in the office environment. Office workers must learn to listen attentively, to read slowly and precisely, and to translate directions into prudent action. Too often office workers who fail to question and to reread written directions do not completely understand what they are to do. To help in alleviating this problem, office workers might consider and answer the following questions: (1) Do I understand the meaning of every word in my directions? (2) What task am I trying to accomplish? (3) What things will I need? (4) Where do I begin? What are the following logical steps? (5) What have I forgotten to consider? (6) Am I ready to begin the task? (7) Did I successfully finish the task to my satisfaction and to that of my supervisor? Since failure to follow directions in the office environment often leads to serious repercussions, office workers must learn to follow directions carefully if they are to succeed.

Searching and locating information as well as researching are frequent components of office tasks. In order to be successful in these reading-related activities, office workers must be rather knowledgeable about possible sources of relevant information within and outside the working environment. They must learn that many printed sources of information are arranged and/or cross-referenced alphabetically. They must determine the key words under which relevant information is indexed and locate it quickly by using guide words or other markings. Because reference sources often have challengingly high readability levels, office workers must read slowly and carefully to extract the content. When illustrations accompany the reading materials, office workers must double their reading techniques: they must read both the paragraphs and the illustrations, as one reinforces the other. Office workers who do not do so are missing a valuable means of reinforcement.

Office workers are often involved with sorting, filing, and retrieving materials. These reading-related functions require that office workers skim and scan the information in order to determine how the recorded information can best be integrated into the office filing system, decide where the recorded information goes in the storage system via alphabetizing or some other ordering process, place the recorded information where it belongs by quickly and accurately distinguishing among indexing symbols, and reverse the process by locating the stored information at a later date with a minimum of delay. Many office workers can significantly increase their record-handling skills by refining their skimming and scanning skills.

When office workers communicate in writing, they must be certain that their products are readable. To make their communications more readable, they should use short, uncomplicated sentences and paragraphs; precise vocabulary tailored to the target audience; logical, sequential arrangement of content; and subject lines, headings, and underlines to call attention to important information. By carefully structuring communications, office workers can assist others in reading successfully.

To avoid scrambled words, office workers who type must read the material which is to be typewritten at rates only slightly in excess of their actual typewriting rates. They must significantly lower their reading-studying rates to reach their proper copy-reading rates. Office workers who typewrite using combination response patterns are actually reading in two different ways: with short, saccadic eye movements for stroke-by-stroke typewriting and with long, sweeping eye movements for word and unit typewriting. Since the development of typewriting response patterns significantly influences the productivity of typists, the importance of proper reading for typewriting purposes must not be overlooked.

Office workers with shorthand skills have developed several specialized reading skills. They have become expert decoders of shorthand outlines. Shorthand readers look for minute detail in order to differentiate among various outline components. Skilled transcribers make frequent use of contextual clues. Simply stated, they use the words before and after as well as a general sense of the content as aids in decoding and in filling gaps. The skillful use of contextual clues allows competent transcribers to achieve near verbatim transcription accuracy.

The process of verifying the accuracy of recorded information, be it called proofreading, checking, or verifying, is a crucial reading-related activity in the office environment. Since the purpose of the process is to verify absolute accuracy, extreme caution and care are mandated. Reading rates must be extremely low to enhance the probability of success. In many circumstances, office workers use the highly effective paper bail method for proofreading without realizing that the method works so well because it impedes their reading rates. The paper bail method forces readers to slow down and to concentrate on the absolute accuracy of the copy.

Yes, reading-related skills are a basic component of the office environment. Only as business educators realize the importance of and aid in the development of appropriate reading-related skills can they train students to succeed in the changing office environment.

Section C: Speaking

NORMA CARR-RUFFINO

San Francisco State University, San Francisco, California

Alert business teachers are helping their students develop the oral communication skills they will need as office workers in the 1980's. These skills include:

- Giving and receiving information and instructions
- Persuading
- Setting up and participating in conferences, staff meetings, and other small group meetings
- Occasionally making short formal presentations.

Competent office workers should be able to perform all these tasks effectively, and students need to develop skills in the verbal aspects of these tasks. To be completely effective, however, students must become aware of the impact that nonverbal communications and interpersonal relationships have on verbal messages. In fact, much of the recent research in this area indicates that the verbal portion of a message is only a minor fraction of the total message the listener receives. An important goal of many teachers, then, is to help students integrate a knowledge of effective verbal communication with appropriate nonverbal messages that facilitate better interpersonal relationships. One way of accomplishing this goal is to make students aware of the more common barriers to effective oral communication and to help them develop techniques for overcoming these barriers.

BARRIERS TO EFFECTIVE SPEAKING

Here are some common practices that tend to create barriers to effective speaking:

Using vague, unclear terms. What does a secretary mean when she tells a receptionist, "You must improve your communications"? Does she mean written or spoken communications? Telephone or face-to-face conversations? That the communications are incomplete? Unclear? Garbled? Too wordy? Tactless? Or what? Students must learn to choose words that are specific and clear to the listener.

Using terms that are unfamiliar to the listener. "Now, Betty, these rollovers go to the wire desk where the AGP clerk pegs them and passes them on to LEC." Betty is new to this line of work. How well will she be able to follow this explanation? Technical terms, jargon peculiar to a certain industry, abbreviations, and other unfamiliar terms can block understanding of a message. Students must learn to put themselves in the listener's place and to use terms that are likely to be familiar, or to explain questionable terms.

Giving too much information. Some workers talk too much! Listeners can absorb only so much information at a time. When they are overloaded with information, they find it difficult to retain any of it. Students must learn to be concise, to select the most important points, and to give large quantities of information in small doses.

Giving too little information. "Here's the Payton job. Please take care of it while I'm gone this afternoon. 'Bye." Jim sits there wondering, "What's the Payton job? What does she want me to do with it?" The listener doesn't have enough information to act on the message. Students must learn to give information that is complete enough to allow the listener to respond appropriately. Again, students must develop skill in putting themselves in the listener's place.

Exhibiting nonverbal behavior that conflicts with the verbal message. "Sure, Fred, I have time to discuss that problem" (glancing at watch). "It's important to me to get this thing worked out" (drumming fingers on desk). When speakers' actions don't match their words, most listeners rightfully pay more attention to the actions. Students must learn to be clear about their intentions and to convey those intentions sincerely.

Failing to respect basic human rights. Carmen is asking for a long overdue raise. "Well . . . (head down, shoulders slumped) I know you have a budget squeeze right now, but . . . uh . . . do you think there's any way you might be able to give me a raise?" Carmen is not standing up for her personal rights, nor is she being direct in stating her position. When Bill asks for his long overdue raise, he says, "You've been overlooking the fact that I'm not paid enough for the work I do. I think you're taking advantage of me" (jaw jutting forward, hands clenched). Bill is standing up for his rights, but in the process he's attacking and belittling his boss. He's not respecting his listener's basic human rights. Students must learn to express themselves in ways that assert their own rights and at the same time respect the rights of others.

Creating defensive attitudes within listeners. When listeners feel threatened, dominated, belittled, or angry, they put up their defenses. As a result they either hear a quite different verbal message than the one the speaker intends, or they block out important parts of the message.

"Mary, your petty cash account is short again. I just can't have such sloppiness. From now on you'll have to ask me when you need money from the petty cash account." Depending on Mary's level of self-confidence, her past transactions with the speaker, and other intrapersonal and interpersonal factors, she's likely to feel some degree of defensiveness and to block or distort the speaker's words. As a result of an eight-year study, J. R. Gibb found that certain types of behavior tend to create blocks to effective communication by creating defensiveness. He categorized these into the six types of behavior shown in the lefthand column below. He also categorized the contrasting types of behavior that tend to facilitate accurate perceptions of verbal messages and to encourage open responses by creating a supportive climate (shown in the righthand column).

Behavior That Creates *Defensive Barriers*	*Behavior That Facilitates* *Open Communication*
1. Evaluating others' behavior	1. Describing others' behavior
2. Trying to control others	2. Cooperating in solving problems
3. Trying to manipulate others	3. Acting spontaneously
4. Indifferent to others' welfare	4. Concerned with others' welfare
5. Considering oneself superior to others	5. Considering oneself equal to others
6. Knowing it all.	6. Open to others' ideas.

Students must become skilled at creating supportive climes that facilitate open communication if they are to become successful in the business world.[1]

TECHNIQUES FOR OVERCOMING BARRIERS

The principles of effective speaking, as presented in many current textbooks, may be used as the foundation for overcoming the first four barriers mentioned here. In addition, many of the principles of clear, complete, concise, concrete, and courteous writing apply to speaking situations as well.

A comprehensive framework for understanding human behavior can help many students prevent or overcome barriers to communicating effectively. Transactional Analysis provides such a framework and does so in everyday language students can understand. A basic text for beginners who are unfamiliar with Transactional Analysis is *Born to Win* by Muriel James and Dorothy Jongeward (Addison-Wesley Publishing Company). More detailed explanations and examples may be found in *What Do You Say After You Say Hello?* (Grove Press) by Eric Berne, the originator of Transactional Analysis. *Egograms* by John M. Dusay (Harper & Row) provides some especially helpful ways to implement behavior change, and *The OK Boss* by Muriel James (Addison-Wesley Publishing Company) applies the concepts of Transactional Analysis to the office environment.

For many students it is helpful to understand how assertive speech and behavior facilitate effective communication while nonassertive and aggressive behavior create barriers. Assertiveness training has been especially effective in preparing women to move into the business world and to be promoted into supervisory and managerial roles. There are many assertiveness training books on the market that can provide helpful background reading for students. An indispensable text for teachers is *Responsible Assertive Behavior* by Arthur Lange and Patricia Jakubowski (Research Press Co.).

CONCLUSION

By helping students become aware of the impact nonverbal communication and interpersonal relationships have on the effectiveness of their verbal communications, business teachers can help students develop the speaking skills they need to function in the office of the 1980's. Such awareness must be integrated with a solid foundation in the principles of verbal communication.

---

[1]For further information see Gibb, J. R. "Defensive Communication." *Journal of Communication* 3:141–48; September 1961; and Carr-Smith, Norma. "Overcoming Defensive Barriers to Communication." *ABCA Bulletin* 41:12–15; March 1978.

Section D: Listening

OSCAR H. SCHUETTE

Metropolitan State College, Denver, Colorado

"Did you misunderstand what was said?" "We must have had a communications problem on this matter." "That is not what was said." Are these statements familiar? How frequently have we heard similar ones in business offices or in educational settings? Regardless of how each is stated, the implication is that a listening problem prevailed; a primary communication skill was exercised with negative results. How important is good listening ability to individuals in both personal and business settings?

Both vintage and recent research statistics reveal that the amount of time spent for each of the four conventional communication skills is as follows:

1. Of his/her total waking hours, the average person spends 70 percent in some form of communications. The total communication time consists of:

   Writing 9%
   Reading 16%
   Speaking 30%
   Listening 45%

2. The average business executive spends 90 percent of his/her working time in communications. The average communications hour consists of:

   Writing .... 5½ minutes
   Reading .... 9¼ minutes
   Speaking .... 18 minutes
   Listening .... 21 minutes

While these statistics appear to be rather general and reflect the past, they have, nevertheless, been corroborated by various recent studies and in different situations.

INSTRUCTIONAL EMPHASIS RECEIVED

If we compare the relative positions of each of the fundamental communication skills listed to the emphasis given them in public educational institutions, we find that an inverse relationship exists. Reading and writing are given a much greater emphasis than is given to speaking and listening in almost all educational institutions. Most likely no formal emphasis is given to listening. The two most used communication skills, then, receive less attention than do those used less frequently. Has our educational system been built upside down? To accentuate this negative situation even more, a high majority of people have had absolutely no personal training to develop any listening ability. They develop their own listening habits and constantly repeat them.

The business world has been much more cognizant of the need for special listening training than has the educational sector. Although slow in being recognized, listening training is now being included as units in miscellaneous business courses or as separate courses in communications departments.

COST OF POOR LISTENING

The price paid annually for poor listening ability in the business world, and especially in offices, is quite high; actually, it grows into millions of dollars. This cost grows out of various communication activities of which listening is a part. Poor listening leads to mistakes that require remedial activities, repetitive efforts, and multiplied time usage. Some business organizations actually add to the cost by funding listening improvement seminars for their employees. Offices are normally not considered as profit making; however, good communications contribute to the profit of a company and poor communications are considered hidden costs.

CRITICAL PROBLEMS

Inherent in the overall listening problem is the unawareness of specific bad listening habits and the fact that all listening activities are not alike. Distinct and separate types of listening activities have been identified, and each one requires a different self-discipline. The specific types that have been acknowledged are administrative briefing, educational listening, social listening, and nondirected listening. Playing an affiliate role in each of these types is nonverbal communication, which contributes from 55 to 80 percent of the actual message received. Listening then also has a "seeing" aspect.

The two types of listening activities that are most critical in the business world and in office settings are administrative briefing (listening to instructions) and educational listening. The former is prevalent during each work day, while the latter is heavily used in scheduled training sessions, orientation to employment processes, and for regulations instituted. Retention is the expected result of any listening activity. For administrative briefing, this retention should be evident through proper fulfillment of the instructions; for educational listening there should be a high percent absorption of information. The national retention average of individuals for educational type of listening is only 25 percent and is reached within 24–48 hours. The prevailing effectiveness of administrative briefing listening activities can easily be seen through the resultant costly mistakes referred to previously.

Listening ability is frequently confused with hearing ability. The former is mental, while the latter is physical only. The two chief distinguishing characteristics of good listening ability are those of thinking and concentration. Concentration is directly affected by the individual's curiosity about any subject. During the maturation years, one's curiosity diminishes as a result of increased interests in other activities; peer conformity; and the decision, due to past failures, that some topics are not to one's liking or are too difficult.

Both thinking and concentration are influenced by such factors as one's personal background, emotionalism, ability to detect central ideas, handling of distractions effectively, and evaluation of messages received. While all of these factors are important in their effect on good listening ability, the most significant one is that of evaluating messages. An existing human tendency is to evaluate before all the information is received and inadvertently divert the mind's efforts toward a rebuttal based on what is liked or disliked. Emotionalism can be either overly supportive or negative in nature.

In administrative briefing activities a very regimented, nonevaluating listening ability must be employed. It should be a *verbatim* acknowledgement of what was said followed by a recapitulation of the information given. For many persons this requires a strong self-discipline. The intent of any instructions is to promote explicit action rather than self-modified effort.

In educational listening, evaluation should be delayed. Evaluation in such situations, however, should be carried out formally with the characteristics of critical thinking, such as distinguishing between concepts and facts, separating fact from opinion, identifying fallacies of reasoning, understanding the nature of arguments, drawing proper inferences, etc. Employing these learned activities while listening usually helps to avoid distractions and takes up much of the differential between the high average thinking speed of some individuals and the much lower speech speed of others. Good listening ability then requires critical thinking, promotes learning, and increases retention.

EMPHASIS NEEDED

Listening skill is fundamental to an employee's effectiveness in business, but little training has been provided. Office employees cannot afford to say that they have been listening all of their lives and don't need listening training now, can hear all right, think that reading is more important, or that listening ability is mostly a matter of intelligence.

Educational institutions must provide relevant instruction for students at a sufficiently early age so that greater mental growth than in the past is possible on the way toward an occupation as well as greater receptivity while in a position. Crash seminars or a 1- or 2-hour emphasis, whether in a business establishment or in an educational institution, can at best only enable an individual to be aware of the importance of good listening ability but do very little in remedying what has been in the making for 20 or more years. Teachers at various institutional levels and in miscellaneous academic areas, both vocational and nonvocational, need to become more personally informed as to how good listening skill is developed. It must be realized that listening training is as essential as is that for other conventional communication skills. This requirement will necessitate formal training for the teachers themselves before they can hope to be of assistance to their students. No doubt, there will be resistance to this course of action. However, if there is a genuine concern for the accumulation of knowledge and a worthwhile thinking ability for our students, such resistance can hardly be justified.

Cost effectiveness procedures are always of concern to business establishments, and conventional listening ability as a basic communication skill has not measured up. In the future more attention will be given to the cost of each individual's level of the total basic communication skills. This attention will be followed by a greater awareness of the role played by each facet of communications skill. Seminars, formal courses, and a repeated emphasis on the personal improvement of listening skills should become more common. The payoff of good communication skills demands, though, that these emphases be accelerated to catch up with the lost years. Currently, collegiate and public school students are being introduced to listening instruction, although fragmented in many cases. Nevertheless, these students will have an advantage over their predecessors who are already in business positions.

CHAPTER 16

Special Competency Requirements
Section A: Data Processing Personnel

JUDITH J. LAMBRECHT

University of Minnesota, Minneapolis

The keen importance of computerized data processing for today's business needs little elaboration. It is assured that all office workers will continue to encounter an increasing number of computerized applications in their jobs. Increased automatization of administrative office functions through the development of word processing systems is one illustration of the potential merging of traditional office information systems and data processing systems.

The data processing counterparts of typewriters, calculators, and dictation devices are keypunches, data entry units, interactive terminals, remote job entry stations, minicomputers, voice-response units, and OCR devices. Further, the data processing counterparts of manual filing systems are automatic filing and information retrieval systems plus manual and semiautomatic storage and filing systems for tapes, cards, disks, printouts, and computer-output microfilm and microfiche. In short, the administrative office services functions will continue to become more intimately connected with business data processing functions. Long-range predictions are that administrative services may become part of data processing in some firms.[1]

Because of the growing pervasiveness of computers in business as well as other aspects of our daily lives, there are two areas appropriate for the development of data processing competencies at the high school level in particular: basic computer literacy and specialized data processing skills for entry-level data processing jobs in the office area. Several reports have documented the general knowledges all office employees should have to be literate about data processing; those general data processing competencies considered basic for all business employees include the following:

1. Recognize that the processing of business data is the transformation of business facts into useful information in order to show what has occurred within the business and to provide a basis for future decisions.

2. Understand the role of computers in facilitating the basic functions of a business, namely, the functions of manufacturing or producing a service,

---

[1]Dolotta, J. A., and others. *Data Processing in 1980-1985*. New York: John Wiley and Sons, 1976. pp. 134–36.

sales and marketing, purchasing, accounts payable, personnel and payroll, and billing and payments received on account.

3. Understand the role of computers for society in general, such as applications in science, government, education, recreation, and personal use.

4. Understand the differences in manual, mechanical, punched card, and electronic data processing.

5. Describe or provide examples of the following steps in the data processing cycle: recording, classifying or coding, sorting, calculating, summarizing, communicating, and storing.

6. Describe the basic components of a computer and their interrelationship, namely, input control, processing, storage, and output.

7. Recognize the capabilities and limitations of computers, such as:
   a. Ability to execute arithmetic operations at high speeds
   b. Ability to perform logical operations on data
   c. Ability to store and retrieve vast amounts of data
   d. Ability to simulate complex business situations, such as inventory control, to project the possible effects of different decisions or events
   e. Necessity for all instructions to the computer to be supplied by programs prepared by persons
   f. Need for the use of computers for business applications in which there is a large volume of data and repetitive operations
   g. Inability of the computer to make value judgments without human intervention.

In this short summary, the data processing competencies necessary for job use have been limited to those appropriate for the entry-level positions, commonly considered clerical jobs, with brief descriptions of other data processing jobs. Typically, the hierarchy of data processing occupations includes those ranging from data processing manager to systems analyst, programmer, computer operator, and data entry clerk.

Computer operations and data entry are two data processing career areas where high school preparation plus on-the-job training are sufficient for employment. In fact, Johnson has identified the three areas of keyboard specialist, technical machine operator, and data control clerk as data processing production occupations for which high school preparation is adequate to start a trainee up a career ladder.[2] Greater career advancement opportunities exist in the data control and technical machine operations areas than in the data entry field, where supervisor is likely to be the top position obtainable. Job opportunities, however, will continue to be abundant for several years in the keypunching field.

Johnson further reported that the educational, on-the-job, and prior work experience requirements for the entry-level jobs do not differ significantly for the data entry, data control, and console operator trainee positions. Because Johnson's job descriptions and training recommendations for entry-level data processing positions are both more current and comprehensive than other similar task analysis studies, the job require-

[2]Johnson, M. F. *Job Specifications for the Computer Production Operations and Skill-Related Data Processing Job Cluster.* Doctor's thesis. Philadelphia: Temple University, 1976.

ments Johnson identified are the basis for the competencies summarized here.

Each of the three entry-level DP occupations, computer console trainee, data control clerk, and data entry clerk, can be said to have the following competencies and trait requirements in common:

1. Skill in operating a 10-key adding machine and possibly the typewriter
2. Familiarity with clerical routines and filing procedures
3. Familiarity with basic data processing concepts and terminology
4. Basic arithmetic skills that will permit comparing control totals, maintaining work logs, and interpreting numerical information such as data field lengths and formats
5. Sensitivity to the importance of accurate work and ability to check carefully for discrepancies in jobs processed or incompleteness of data
6. Care in handling source documents, punched cards, or magnetic media
7. Willingness to work in circumstances requiring time-critical assignments
8. Possessing a preference for activities dealing with machines, techniques, and processes which involve routine, concrete, organized procedures
9. Ability and willingness to take and follow written and oral job instructions.

Data entry operators using either keypunch/key-verifiers, stand-alone buffered data entry devices, or computer-assisted data entry devices need the following additional competencies or traits:

1. Ability to typewrite at a minimum of 40 wpm
2. Skill in keypunch/key-verifier operations and preferable buffered stand-alone data entry device operation (tape cassette, diskette, and buffered dual-function card machines)
3. Sufficient keystroking skill to meet production requirements of approximately 8,000 keystrokes an hour on unbuffered machines to 10,000 keystrokes an hour on a buffered machine. Error ratios of 1 percent to 2.5 percent must be maintained on this work. Trainees may be expected to attain 75 percent efficiency within three months
4. Special awareness of the importance of accurate work
5. Willingness to perform continuous machine operation requiring sitting for long periods of time
6. Willingness to accept a production environment with tension, time pressure, and monotony.

Computer console operators need the following additional competencies or traits:

1. General preparation in clerical operations and data processing, also possibly accounting
2. Knowledge or familiarity with electronic and mechanical business data processing equipment
3. Motor coordination and digital dexterity necessary to manipulate equipment
4. Willingness and ability to learn rapidly the intricate operation and control of a computer system, such as the computer console, punched card, magnetic tape, direct access I/O devices, and high speed printers.

Job competencies have not been included for electric accounting machine (TAB) operators since this position, along with unit record operations as a whole, is disappearing from most firms. New data processing job titles in specialized industries, such as banks, or with specialized equipment, such as computer-output microfilm, continue to appear. While on-the-job training may initially be more feasible for such specialized jobs, students can benefit from knowing of the wide variety of data processing jobs available. Teachers will notice from the above competency lists that continued attention needs to be given to basic office skills and knowledges. The challenge for the business teacher is to relate these fundamental skills to current data processing applications.

Section B: Word Processing Personnel

ANNE M. EGRY

Brashear High School, Pittsburgh, Pennsylvania

Office automation and word processing technology have made an extraordinary impact on the secretarial profession. The most dramatic change has been made in the structure of the work station and of the work group. Reevaluation of the functional characteristics of the traditional secretarial role has led to the development of two specialized career paths—the correspondence secretary whose job tasks involve the typing or mechanistic functions and the administrative support secretary whose job tasks involve the nontyping or organic functions. Either one of these career paths may lead to middle management positions. Too, the trend toward work groups, reported in Chapter 6, will no doubt lead to other specialist positions within the total structure.

STRUCTURE OF CAREER PATHS

According to current labor statistics, office workers comprise the second-largest employment group in the United States with clerical jobs projected to increase faster than employment.[1] The use of word processing equipment is also increasing rapidly so that by the end of 1980, it is projected that the word processing industry will encompass a $6 billion market.[2] The types of businesses utilizing word processing applications are *government*, e.g., courts, probation offices, welfare departments, and police departments; *service*, e.g., law offices, airlines, insurance companies, banks, hospitals, and utility companies; *manufacturing*, e.g., engineering departments and meat-packing plants; and *retailing*, e.g., department

---

[1]Bergerud, Marly, and Gonzalez, Jean. *Word Processing: Concepts and Careers.* New York: John Wiley and Sons, 1978. p. 20.

[2]Moody, Patricia Ginn, and Matthews, Anne Lamb. "WP: More a Matter of Skills than Equipment." *Balance Sheet* 54:204; February 1978.

stores and sales offices.[3] Few businesses remain untouched by word processing.

While the organizational structure of word processing, as well as terminology, is changing, Figure I lists the career paths and average weekly salaries of word processing/administrative support personnel employed by these types of businesses in 1978.[4]

Management	
Manager Word Processing $313	Staff Analyst $360
Manager Correspondence Center $315	Manager Administrative Services $342
Supervisor Correspondence Center $263	Manager Administrative Support $315
Proofreader $196	Supervisor Administrative Support $288
Lead Correspondence Secretary $222	Lead Administrative Secretary $265
Senior Correspondence Secretary $205	Senior Administrative Secretary $247
Correspondence Secretary $182	Administrative Secretary $209
Associate Correspondence Secretary $162	Associate Administrative Secretary $165

FIGURE I. Career Paths and Average Weekly Salaries of WP/AS Personnel

STRUCTURE OF COMPETENCIES

The three specialized groups involved in a word processing/administrative support function are correspondence personnel, administrative support personnel, and middle management personnel. The general characteristics of the overall group may include the following: positive attitude, machine oriented, team oriented, detail oriented, technically oriented, self-directive, flexible, and innovative with analytical and abstract reasoning.[5]

Collecting, prioritizing, transcribing, proofreading, correcting, distributing, and filing documents are the general competencies of the correspondence personnel. Telephoning, scheduling, researching, composing, dictating, proofreading, editing, duplicating, and coding documents as well as mail handling are the general competencies of administrative support per-

---

[3]Bergerud, Marly, and Gonzalez, Jean, *op. cit.*, p. 20.

[4]International Word Processing Association. *Fourth Salary Survey Results 1978.* Willow Grove, Pa.: the Association, 1978. p. 9. Reprinted with permission.

[5]Bergerud, Marly and Gonzalez, Jean, *op. cit.*, p. 168.

sonnel. Employing, evaluating, and promoting workers and planning, coordinating, analyzing, and reporting workloads are the general competencies required of middle management personnel.[6]

IMPLICATIONS FOR EDUCATION

Word processing is a rapidly expanding technology encompassing many businesses and industries. Although the concept of word processing is not new, the systematic approach to word processing as an administrative function is innovative and should be considered a systems approach to internal and external communication services.[7] The three basic elements of a word processing system are procedures, equipment, and people. It is the personnel of a word processing environment who make the system work, and their characteristics and competencies are technical and specialized.

In order to prepare personnel for entry-level positions in a word processing environment, educators must (1) incorporate word processing concepts and terminology into already existing programs, i.e., typing, shorthand, secretarial office procedures, business English, and office management courses; and (2) implement new word processing curriculum in order to train initial entry-level workers for this new area of specialized communication services. See Chapter 6 for a detailed discussion of curriculum considerations in developing competencies for word processing personnel.

Section C: Secretarial Personnel

BETTY L. WOODEN

The National Secretaries Association (International), Kansas City, Missouri

Secretarial jobs are as varied as the secretaries themselves—no two are exactly alike. In large offices with many secretaries, there may be strict guidelines for every procedure, while in smaller offices, the secretary may have a greater degree of discretionary responsibility.

Neither can it be said that *all* secretaries must type at a certain speed, or take shorthand at so-many words a minute (or perhaps even take shorthand at all). These requirements are generally determined by the immediate supervisor, who basically wants the job done properly and in the least amount of time possible!

Teamwork between secretaries and executives has become the hallmark of more and more progressive businesses. Today's executives want, and need, secretaries who understand the purposes of the organization and who are prepared to assist in accomplishing these purposes. To fulfill these needs, career-minded secretaries must have a wide range of knowledge and

---

[6]*Ibid.*

[7]Denick, Joanne. "The Impact of Word Processing on Secretarial Education." *Balance Sheet* 60:156; December/January 1979.

skills, and be prepared for the "next" job as well as for the present one. Of primary importance is the secretary's ability to set priorities and make decisions on what must be done immediately, what may be delayed for a few hours or a day, or even what need not be done at all.

Whether the executive dictates material to be typed or the secretary composes on her own initiative, the finished product must meet the highest standards in regard to appropriate style, correct spelling and grammar, sentence structure, and punctuation. Some executives will not permit the secretary to make the slightest change in what was dictated, but fortunately, the majority of executives depend upon the secretary to "clean up" their correspondence and are grateful when they are made to "look good" on paper. They may even say, "Please answer this—you know what I want," feeling confident it will be done well. This kind of working arrangement takes time to develop, but can be most satisfactory to both the executive and the secretary.

Although most secretaries would list filing as their least-liked duty, a no-fail filing system is extremely important in a well-run office. Whether simple or elaborate, the system must enable the secretary to quickly retrieve correspondence, reports, documents, or whatever. In large companies, there may be a central file room, but the secretary must be familiar with the system used for coding, requesting files, and seeing that files are returned as soon as they have served their purpose.

The secretary should be familiar with the newest office machines and equipment. Possessing factual information on the advantages and disadvantages of various equipment and supplies may often save the employer money and improve the efficiency of the operations.

The secretary should be knowledgeable concerning various duplication/reproduction processes. The method chosen will depend upon the cost, the speed required, and the quality of the finished product. For example, a general in-house memo to 30 people could be reproduced by mimeograph or photocopy, but the annual report to the stockholders would usually require the services of a first-class printer. Someone else may be responsible for selecting the printer, but the secretary may be required to prepare the material itself.

Even if the organization has a central mailroom, the secretary should know the latest postal information regarding types of services available, such as insured, registered, certified, special delivery, special handling, express mail, mailgrams, etc., and which would be applicable to a given situation.

Teletype or telex services are available in many offices. The secretary may be required to operate these machines and should become familiar with them. These services are quick, and less costly than long-distance telephone calls.

Of course, good telephone technique is very important. Often the secretary is the only image of the company that customers or clients may have. Knowing how to handle the important client, or the irate customer, or the "pesky" salesman (without making anyone angry) is a valuable asset to the organization. The trend today is for the executives to place their own calls and to receive calls direct, rather than through the secretary, but if the secretary customarily screens the executive's phone calls, it must be done in such a way as to make the caller feel the call has received prompt, courteous attention.

Frequently a secretary may be called upon to research material for a speech or various reports for which the executive is responsible. The material may be in the office files, the company library, or perhaps the public library. Knowing how to find the material needed is an invaluable help to the executive.

Another important area of secretarial duties is preparing agendas, planning meetings, meal functions, company parties, etc. Even if a travel agency is used for airline or train travel, the secretary will need to know the kinds of hotel accommodations referred, whether the executive's schedule is flexible or if he *must* be in a certain city at a certain time for an important appointment, and whether he prefers first-class, coach, or "economy" travel arrangements. The secretary should know how to read an airline schedule and will find the Official Airline Guide very helpful.

If the secretary has the responsibility for making appointments for the executive, it is important that the calendar be posted and the executive made aware of what has been scheduled.

The secretary should be familiar with company policies and their implementation. Many companies have standard procedures covering every conceivable phase of the business; others are more flexible in the day-to-day operations, but the secretary must know the limits of authority granted her.

Depending upon the size of the organization and the types of products and/or services it provides, the secretary will often find it necessary to be familiar with data processing terms and procedures and to provide input for the computer.

Some knowledge of business law is often required, concerning such matters as contracts, product liability laws, insurance, etc.

Many secretaries have the responsibility of supervising other employees and *may* have the authority to hire or fire. (Knowing the latest EEOC rules and regulations is extremely important in this instance.)

The secretary must, of course, understand the importance of confidentiality as it pertains to the executive's work and hers. This may include maintaining personnel files, salary information, job openings due to promotions, retirements, terminations, etc. It is the executive's prerogative to release this kind of information, and a secretary must never forget that!

All of the above duties can be learned, either through formal schooling, on-the-job training, or through trial-and-error experience. Another important asset worth mentioning is for the secretary to *look* the part, which means appropriate grooming in good taste for the office.

But an all-important secretarial asset is the ability to get along with the executive, fellow employees, customers, and the public in general. Knowing everything about the job itself is important, but if *human relations* are neglected, the secretary will be more of a liability than an asset. Having a positive attitude, and willingness to cooperate in resolving conflicts, along with a good sense of humor, will almost certainly ensure secretarial success.

The National Secretaries Association (International) has based its general outline of secretarial assignments and responsibilities on its long-standing definition of a secretary as "an executive assistant who possesses a mastery of office skills, demonstrates the ability to assume responsibility without direct supervision, exercises initiative and judgment, and makes decisions within the scope of assigned authority."

In the context of NSA's definition, the following has evolved [reprinted with permission from the May 1978 issue of The Secretary magazine, published by The National Secretaries Association (International), Kansas City, Missouri]:

NSA PROTOTYPE SECRETARIAL JOB DESCRIPTION

A secretary relieves executive of various administrative details; coordinates and maintains effective office procedures and efficient work flows; implements policies and procedures set by employer; establishes and maintains harmonious working relationships with superiors, co-workers, subordinates, customers or clients, and suppliers.

Schedules appointments and maintains calendar. Receives and assists visitors and telephone callers and refers them to executive or other appropriate person as circumstances warrant. Arranges business itineraries and coordinates executive's travel requirements.

Takes action authorized during executive's absence and uses initiative and judgment to see that matters requiring attention are referred to delegated authority or handled in a manner so as to minimize effect of employer's absence.

Takes manual shorthand and transcribes from it or transcribes from machine dictation. Types material from longhand or rough copy.

Sorts, reads, and annotates incoming mail and documents and attaches appropriate file to facilitate necessary action; determines routing, signatures required, and maintains follow-up. Composes correspondence and reports for own or executive's signature. Prepares communication outlined by executive in oral or written directions.

Researches and abstracts information and supporting data in preparation for meetings, work projects, and reports. Correlates and edits materials submitted by others. Organizes material which may be presented to executive in draft format.

Maintains filing and records management systems and other office flow procedures.

Makes arrangements for and coordinates conferences and meetings. May serve as recorder of minutes with responsibility for transcription and distribution to participants.

May supervise or hire other employees; select and/or make recommendations for purchase of supplies and equipment; maintain budget and expense account records, financial records, and confidential files.

Maintains up-to-date procedures manual for the specific duties handled on the job.

Performs other duties as assigned or as judgment or necessity dictates.

Section D: Support Personnel

J. HOWARD JACKSON

Virginia Commonwealth University, Richmond

In the 1959 American Business Education Yearbook, Satlow identified seven types of activities performed by clerical support workers:[1]

1. Typewriting and preparation for duplication
2. Filing
3. Recordkeeping
4. Handling the telephone
5. Operating adding-calculation machines
6. Operating miscellaneous office machines
7. Nonspecialized activities such as:
   a. Classifying and sorting
   b. Checking for accuracy
   c. Filling in forms
   d. Stuffing and sealing envelopes
   e. Collating and stapling
   f. Addressing envelopes by hand
   g. Operating a folding machine
   h. Ordering supplies
   i. Relieving other workers.

Despite the impact of computer technology and word processing over the past 21 years, jobs requiring these same skills still exist. Office terminology and technology have changed, but the responsibility of equipping students with competency in these support areas remains. The following paragraphs will explore the competencies in the areas where office technology has made the greatest impact.

REPROGRAPHICS

Reprographics involves the use of two types of equipment, copiers and duplicators, to reproduce multiple copies of typed, written, or drawn images. The competencies required for effective use of reprographic services are:

1. Preparation of camera-ready copy
2. Proofreading and the ability to judge quality copy
3. Operating copying and duplicating machines

[1]Satlow, David I. "Routine and Nonspecialized Skills." *The Clerical Program in Business Education.* Sixteenth American Business Education Yearbook. Somerville, N.J.: Somerset Press, 1959. Chapter 9, pp. 107-08.

4. Selecting the appropriate process to save time, effort, and money
5. Identifying and using special features of copying and duplicating machines, such as:
   a. *Duplexing*—the process of reproducing copy on both sides of a sheet of paper
   b. *Reduction*—the ability of a copier to reduce the size of the original copy
   c. *Color*—because of the high per-copy cost, use of color copiers limited in most offices to jobs where color is essential.
6. Preparation of special imagery processes: Copy to be duplicated can be transferred to an offset stencil or spirit master in a number of ways, and although recent developments have eliminated the necessity for typing the original, typing a stencil or master is still the most widely used method of producing an image to be copied or duplicated.

   Four major imagery processes have emerged in the past two decades. Students should be competent in their use because of the tremendous savings in time and effort. *Thermal imagery or heat transfer* is used to image stencils and spirit masters. *Facsimilie imaging* refers to the electronic scanning method of preparing stencils and offset masters. *Photo imaging* permits the rapid transfer of original copy to offset masters. No film is required, but a chemically sensitized master is used. *Electrostatic imaging* is the fourth method with which students should be familiar and it involves substituting a sensitized offset master for copy paper in a copier. The original is copied on to the master to be reproduced on an offset duplicator.
7. Other miscellaneous competencies needed for effective performance in reprographics are:
   a. Collating
   b. Stapling
   c. Drawing on a master and stencils
   d. Making corrections on stencils and masters
   e. Preparing guide copy
   f. Selecting the proper paper and quality of masters and stencils
   g. Placement of copy on masters and stencils
   h. Cleaning and identifying stencils.

MAILROOM

Mail is a major concern to most businesses. Since the Postal Reorganization Act of 1970, postal services have changed and the cost of their services has increased. There has been increased use of mechanization but a decrease in the volume of mail handled by the post office because of the popularity of the telephone and alternative ways of sending messages. Business teachers preparing clerical support personnel should insure that students have the following competencies:

1. Identify and use the proper classifications of domestic mail and the most efficient use of postal services.
2. Identify and use other appropriate classifications of mail such as priority mail, official and free mail, mixed classes, and mail for the blind.
3. Identify various services offered by the post office including: registered and insured mail, COD service, certified mail, certificates of mailing, special delivery and special handling, metered mail, forwarding, returning and re-

mailing, recalling mail, change of address, zip codes, presorting, mailgram, Vertical Improved Mail (VIM), general delivery, international mail, money orders—foreign and domestic, reply postage.

4. Identify and select appropriate domestic shipping services. The major services with which office workers should be familiar are United Parcel Service; railway, air, and bus express; rail, motor, water, and air freight.

The role of the teacher should be to provide background that will enable the student to determine the savings in time and money that can be made by comparing costs and delivery times of the different services. Other competencies needed by support personnel assigned to the mailroom include briefly:

1. Filling in forms by hand
2. Stuffing, sealing, and stamping envelopes
3. Classifying and sorting internal mail
4. Checking for accuracy
5. Addressing envelopes by hand
6. Sealing, stamping, folding, opening letters mechanically.

TELEPHONE

The competencies needed to handle the telephone are essential to every office worker's success. Technology has changed this important facet of office support services. A brief listing of the competencies needed by students in handling the telephone includes the following:

1. Ability to handle all aspects of telephone conversation—greeting, identification, voice modulation, ending a conversation, message taking, screening calls, and the use of phonetic techniques in helping callers understand names and numbers—e.g., "A" as in apple, "B" as in boy
2. Ability to use equipment properly—there are several new developments here that make telephone service more efficient. These are:
   a. Dimension—an electronic system with a display board that indicates the calling number and the class of service employed by the caller. This is the latest model of the Bell System's PBX (Private Branch Exchange), but it has many new features.
   b. Com Key—a small desk switchboard with many new features
   c. Centrex—a system permitting an outside caller to dial direct to the extension without going through that switchboard
3. Ability to use special telephone services, including the directory, message-taking services, toll-free numbers, direct distance dialing, operator-assisted calls, telephone credit cards, telegrams, and mailgrams
4. Ability to determine the relative costs of the various telephone and telegraphic services
5. Ability to determine the proper time to make calls according to the time zones and the application of special rates.

Proper telephone technique is essential to business success, and considerable help to the teacher developing these competencies is available through local telephone companies.

Although the activities listed by Satlow in 1959 still exist as a part of the administrative support services in the office of 1980, new developments in this area have been tremendous. Only a few of the major competencies required as a result of these changes have been included here, and no attempt was made to give an in-depth analysis of the teacher's role in providing future officer workers with the required competencies to cope with the support services needed in the office of the eighties.

Section E: Records Management Personnel

DOUGLAS A. GOINGS

McNeese State University, Lake Charles, Louisiana

Records management personnel may be classified into two groups of job competencies according to the degree of difficulty and specialization associated with their job tasks. The first, the job-entry personnel group, works primarily as records room clerks and couriers. More than likely, their tasks center around alphabetic and numeric records management methods. The second, the promotional records management group, works with all methods of records management. Their tasks involve work with alphabetic, numeric, geographic, chronologic, and subject records management methods. Where job-entry personnel are concerned primarily with filing and finding, promotional personnel are concerned with records retention and disposition, creation and expansion, and supervisory tasks.

In examining these two groups of records management personnel, a survey of competencies for each group will help define more clearly the various tasks involved with the two groups.

JOB-ENTRY RECORDS MANAGEMENT PERSONNEL

Entry-level personnel should be expected to have competence in records management in three areas: knowledge, skill, and human relations. If these three areas are at acceptable levels, little time and effort will be wasted in the records department. These competencies should indicate how well entry personnel can handle tasks usually associated with their positions.

For the largest number of business offices, all tasks in the records department center around the alphabetic or the numeric records management method. Entry personnel should be expected to have a proper understanding of these two methods, as defined by company policy; be able to follow the procedures associated with each method, including retrieval procedures; and possess acceptable human relations skills for the records department.

Knowledge competencies. Job-entry personnel usually work as records department clerks, filing and finding materials stored by the alphabetic method. The most critical factor, therefore, is that these personnel fully

178

understand the rules for alphabetic indexing. All personnel must be adequately prepared for alphabetic indexing since records management theory is based upon these rules. Entry-level personnel who are aware of the advantages and disadvantages of the alphabetic and numeric methods demonstrate better job performance than personnel lacking this awareness.

A clear understanding of the procedures for alphabetic and numeric methods should be expected of all personnel in the records department. Each step—indexing, coding, inspection, cross-referencing, sorting, and filing—should be fully understood and locked into proper sequence for each member of the department. Each person should fully understand the theory and mechanics of retrieval procedures. Proper care must be taken so that each step in the retrieval process becomes as active a part as possible of the job performance of the department personnel. This process is important if the records department is to provide full service for its company.

Skill competencies. The skills competence area of records management should include the speed and care involved in the ordering and sorting of supplies and equipment for the records department. Typing of labels and preparation of file folders, file cabinets, and file guides is important because of the time saved with easily read file materials. Personnel must be able to read quickly, with good comprehension, so that filing and finding time is kept to a minimum. This skill is required for proper inspection, indexing, cross-referencing, and sorting. Listening is an important part of records management work. Records department clerks must listen closely when requests for filed materials are made by telephone, in person, or by courier. Good color distinction is necessary if color-coded systems are used in the records department.

Human relations competencies. If the records department is to function properly and to its purpose, the personnel must be able to relate to other departments in the company. Good human relations skills must be actively employed to ensure that the records department is seen as an important, active part of the company. Proper communication with other personnel in and outside of the department expresses concern for good human relations.

PROMOTIONAL RECORDS MANAGEMENT PERSONNEL

As records department personnel mature in the performance of their job tasks, they may be assigned more specific and demanding records management tasks. These tasks include making decisions about records transfer and storage, supplies and equipment purchases, maintenance programs, system design and expansion, and supervision of department activities and personnel. These tasks are the natural promotion work for former entry personnel after they have had a sufficient internship as records department clerks and couriers. Promotional records management personnel can effectively function at a more advanced level of job activity if they achieve competence at the required levels of knowledge, skill, and human relations.

Knowledge competencies. Records department personnel perform a variety of decision-making functions. Examination and design for new records management systems and system expansion require knowledge of available supplies, equipment, methods, and systems. If the personnel in the records department are to be held responsible for the safety of filed materials, then requisition, charge-out, and follow-up procedures must be fully understood. Supervisory tasks require complete understanding of records management philosophy and personnel management theories.

Skill competencies. For the higher level of records management job performance, personnel should be able to demonstrate the same skills required of entry-level personnel. Skills in reading, typing, completing forms, listening, filing, and finding are needed by everyone in the records department. The most critical for promotional records personnel is reading. These personnel are expected to make decisions on numerous functions, records cycles, retention and disposition programs, subject method indexes, etc., all of which require excellent reading and comprehension skills.

Human relations competencies. Because of the more complex and demanding job performance of promotional records management personnel, excellent human relations skills are essential. Supervisory tasks require top quality communication for smooth operation of the records department. Just as good human relations skills are required of records department clerks for proper records department recognition, these skills are equally important for the promotion personnel. Records department supervisors and purchasing agents work more closely with the company than do clerks and couriers; therefore, such positions require well-developed human relations skills.

FUTURE RECORDS MANAGEMENT

The records department of the future will consist of highly technical equipment, computer-assisted file devices, and personnel who resemble computer programmers. The days of the "letter in the file folder" are disappearing. Tomorrow's records management practices and procedures will center around computers and CRT units. Personnel required for the future must have word processing skills, computer programming skills, and superior human relations skills. The work of the future records department personnel will be much more attractive but will be much more demanding because of the expected increases in materials, personnel requirements, and government policies.

CHAPTER 17

Emerging Office Occupations

G. W. MAXWELL and JUDITH KNIGHT O'HARE

San Jose State University, San Jose, California

If they are to be relevant, office education programs must accurately reflect the office environment that exists in the real world of business. But successful fulfillment of this requirement in the midst of a situation where offices are in a state of continual change presents a challenge to any curriculum designer.

With this situation in mind, the business education personnel in the vocational unit of the California State Department of Education collaborated with the business education department at San Jose State University to design a research project. A major portion of the goals of the research was to (1) identify new and emerging office occupations, (2) analyze circumstances that led to development of these occupations, and (3) gain insight into the effect of the findings upon the business education curriculum. Concurrent goals also concerned the handicapped and the disadvantaged as well as sex equity.

The report presented in this chapter deals only with the findings related to the first two goals listed above. It is based upon completion of most but not all of a series of interviews scheduled with California business firms and selected informed persons.

The research was concerned with entry-level office occupations. Management type office positions were excluded from consideration in the research. An entry-level occupation was defined as a beginning job acquired by a person with little or no prior work experience and with little or no formal education or special training beyond the secondary school. Office occupations generally included such titles as clerk, typist, secretary, accounting clerk, word processor, data input operator, and stenographer.

PROCEDURE

At the beginning of the research study, it was decided that information regarding emerging office occupations could be gathered from related literature and from companies employing large office staffs. A review of the printed material was helpful in determining what other researchers had concluded about office jobs and in focusing the emphasis of the interview questions. The interviews, however, provided most of the information for the study.

Approximately 40 companies throughout California were chosen for the interviews. Most companies selected were chosen because they employ a sizable number of office personnel and are well-known in their industry. A few smaller companies were included because their reputations earmarked them as being innovative within their industry.

In addition, interviews were conducted with seven individuals who have been studying and investigating jobs and offices of the future. Three temporary employment agencies were also interviewed because of their role in meeting clerical needs in offices.

The respondent companies employed from 300 to over 10,000 people in occupational fields that include legal, oil, medical, manufacturing, financial, utilities, insurance, scientific, electronic, and travel industries. Employment or personnel representatives were usually the persons contacted for the interview, and they were asked the following open-ended questions:

1. How many people do you employ?
2. How many are in clerical positions?
3. (A) How are job skills and job competencies in clerical occupations changing?
   (B) Are there new components in these occupations?
4. Are any of these skills or competencies becoming so complex that they are creating or will create new jobs?
5. What clerical jobs do you think will not exist in five years? What will replace them?
6. (A) What kind of training and/or educational background is necessary for someone to enter a clerical occupation?
   (B) What basic skills do you require for these jobs?
7. (A) What opportunities are available in clerical positions for handicapped people?
   (B) What opportunities are available for academically or economically disadvantaged people?
8. What is being done to eliminate sex bias and discrimination in clerical occupations?
9. Can you identify any new occupations? If so, identify and describe.
10. Are job openings a result of growth, replacement, or both?

Although each person was asked the same questions, additional information was often volunteered by the company spokesperson. This information usually was indicative of the specific needs and emphasis of the individual company and/or representative.

After completion of the interviews, the actual responses as recorded were developed into sets of "standard" responses. For example, the actual responses "skilled, qualified, clerical employees are difficult to locate" and "word processing operators and secretaries are hard to get" became the standard response of "there is a shortage of good/qualified secretaries and/ or clerks or tellers." Each actual response was then fitted into one of the standard responses and frequency tallies were made. The sets of standard responses along with their frequency tallies appear in the "Findings" portion of this chapter. Only portions of the findings appear in this article.

FINDINGS

Since the interview questions were open-ended, and all additional volunteer information was welcome, the scope of the responses was quite broad. If time and finances had permitted, a follow-up questionnaire could have been developed from the responses and submitted again to the participating companies for their agreement or disagreement with the standard response statements. This probably would have altered the findings and given stronger support to particular trends.

For example, some companies volunteered information pertaining to what schools could do to prepare students for the working world. Approximately 13 companies mentioned a need for business English. If the follow-up questionnaire had been distributed to companies and included a question such as "Do you think business English should be taught in schools?" more than 13 of the 40 companies probably would have responded positively. It is necessary to keep this in mind when interpreting the findings presented below.

The numbers on the right indicate the frequencies of the responses.

1. How many people do you employ?
   a. 1000–4999   12
   b.   600– 999   5
   c. 10,000+   5
   d.   300– 599   3
   e. 5000–9999   3

2. How many are in clerical positions?
   a. 1000–4999   10
   b.   600– 999   6
   c.   100– 299   4
   d.   25– 99   2
   e. 10,000+   2
   f.   300– 599   1
   g. 5000–9999   0

3. (A) How are job skills and job competencies in clerical occupations changing?
   a. New skills needed for new technology in the office (word processors, computers, telephone systems, etc.)   12
   b. No great changes, but a refinement and/or sophistication in jobs because of new automated information systems (technology)   11
   c. Automation has relieved some of routine or rote work of secretaries and typists   11
   d. More technical and specialized   6
   e. Secretaries are expected to work for more people   4
   f. More behavior and interpersonal skills development so employees will get along better with each other   3
   g. Clerical positions going on-line; therefore, clerks need to acquire some data processing skills   3
   h. Not changing—still use large clerical staff for same jobs   3
   i. Fewer skills needed   3
   j. More complex due to government regulations   2
   k. People need to be more detail oriented and analytical   2

3. (B) Are there new components in these occupations?
   a. Clerks going on-line (learning to use computers) 8
   b. Some secretaries are doing more administrative duties 6
   c. Secretaries doing paralegal work 1
   d. New equipment and demand in the credit field could lead to new jobs 1

The responses to question number three indicate that new technology in the office is relieving workers of some routine and uninteresting work as well as demanding new skill, knowledge, and capabilities. Rather than causing unique new jobs to surface, the technology of the automated office is bringing about a refinement of existing jobs.

4. Are any of these skills or competencies becoming so complex that they are creating or will create new jobs?
   a. Secretary moving into administrative assistant position 8
   b. Clerk typists moving into the role of word processor 5
   c. In stock brokerage, a wire-operator (who places orders) is now considered a computer operator because of technical advancements 2
   d. File clerks becoming records managers—gaining new emphasis, not low level clerical jobs any more 1

Again, it can be seen that the responses do not per se indicate that new jobs are emerging. Rather, they seem to depict a change in the nature and characteristics of existing jobs. There also appears to be a rise in the status of some clerical positions.

5. What jobs do you think will *not* exist five years from now?
   a. Keypunch operators 7
   b. Clerical jobs (routine, nitty-gritty) that machines will be doing 5
   c. File clerks 4
   d. Word processing changing the traditional role of secretary 3
   e. Steno-clerk duties being taken care of by word processing 3
   f. Fewer accounting clerks, since computerization 1
   g. Newspaper stereotypesetters 1
   h. Entry-level (no prior experience) 1

The common characteristic of office jobs that may be disappearing is repetitive and routine work. This is almost certainly due to the increasing role of automation in the office in performing this type of task.

6. (A) What kind of training and/or educational background is necessary for someone to enter a clerical occupation?

Accounting clerk
One or more years of experience and education in accounting 4
Ten-key adding machine 1

Intermediate clerk (training to be bank teller)
No work experience necessary 1

Receptionist-medical
Elementary medical training 1

Insurance—entry level
No work experience necessary 2
Does not have to be high school graduate 1

Legal secretary
One and one-half years of legal experience   1

Banking secretary
Six months to one year of clerical experience   1

Entry-level banking
No work experience necessary   2
Does not have to be high school graduate   1

Entry-level general
Does not have to be high school graduate   2
No work experience necessary   2
Cash handling or public contact experience   1

General secretary
Two years secretarial experience   2
No work experience necessary   1

Entry-level computer
Computer familiarity   1

Tellers
Ten-key adding machine   2
Cash handling and public contact   1

Companies such as banks and insurance agencies frequently require neither a high school diploma nor prior work experience. The clerical jobs in these two businesses are excellent stepping stones into the company and eventually into management positions.

6. (B) What basic skills do you require for this job?

According to the responses, typing skill is most often required by businesses for secretarial and clerical positions. The next most frequently asked for skills are machine transcription skill, shorthand, and good communication skills. It is important to note conflicting responses concerning shorthand. Nine companies said that there is a reduced need for shorthand, while eight noted that shorthand is required for most secretarial positions. For higher level secretarial jobs, shorthand is still important, especially if the secretary wants to work for an executive. Word processing skills are not in high demand because not all of the companies interviewed are making use of word processing equipment at this time. Since there are so many different types of equipment, good typing and editing skills are more in demand because people with these skills can be trained on the equipment. As more businesses make use of word processing equipment, trained operators undoubtedly will be in greater demand.

7. (A) What opportunities are available in clerical positions for handicapped?
    a. Company works with department of rehabilitation or other
       agencies for disabled   8
    b. Commitment to employing handicapped   6
    c. Not many (or any) disabled apply for the jobs   4
    d. Facilities are adaptable to handicapped needs   3
    e. Identifying jobs that specifically can be filled by handicapped   2
    f. No specific programs   2
    g. Good clerical jobs available   2

h. Facilities available but must meet company specifications for job 2
i. Hired for some departments but not others 2
j. Takes care of own people disabled on the job 1
k. Repetitive jobs available 1
l. Arrangements for handicapped students to be in work experience programs 1

7. (B) What opportunities are available for academically or economically disadvantaged people?
a. Work experience programs 5
b. Training classes for minorities to help them get better jobs 4
c. Working with inner-city schools to convince students not to drop out 2
d. Work with organizations that help "disadvantaged" people 2
e. Classes for disadvantaged minorities to fulfill high school diploma requirements 1
f. Not many apply 1
g. Jobs designated 1

Most companies make an effort to assist disabled and disadvantaged workers in finding office jobs. The number of handicapped office employees is not very large. However, the trend of the future seems to be to hire more handicapped people in order to meet government affirmative action requirements and because employers are realizing the potential of handicapped employees.

A number of companies are spending time and money to work with economically disadvantaged students to convince them to stay in school. Businesses are also working with schools to provide employment for students from inner-city schools through work experience programs.

8. What is being done to eliminate sex bias and discrimination in clerical occupations?
a. More males in clerical positions 16
b. Increase of male word processors 8
c. No significant increase in male clericals 6
d. Women and men encouraged to try nontraditional jobs 4
e. Breaking down opposition to male secretaries 2
f. Committed to fairness 2
g. Higher predominance of men in clerical positions in San Francisco 2
h. Government demanding more males 1
i. Speaking at schools to tell students jobs are not limited to one sex 1
j. As wages in clerical jobs increase, both men and women choosing these jobs 1

There is an indication of an increase of males in some clerical office positions. Word processing seems to have more appeal to men than other clerical jobs. This seems to be consistent with both males and females working in so called nontraditional jobs throughout our society.

9. Can you identify any new occupations? If so, identify and describe.
a. Word processing operators 9
b. Input/output clerks (stock brokerages) 2
c. New positions and new job titles being tied to new products offered by companies 2

d. New occupations in specific companies, but not new to offices 2
e. Microfilm processors 1
f. Liaison representative (credit card division go-between for collectors, managers, and customers) 1
g. Office manager overseeing a group of secretaries and word processor operators 1

Most of the jobs new to particular companies are in the area of word processing, which in itself is not a new occupation. Other jobs that some businesses consider new are already in existence elsewhere.

10. Are job openings a result of growth, replacement, or both?
    a. Growth 9
    b. Replacement 6
    c. Both 2

Although only ten formal questions were asked, the following information was volunteered.

11. What can schools (education) do to meet your future needs?
    a. Students should learn business English (grammar, spelling, punctuation and editing). 13
    b. Students should learn typing. 7
    c. Schools should offer a course in data processing. 7
    d. Students should improve communication skills (written and oral). 5
    e. Students should learn shorthand. 4
    f. Students should learn basic math and other basic skills. 4
    g. Students should be taught telephone techniques. 4
    h. Students should be taught techniques for getting and keeping a job. 4
    i. Teach basic business etiquette. 4
    j. Stress the future need for a combination of technical skills and human relations skills. 3
    k. Students should learn accounting and bookkeeping. 3
    l. Provide word processing training. 3
    m. Students should learn computer language. 3
    n. Teach students how to accept change and work with it; to be flexible and know trends. 2
    o. Schools should offer a course in merchandising. 2
    p. Teachers should work in offices to keep abreast of changes. 2
    q. Teach vocabulary (jargon of various industries). 2
    r. Students need to learn to be creative thinkers and how to make decisions. 2
    s. Instill good work habits and work ethics of loyalty and responsibility to employer. 2
    t. Students should learn medical terminology. 1
    u. Prepare students for future technology. 1
    v. Move the stress away from college preparatory. 1
    w. Learn machine transcription. 1
    x. Help students set career goals. 1
    y. Teach survival skills. 1

12. What will the office of the future be like and how will it affect jobs?
    a. Paperless—computerized filing and retrieval 3

      b. Work more interesting   3
      c. More job satisfaction   2

The following list begins with lettered sub-items:

    b. Work more interesting — 3
    c. More job satisfaction — 2
    d. Electronic mail — 2
    e. More in-plant printing — 2
    f. Everyone in the office connected to a computer — 2
    g. Competition among companies to provide best customer service — 2
    h. Terminals at home—call work into the office — 1
    i. Computationless—computer does computations — 1

13. Other unsolicited information
    a. There is a shortage of good/qualified secretaries and/or clerks or tellers. — 10
    b. Some companies (banks and insurance in particular) are experiencing high turnover. — 5
    c. Business people are going out to high schools and junior high schools to convince students to stay in school, and to tell students about various career opportunities. Personnel people in particular will talk to students about job seeking and job keeping techniques. — 5
    d. Automation is not reducing the number of clerical and secretarial jobs. — 4
    e. A small number of companies are resorting to in-house training programs because many of their entry-level clerical applicants and employees do not have basic English and math skills. — 4
    f. There is a trend to change job titles rather than to actually change the job itself and the skills required to carry out the job. — 4
    g. Fewer women are going into secretarial careers. — 3
    h. There is a rise in status and caliber of secretaries. — 2
    i. There are an increasing number of re-entry women in the job market. — 2
    j. Some companies are converting their paper files to microfilm or microfiche. — 2
    k. Automation has reduced the number of clerk typists and secretaries. — 1
    l. Medical clerical jobs are available. — 1
    m. The position of executive secretary is still a valuable one. — 1

The shortage of qualified clerical employees was expressed by a number of companies and seems to be a problem for employers throughout California.

CONCLUSIONS

One of the primary goals of the research study was to identify new and emerging office occupations. However, interestingly enough, the findings do not appear to indicate any new occupations in this area of business. Rather, office occupations appear to be in an evolutionary transition rather than part of a revolutionary overhaul. Some companies did identify some occupations which they labeled as new; however, it appears that these were actually new to the company rather than new to offices in general. In some cases, new job titles were being used, such as administrative assistant instead of secretary; however, a new job title by itself does not necessarily indicate a new occupation with new job skills being used.

Although new office occupations do not appear to be emerging within the foreseeable future, an awareness of trends relating to office workers is nevertheless vital to business and business educators so that they can be prepared for evolutionary change. Some trends that appeared to surface from the interview findings were:

1. There is a continuing need for clerical personnel in most industries. There is a shortage of skilled, qualified secretaries throughout the state, as well as people to fill the many job openings for other types of clerical positions. The Department of Labor predictions verify this finding and foresee a growing need for office workers over the next five years. The only industry interviewed that did not have any problems finding applicants was the airline industry, which has an abundance of applicants for all positions.

2. As new technology is introduced into the office, jobs are becoming more specialized and more sophisticated. Many clerical jobs require a higher skill level in order to meet the specialized tasks. New skills are necessary to carry out jobs on equipment such as computers, word processing equipment, and telephone systems. However, the traditional keyboard skills are still mandatory for most office jobs, since computerized and other types of automated equipment that are being used in offices require use of a keyboard. Jobs are becoming more interesting and less routine in the office since automation has eliminated many of the boring tasks.

3. Since many of the routine (and often time-consuming) tasks no longer need to be done by secretaries, they are assuming more responsibility for decisions and tasks formerly handled by their bosses and managers. This definite trend will probably make the secretarial job more interesting and appealing to both men and women.

4. Information is being recorded and stored on microfilm and microfiche, or is being fed directly into computers. This trend has raised the status of the file clerk job to that of records management and microfilm processing, with new skill levels required to store and retrieve information.

5. Although not an original objective of the research project, findings pertaining to the office of the future emerged from some of the interviews. More and more work will be done by machines interacting with each other. However, there does not seem to be any indication of a reduction in the number of clerical workers needed in the office. A solid combination of technical skills and human relations skills will become more essential in the computerized or automated office.

IMPLICATIONS FOR BUSINESS EDUCATORS

What are the implications of these findings for business educators? What effect should the findings have on the business education curriculum? Should new offerings be incorporated into the business education curriculum?

The findings indicate a need for students to become familiar and comfortable with computers and other new office technological equipment. Therefore, if data processing classes are *not* part of the present business education curriculum, the findings suggest that these classes should be added. This might pose a problem of cost for educational institutions since most cannot afford to install and update the latest office equipment. Perhaps the answer lies in more cooperation between business and education. Many equipment companies can demonstrate new lines of office equipment, and tours of innovative companies would provide exposure of the students to office technology.

A revision of some existing courses to include aspects of such areas as micrographics and reprographics may be more reasonable than expansion of the entire curriculum. Also, new materials are constantly being published that enable instructors to teach the terminology and basic concepts of data processing without any equipment. Classes such as filing could be updated to include newer and more sophisticated methods of records management. Office or secretarial practice classes could contain assignments that require decision-making techniques that might be used by an administrative assistant.

Business English was mentioned emphatically by numerous companies as the class most needed in schools. If business English is already an offering in a business education department, incorporating terminology from various types of businesses would be a relevant revision.

Should the business education offerings be moved to a different grade level? Are they being taught too late in a student's school career, or should the more technical and specialized instructions needed for tomorrow's jobs be taught in postsecondary institutions? Students at all educational levels benefit from business education, since most of them will work at some point in their lives and can put more sophisticated information to use as they go through school and make their career choices.

What about the possibility of reducing the number of offerings? This is not consistent with the findings of the study. Students need *more* exposure to the business world, not less, if they are going to be prepared to survive and succeed in a changing technological environment.

CHAPTER 18

Career Opportunities

B. JUNE SCHMIDT

Virginia State Department of Education Regional Office, Radford

The processing of information has always been the basic function of the office work force. The office serves as the physical facility where information is classified, sorted, coded, recorded, analyzed, and reported. Through the operation of the office, management of an organization is able to interact with information, an activity essential to sustain the life of an organization.

Work force projections indicate that over the next several decades a larger and larger proportion of the work force will be employed as office workers. This increase will not result from a change in the basic function of the office. Instead, it will occur because of increased demand for more, more timely, and more accurate information on the part of management. Readily accessible information will serve as a major factor in an organization's meeting competitive demands.

The ability of the office worker to provide the required information will be dramatically affected by emerging office technology. The key technological impact will most likely come from expansion of telecommunications capabilities rather than from expanded electronic data processing capabilities as typically perceived. Telecommunications advances will facilitate the transfer of information between and among office systems such as word processing, micrographics, and reprographics.

The new office technology may be viewed as a threat to the typical office worker of today. Assumptions are often made that sophisticated equipment can replace workers. Experience, however, has shown the reverse to be true. The more information that becomes available, the more information is desired; hence, equipment that facilitates information processing tends to expand office job opportunities.

The most pressing problem to surface as the impact of office technology is felt will be that of humanizing the technology. Those who manage the office of the future will be continually confronted with the problem of developing human resources to cope with more and more sophisticated equipment. Management's aim will be speeding information flow while reducing office costs and providing office workers with more meaningful work experiences. One way these experiences will be provided is through the development of career opportunities for office workers.

THE OFFICE: THE ADMINISTRATIVE SERVICES
DIVISION OF AN ORGANIZATION

The position of the office work force in the organizational structure naturally affects the potential of the office worker for meeting the needs of management. The current trend is for the office to be recognized as the administrative services division of an organization, a division on equal footing with other divisions such as finance, personnel, production, and sales. This relationship is illustrated in Figure I. The administrative services division is generally responsible for providing communication, data processing, information storage and retrieval, and word processing services.

Communication services. Three systems that operate as the means for providing communication services are detailed in Figure II. These systems, telephone, mail handling, and reprographics, although currently functioning in most offices, will develop to a higher level as the impact of information transfer technology is realized. Particularly important developments will occur in telecommunications networks, electronic mail processing, and intelligent copiers interfaced with data and word processing systems.

The reprographics system is one for which a career ladder may have already evolved. The relationship of some of the possible jobs in the ladder is depicted in Figure III. The reprographics system will be comprised of both decentralized copiers and centralized high speed copiers that are computer controlled. Further, for many large organizations, in-house printing has proven economically practical and will continue to expand to other and smaller organizations. Typical entry-level jobs in the reprographics system include equipment operator, copy machine operator, and copy preparation clerk. Employees who want to advance on the reprographics ladder will need, among other qualifications, an ability to realize the relationship of this system to other office systems and a knowledge of what technological advances can mean to reprographics: for example, how electronics can affect duplication processes.

Data processing services. Data acquisition, data conversion and storage, and data distribution systems comprise the data processing services of the administrative services division of an organization. Current technological developments of importance for data processing are enumerated for each of these systems in Figure IV. A key advance in data processing services will be the ability to interface with other office systems such as word processing, micrographics, and reprographics. Data processing operations will not be viewed as isolated and mysteriously remote, but rather will become an integral part of all office systems. In the data acquisition and data distribution phases, video display and portable terminals accessible to every office worker will facilitate the input and output of data. Advances in optical character recognition capabilities will also play a major role in involving all office workers in data processing services.

Expansion in the applications for and use of computers has been and will continue to be limitless. Likewise, job opportunities for employees in data processing will continue to expand at an increasing rate. Possible career ladders for data processing employees are presented in Figure V. Beginning workers will find opportunities in computer, control, and data entry operations. Many entry-level jobs will also be available as terminal operators, sometimes identified as remote-job-entry (RJE) operators. Advancement in data processing will depend on a combination of experience, advanced level training, and ability to work with information systems.

Information storage and retrieval services. Storage and retrieval of stored information have always been critical to the operation of an organization. With the impact of technological advances such as microfilm and microfiche files accessible through computer terminals, the importance of information storage and retrieval operations will be increased. As shown in Figure VI, two systems, records management and micrographics, operating interrelatedly will provide information storage and retrieval services.

New office career opportunities have already become available through technological advances in micrographics. In Figure VII, possible career ladders for micrographics system employees are identified. Rotary/planetary camera operators, micrographic duplication technicians, and micrographic production clerks are current entry-level opportunities. An awareness of and keen interest in applications for technological innovations will be essential for advancement in the micrographics systems.

Word processing services. The word processing services area of the administrative services division is the one that can be characterized as having "come of age." No question exists as to the impact that technological advances in dictation and word output equipment have had on the office work force. One of the key advances in this area is word processing equipment with data processing functions available at affordable prices. This and other technological advances that will affect the word processing services systems of dictation and word output are listed in Figure VIII.

A typical career ladder for a word processing center operation appears in Figure IX. Currently, a two-track career ladder, one for correspondence and one for administrative secretaries, is commonly recognized. As word processing equipment becomes available at more and more work stations as a result of reduced cost of the equipment, the word processing career ladder may change. The result of the less expensive equipment is a trend toward decentralization of word processing operations. Decentralization also reflects the need of both executives and secretaries for varied organizational configurations. Entry-level requirements for secretaries may well revert to traditional expectations—the need for both correspondence and administrative skills. Therefore, preparation for entry-level jobs in the word processing service area will require, in addition to traditional word output and administrative skills, a knowledge of word processing equipment—how to operate the equipment as well as potential applications for it.

OFFICE CAREERS, THE BUSINESS EDUCATOR
AND THE BUSINESS STUDENT

In the preceding discussion career opportunities for the office worker in a large organization have been examined. The impact of advances in

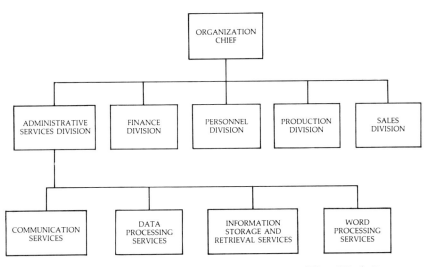

FIGURE I. The Administrative Services Division, or Office Work Force, in the Organization Structure

*A slightly different breakdown of Administrative Services is presented in Chapter 2.

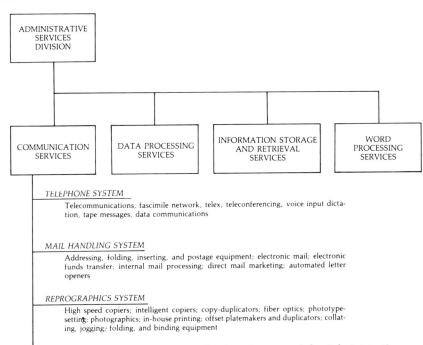

FIGURE II. The Communication Services Systems of the Administrative Services Division

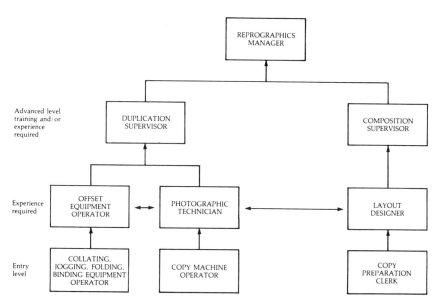

FIGURE III. Possible Career Ladders for the Office Worker in the Reprographics System

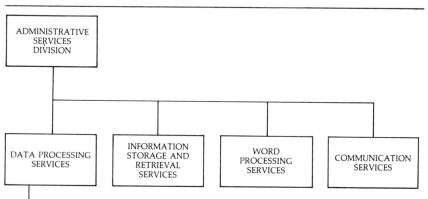

DATA ACQUISITION SYSTEM

Video display terminals, portable terminals, intelligent terminals optical character recognition (OCR), key-to-disc data entry, distributed data entry

DATA CONVERSION AND STORAGE

On-line and off-line storage, high-speed random access, expanded central computer capability, data-base management, software designed for ease of accessibility to information

DATA DISTRIBUTION SYSTEM

High speed printers; computer output microfiche (COM); remote terminals; interface with word processing, photo composition, and microfilm library

FIGURE IV. The Data Processing Services Systems of the Administative Services Division

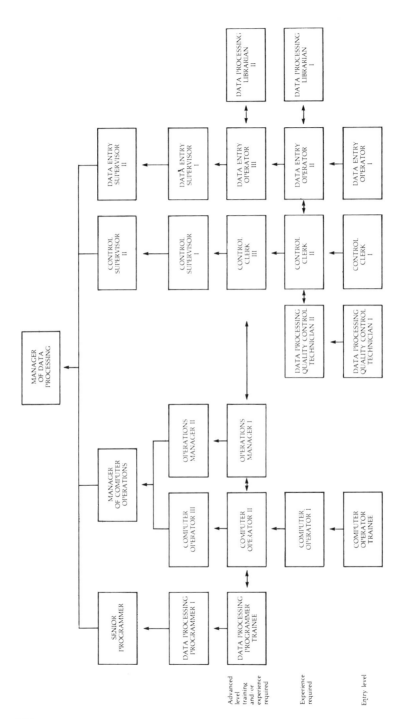

FIGURE V. Possible Career Ladders for the Office Worker in the Data Processing Services Area

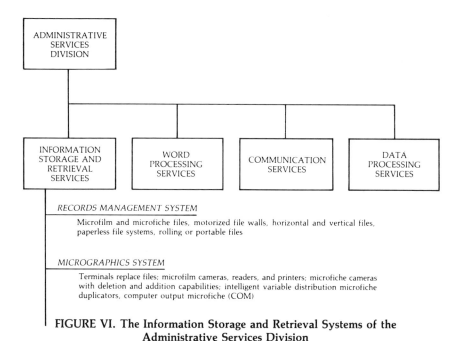

FIGURE VI. The Information Storage and Retrieval Systems of the Administrative Services Division

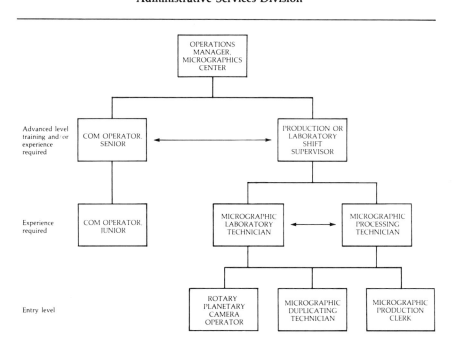

FIGURE VII. Possible Career Ladders for the Office Worker in the Micrographic System

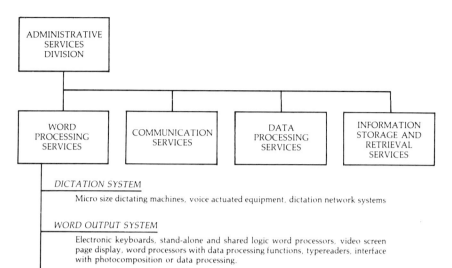

DICTATION SYSTEM

Micro size dictating machines, voice actuated equipment, dictation network systems

WORD OUTPUT SYSTEM

Electronic keyboards, stand-alone and shared logic word processors, video screen page display, word processors with data processing functions, typereaders, interface with photocomposition or data processing.

FIGURE VIII. The Word Processing Systems of the Administrative Services Division

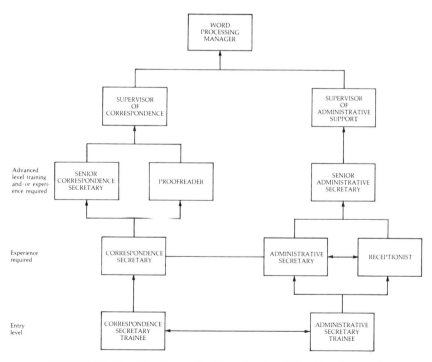

FIGURE IX. Possible Career Ladders for the Office Worker in the Word Processing Services Area

office technology that will help create career ladders for office workers in large organizations will also be felt in smaller organizations. Essentially, the same career ladders will exist, sometimes with combined steps. Even small offices, those with only one or two workers, will be affected by cost breakthroughs in the electronic processing and communicating of information. Experiences gained in smaller offices will help the office worker interested in advancement to understand the interrelationship of the many systems operating in larger offices where career advancement opportunities for the office worker will most likely be found.

To meet the challenge of preparing students for potential office careers such as the ones identified in this chapter, business educators must find answers to a number of questions. Some of the more pertinent ones follow:

What career opportunities will be available for the office worker? How will known career paths be affected by advances in office technology? What skills and knowledges will students need in order to climb office career ladders? How, when, and where can these needed skills and knowledges best be taught?

How can students be informed of office career opportunities? How will evolving office careers affect the recruitment of students for business programs?

How can employers be informed of the importance of career ladders and advancement opportunities to the office worker? How can employers participate in providing opportunities for students to gain the skills and knowledges required for career advancement?

Part V

CURRICULUM CHALLENGES OF THE CHANGING OFFICE ENVIRONMENT

CHAPTER 19

Curriculum Challenges of Secondary Business Education

MERLE W. WOOD

Oakland Public Schools, Oakland, California

Prior to the first space shot in 1957 secondary business education was a very stable, strong instructional component in the secondary schools. There was little call for change; thus few modifications were made. Subsequent to the successful launch of that first satellite, secondary schools responded to government and community influence and focused attention on guidance, science, and mathematics. Schools modified their educational priorities to ensure that this country did not lose the race into space. These events tended to have a negative effect upon business education.

With the availability of money under the Vocational Education Act of 1963 a new influence was felt, and it brought about additional change in business education. Shortly thereafter, the social revolution had its genesis on the college campuses. Soon this influence, and a new, liberalized attitude toward many basic values, permeated into secondary schools. Business education courses and programs found it necessary to compete with an entire range of social and liberal arts programs and a new laissez-faire attitude toward secondary education.

Our field has moved all the way from "typing, shorthand, and bookkeeping" to a range of courses, programs, and instructional procedures that were beyond our wildest imagination 25 years ago. Not all of the change has been good. Yet, because of these outside influences we have been intensely active. We have broken the bonds of tradition. We not only survived, we prospered. With this prosperity our students and communities have gained.

There is no question at all that change is going to continue to occur in the secondary business education curriculum. We will still be responding to many external pressures. However, there are several emerging outside influences that are quite compatible with the philosophy of business education. Much of our activity in the recent past has been reactive and competitive. Many of our curriculum modifications were made in order to survive. We found ourselves, as teachers in other disciplines found themselves, lowering standards and watering down courses, taking one year's time to teach one semester's content, permitting severe absenteeism because it was impossible to do otherwise, and accepting student behavior that would have been intolerable in the home or on the job.

There are a number of ways that one can approach an assessment of the causes for change that will occur in our curriculum over the next decade. The focus of this yearbook is on those changes that will be brought about because of changes in the office environment. There will be technological causes of several sorts, and they do represent one important change agent. However, the major change to secondary business education curriculum will be initiated because of a set of interrelated financial, social, and political factors.

MINIMUM GRADUATION REQUIREMENTS

Perhaps the single largest external influence that will be felt upon the business education curriculum, in fact all public school education, is that of accountability. At the time of this writing 40 of the 50 states have already passed some sort of legislation that demands that students reach a specified level of competency in basic skills before they may be granted a high school diploma by a local school board. Too many students have been graduated with deficiencies in reading, writing, and calculating. Test scores in basic skills have fallen, year after year, all across the country. The high school diploma has been cheapened beyond toleration. These facts, along with the increasing costs of public education, have finally brought about intense community and political interest in forcing the schools to do a better job.

The attitude of school staffs toward graduation examinations has been positive, supportive, and even enthusiastic. While the job of accommodating these new laws will be difficult, schools see them as tools that will help to bring about a renaissance in education. Also, by virtue of such laws, it appears that the years of public and social permissiveness are coming to an end as far as public school education is concerned. Schools see such laws as permitting them to get back to the job they were designed to do and, indeed, want to do: to teach students.

This same monumental force, establishing standards of achievement for graduation, is coupled with an intense national concern about the high cost of government. Business education in the secondary schools represents a part of this cost. The now famous Proposition 13, the property tax reform act of California, is being considered by cost-conscious people in many states across the country. California schools expect more and severe cuts in funding. People throughout the country are conscious of inflation and high taxes. Reducing local property taxes is an appealing way to reduce tax; however, if cuts in school budgets are severe and widespread, they cannot help but have an adverse effect upon curriculum.

Graduation proficiencies. Many of the newly legislated proficiency standards for graduation deal with the applications of basic skills (reading, writing, and computing) to so-called living skills. California, for example, has legislated that each school district establish its own proficiency standards and level of proficiency and that these must be developed with a high degree of input from the community. As one looks at these district-developed listings, their similarity is immediately apparent. Further, a large percentage of the items listed deal with topics and skills that business education has been teaching for the last 30 years or more. Generally, we can expect business education to be highly involved in helping students to develop graduation proficiencies.

In some states the graduation proficiencies must be articulated with lower level proficiency standards. Again, using California as an example, schools must evaluate students' proficiencies at least once during the fourth to sixth grades, at least once during the seventh to ninth grades, and twice during the tenth and eleventh grades. These examinations, and the instruction that precedes them, must be articulated. Any students who fail to pass the proficiency assessment at any level must be provided remediation following a strict, state-designed procedure. The articulation feature was included in the law to assure that students would have a progressive series of educational experiences that would help to assure passage of the graduation test at the high school level.

Here is one proficiency taken from a large school district's locally designed listing. It shows the progression whereby students move from proficiency in filling out a simple form to skill in completing a more complex form. The process used in developing these proficiency standards was to develop the highest level first. Literally, community members said they wanted their children to be able to fill out a job application form as a graduation requirement. Next, the lower level skill standards that would lead to this graduation standard were developed. This is one of 76 proficiencies over which students are assessed at three levels in their school career in this particular school district.

Grade range during which assessment is made	Stated in simple terms	Stated in performance terms
Between grades 4-6	Fill out a public library registration card:	Given a local public library registration card, the student will be able to correctly fill in the information requested.
Between grades 7-9	Fill out a local school registration card.	Given a local school registration card, the student will be able to correctly fill in the information requested.
Between grades 10-11	Fill out a job application form.	Given a paragraph of biographical data and a job application form, the student will be able to answer a series of multiple choice questions relating to the job application and fill in selected items on the form with at least 80 percent accuracy.

Proficiency listings. While public schools by the thousands will undoubtedly specify exactly which dicipline is to teach the various proficiency standards, entire staffs will be alerted to the total school responsibility. Using the proficiency standards from this same California school district again, and showing the standards in simple statement form, here are the competencies in which business educators have a vested interest. Literally, before a high school student in this community may be granted a high school diploma, he or she must, with at least 70 percent accuracy, demonstrate the ability to—

Reconcile a bank statement.

Figure sales tax.

Find the interest on a loan.

Use a dictionary.

Verify the accuracy of a grocery bill.

Verify that change is correct.

Multiply mixed numbers.

Subtract whole numbers.

Multiply whole numbers.

Read graphs and tables.

Figure interest on a consumer loan.

Figure pay earned on the job.

Keep a checkbook record.

Divide mixed numbers.

Complete the 1040A income tax form.

Divide whole numbers.

Purchase a money order.

Read labels on merchandise.

Read an informational chart.

Read a newspaper article.

Read a sales contract.

Use the yellow pages of the phone book.

Understand auto insurance.

Read a paragraph and understand it.

Understand a charge account statement.

Read math statements accurately.

Read an editorial.

Read operating instructions.

Read and understand a utility bill.

Read a lease.

Figure discounts on purchases.

Write a check correctly.

Verify a sales slip.

Read and understand a job want ad.

Figure miles per gallon.

Fill out a job application form.

Prepare written notes based on verbal message.

Write a paragraph.

Use correct word usage.

Capitalize words correctly.

Use correct punctuation.

Spell correctly.

Write a report of an incident.

Answer a help-wanted ad in writing.

Write legibly.

Write a personal letter.

Properly address a letter.

Use the telephone directory.

Locate legal assistance.

Read a street map.

Use synonyms.

Put words and names in alphabetical order.

Use reference materials.

Use a road map.

Use a library card catalog.

Use emergency telephone numbers.

Read and understand signs.

Read a newspaper classified ad.

Read consumer information sources.

Fifty-nine of the 72 proficiencies over which these students will be tested for graduation are integral parts of the curriculum of business education as we have been teaching it for over 30 years. The other significant factor is that these 72 graduation performance standards were developed, not by school staff, but rather from community input. Thus, this particular community and many like it are calling for development of the very skills, understandings, and knowledges that we in business education are prepared to teach and eager to teach. The community call for these skills cannot help but have a deep, lasting, and positive impact upon our curriculum.

Business education publishers. Most of the graduation proficiencies will deal with the application of basic skills to some sort of survival application. Students must have basic math skills in order to keep a checkbook. They must have basic reading skills in order to read a sales contract, and so on. Because of the widespread legislation establishing requirements in the survival skills, publishers of business education materials can be expected to analyze these requirements and to modify the content of instructional materials that they produce. Already some districts, while they may mandate that certain graduation proficiency content be taught in certain, selected courses, are requiring all disciplines to give increased attention to instruction in these proficiencies.

We can expect to find then, fused into many of our texts, structured content dealing with survival skills. This feature will be attractive to text material adoption committees. Indeed, we may find, because our discipline does cover such a large percentage of the kinds of proficiencies that are being required, that we will even have newly designed material developed specifically to meet proficiency requirements and perhaps offered in an entirely new course framework.

Stronger backgrounds. All of this activity dealing with proficiency standards bodes well for business education. We can expect more support for instruction from the homes because students must develop skills and pass an examination in order to graduate. We can expect more support from school administration because our programs do contribute so obviously to the community-developed proficiency requirements. We can expect students to come to us with more carefully developed basic skills. Thus we can more quickly get about the technical instruction required in vocational training programs. Students who can spell, punctuate, use words properly, and do basic math with proficiency are going to be a boon to our instructional programs. We can turn out a better product because our entering students will have a stronger basic education. We can look forward to being able to move students ahead more efficiently. What is more important, students will be able to gain more from their public school education.

MODULAR, FLEXIBLE INSTRUCTION

A second major external pressure is building from this same general insistence that public schools be more accountable for quality instruction. The talk of voucher systems is not idle commentary. We must become accountable. Until we do we can expect to be under continuing and intense pressure. Our current system of lockstep instruction, one hour per day for a semester or a year, is rightly under suspicion if not outright attack. We will find more and more programs where instruction is individualized in some way to accommodate student differences.

Flexible instruction will provide for independent progress. Programs will be broken into manageable subunits. There will be pretesting and post-testing. Students who drop out can simply drop back in when they are able, and they can continue with their training right where they left off. We will see differentiation of staffing. Multimedia instruction will be improved and increased. Alternative systems of instruction will be encouraged and expanded. We may find many students studying at differing times during the day and at widely scattered centers: public libraries, community centers, at home, and at drop-in centers. We can also look forward to establishing and maintaining higher scholastic standards.

Focus on efficiency. The focus will be on efficiency in instruction. If a student can accelerate, he or she will be encouraged to do so. Students will not be locked to an hour per day for a semester to cover a semester of content. We will see students, upon successful completion of a unit pretest, being given credit for the unit and moving on to the next sequential unit. The instructional programs will be modified to fit the students, rather than the traditional pattern where the student must modify themselves in order to fit the program. By virtue of the modularity of the program and the fact that students can move at their own pace, more and more students will be doing homework in order to cover more material in a shorter period of time. All of this flexibility means that we will be delivering instruction differently. We will either modify our traditional instructional materials to fit this new pattern, or we will adopt materials that were specifically designed for individual progress. Even now, more and more of these materials are available on the market.

In the many facilities where modular, flexible instruction is already in use, we find that students are highly motivated. They are learning and, what is more important, they know that they are learning. A vague letter grade, even an "A," does not have the meaning to students that is provided by their successful passage of a posttest over a unit of instruction. Under such an instructional system students know what the performance requirements are. They study and complete the instructional units. After each unit they are posttested. They may move on only if they have reached a predetermined level of proficiency. Such instruction, over relevant material that focuses on specific performance objectives, is most attractive to students. It is attractive to communities because such instruction, while having many other positive features, is measurable. Education, by using this system, can be held accountable.

Flexible, competency-based instruction is not inexpensive. It will cost more than traditional group instruction. However, it will do so much more. In spite of a higher cost, this system of instruction can be expected to expand. Test the theory yourself. If you were operating a business at a substantial profit and could, by increasing your cost 30 percent, increase your profit by 80 percent, would you spend the additional money?

Focus on the classroom. Proficiency standards and competency-based instruction, while they seem to place heavy focus on the classroom teacher, have an implied feature that is certain to produce a major benefit for business education. In traditional, large-group instruction, it has been very easy for the school administration to advise teachers to "do the best you can" when the teacher was confronted with shortages of texts, unrepaired equipment, severe absenteeism, and all of the other details that interrupt instruction or make it impossible. Now, because teaching to graduation proficiencies and competency statements are measurable systems of instruction, administrative support is no longer an option; it is required.

When teachers are asked, and they will be asked, why a student did not learn, an answer must be given. It is possible that the student did not learn because the teacher did not teach. However, if the school district did not provide the tools so the teacher could teach, then whoever failed to provide those tools can expect to be held accountable. We are moving toward accountability for instruction, and there will be wide and sweeping impact upon curriculum and instructional systems. Classroom teachers will now be teaching using a measurable system of instruction. Schools must provide them with the facilities, equipment, materials, and environment where they can succeed. Accountability is for everyone, not just the classroom teacher.

ATTITUDE TOWARD JOBS

At long last the pendulum is swinging back. Public attitude is moving from a philosophy where "everyone who is anyone goes to college" to one where it is acceptable for young people to follow a vocational career. This is a most welcome, healthy, and positive change and it cannot help but improve business education programs in the schools and thus affect our curriculum. For too long we have had bright students shunted off to other programs, often against their will. Now, students are pointing out that they want a quality to their life that vocational training can bring them. Most importantly, parents are understanding the students and are supporting them. Besides having students who are motivated to learn, we will tend to see a larger percentage of students gravitating toward our programs.

Students in high school are hearing the same reports that we hear regarding the inability of many college-trained persons to secure meaningful jobs in their field of interest. Students with technical training are close to, matching, or even exceeding the income of many college graduates. Other students are seeing their parents with college backgrounds in jobs where pressures are often severe and financial rewards and inner satisfaction are not commensurate with the amount of preparation required for the job or the life-style that must be maintained to remain on the job.

MAINSTREAMING, SEX STEREOTYPING, AND CAREER EDUCATION

Several movements are under way within the educational community that will have an effect on the curriculum in secondary business education. One impact will be due to the emerging philosophy that physically handicapped students should, rather than being educated in isolation, join the mainstream of education and, wherever possible, take their vocational training in standard classrooms along with nonhandicapped students. In districts where this has already been implemented one sees some modification to facilities, such as ramps, wide doors, and sometimes special seating arrangements or additional space for students who are confined to wheelchairs. Sometimes equipment needs to be modified. In cases where special intensive instruction is required, teacher aides or teachers of special education come to the business education classroom on a scheduled basis and provide the necessary support to instruction. Where there are several handicapped students in one learning laboratory there may be a special education teacher assigned for the entire period. Adjustments to time requirements, proficiency standards, and so forth are often necessary for such students, and they are made on an individual student basis jointly by the business teacher and special education staff members.

Elimination of sex bias and sex-role stereotyping in business education is already under way. Indeed, our history is full of examples of many efforts and some successes to encourage young men into clerical and stenographic training programs and more representative mixes of male and female students in accounting and distributive education programs. Special minicourses in office filing, keypunch operation, telephone operator training, and similar topics have tended to be composed almost entirely of female students. We will be expected to make maximum effort to eliminate sex bias from our instructional programs. The problem is obviously a very old one, and it is based on broadly accepted perceptions and long-standing practices and traditions in this country.

One of the major sources of help in eliminating sex stereotyping lies with the public media. As we see more and more people working in nontraditional roles, students will be able to envision themselves in such roles. Until students see nontraditional jobs as being acceptable by society, they can hardly be expected to see such jobs as being acceptable for themselves. Instructional materials will continue to reflect this emerging philosophy. Such materials, and the media, can make a significant contribution to reducing and ultimately eliminating sex stereotyping and sex bias.

Along with elimination of sex bias, we can expect to see renewed emphasis on the removal of all bias from our vocational business programs. Location of training sites, recruiting methods, providing opportunities for all races, service to the handicapped, and providing training for students who are not fluent in the English language will all continue to be subject to scrutiny. Providing for these factors will assuredly have continuing impact on our curriculum.

Career education has, in many districts, been approached as a counseling function. While a great deal of good has been done through such career education programs, the current trend is to fuse career education concepts into existing business education programs. We have rich opportunities to do so. Business mathematics can, as it teaches about the mathematics of stock control and inventory work, infuse, even though in small amounts, information about these kinds of jobs: pay, working conditions, advancement opportunities, and so forth. Business law provides a vehicle to integrate additional career information. General business training, with its broad scope of subject content, can be a valuable source of career education information if such content is fused into the subject. Each business course and program can make contributions.

We can expect that we will be called upon to add two distinct types of career education information. One will deal with an emphasis on the features of various jobs: job entry requirements, working conditions, type of work, advancement and spin-off job opportunities, etc. The other, and perhaps the more significant of the two, will be a reemphasis on the work ethic, punctuality, integrity on the job, a day's work for a day's pay, and similar concepts. There has been a decline in the amount of this kind of content in our courses. We will really be returning to a topic that was at one time immutably combined in our curriculum with technical information. Over the past 10 or 12 years it has been difficult, often impossible, to instruct in these important job-related human skills. There seemed to be a resistance to these topics from students because of conditions and attitudes within the society as a whole. Today many educators are sensing a turning point in the attitude of both students and adults. As it continues, we can return this important, basic content to our curriculum.

CHANGES DUE TO TECHNOLOGY IN THE OFFICE

Every once in a while we hear of some technological breakthrough that, when we think of its possible impact, almost frightens us. Yet, when the product or system is implemented we seem to take the change in stride. Many felt this way about space flight just a few years ago. The same was true with the computer; now we take that machine in stride, along with the benefits and problems it has created. Office procedures and equipment are continuing to change dramatically. Besides the technical changes due to new equipment we are seeing changes brought about because of new management philosophies. We even see social forces bringing changes in the office: equal treatment, pay, job opportunities, and working conditions for both sexes, for example. Even court decisions, particularly those dealing with human and personal rights, are affecting the office scene. We are called upon to teach so much to our students to fit them for what is a continually changing work environment. Perhaps the keynote to teaching is to teach students how to be adaptable and how to cope with change.

Banking. One hardly picks up a newspaper today without noting some new announcement by the banking industry. While these announcements are obviously presented as information for customers, they also imply change for those who work in the banks. For example, there are now new "T Plus" accounts. Checking accounts can now, under special arrangements, draw interest. Customers may now arrange for telephone transfer accounts. The list goes on and on.

Banking by computer is a reality with many banks today. Again, this is of interest to both consumers and future bank employees. Many banks now have terminals that allow customers to deposit or withdraw cash at any time of the day or night by use of a plastic card. Almost 10,000 such terminals are in use today. More are forecast for the future.

There are almost 80,000 computer terminals located in retail establishments that are connected directly to various banks. The retailers use them to verify, at the time of a sale, whether their customers have enough money in their accounts to cover the checks they write. It is only one tiny step to reach the point where the funds will actually be transferred from the customer's account to the store's account at the moment of the sale.

There is an increase in the use of checkless payroll systems. This system permits the employer to deposit wages directly into an employee's bank account without the employee's ever even seeing the paycheck. Such a system provides both the employer and the employee with convenience and savings.

In analyzing the changes taking place in banking one senses that, now that equipment is sophisticated enough to handle these applications, banks are trying to offer more customer convenience and savings and are also trying to operate as competitively and efficiently as possible. The cashless society is indeed drawing one step closer. Business educators can expect their curriculums to continue to be modified as banking operations and personal banking continue to be modified.

Speed, miniaturization, and prices. In 1953 an overhead projector cost about $600. Today, even with years of inflated prices, far better overhead projectors cost about $150. The electronic printing calculators of 1965 cost about $1,200. Today they are smaller, faster, more dependable, and frequently sell for about $100. Many business educators are still trying to decide what to do about the fact that students can buy electronic calculators for $7 at the local drug store, thus presenting a problem in the classroom.

Because of new technology many kinds of work are being speeded up. For example, customers now may purchase equipment so they can immediately, through their telephone service, transmit documents across the country almost instantaneously. The U.S. Postal Service advertises next day express delivery of letters and parcels to any city in the country. United Parcel Service, with insurance on lower value packages included in the price, gives high-speed, dependable delivery service. Indeed, this company is providing stiff competition to the postal system. Developments such as these can modify the content of many business education instructional units.

Most people were amazed years ago when they first heard of computer printers printing as many as 10,000 characters per minute. Ten years ago a computer printer was developed that prints at a rate of 60,000 characters per second. To get that figure into the realm of human understanding, convert it to wpm as in typing. This rate, 60,000 characters per second, times 60 (to get one minute's output) equals 3,600,000 characters. Divide this figure by five to get the number of typing words per minute: 720,000 wpm. By dividing this output rate by one hundred we can find the number of 100 wpm typists required to equate the output of this machine: 7,200! Of course, it also means these 7,200 people typed errorlessly and tirelessly just as this amazing printer does.

This machine was in use in 70 facilities shortly after its release, but little has been heard about it in business education. What could its impact ultimately be for the office? How could its use affect the field of word processing? What might it do to jobs related to copy origination, reproduction, transmission, and storage? While such a machine might be viewed today as a frightening aberration, tomorrow it might be viewed with complete calm. It is this kind of technical development that we must watch as we review, modify, and develop business education curriculums.

Miniatures. Over 10 years ago National Cash Register announced their newest microfiche system. On a tiny transparent square measuring two inches by two inches one can record the pages of a 1,245-page book. This particular system, it was announced, could house all of the materials contained in the 270 miles of shelving in the Library of Congress in just six standard file cabinets. Again, while microfiche equipment and systems have been in use for the past 10 years, they have caused only minor impact on business education curriculums. This storage system has the potential, however, of having significant impact. It could revolutionize filing and retrieving much as the office copier modified teaching the use of carbon paper in the typing class. Remember those first sheets of correction paper, then correction fluid, and now we have the correcting typewriter. Each new development in the office, even so-called minor ones, has the potential of affecting the content of our instructional programs.

Eight years ago an executive of one of the major computer companies stated that at that time they had the technical capability to reduce the size of their central processor from approximately 30 cubic feet to one cubic inch. He jokingly said that the day may come when an executive searches through papers on his desk looking for his computer. That day may not come, but miniaturization is here in the form of the silicon chip, and it will affect many machines and systems in the office. A one-chip processing unit may contain over 2,000 transistors in an area one-sixth of an inch long and one-eighth of an inch wide. These chips are so small and inexpensive that they can be incorporated into almost any machine that would be improved with some power to "think." Without doubt, office equipment will be modified because of this amazing, tiny programmable chip.

Surely the time cannot be too far away when the manual typewriter will be a thing of the past. It is not efficient and it is not inexpensive. Typewriter company representatives report that the two major outlets for manual typewriters are schools and government offices. How can schools continue to train students on manual machines when they are becoming more and more scarce in the offices where the students will work?

Robots are at work today. They make castings, weld, spray paint, and do assembly work. It is estimated that there are some 4,000 such computer-controlled machines in use worldwide today. Will they be used in the office? Are there jobs that can be more effectively and economically done through use of robot power rather than people power? If there are, and this is not an entirely remote possibility, we will respond with initial concern and amazement—and then we will adjust our curriculum.

SUMMARY

The greatest impact on our curriculum will not be from technological change, although there will be an unending chain of modifications to office equipment and work systems. The major change will come from social, political, and economic forces. Educators can expect to be held accountable for students' learning. We will be called upon to modify our instructional systems to match the needs of individual students. We will take care of those who have so long been neglected; the handicapped, the less able, and those whose native language is not English, for example. We will slowly modify instruction until sex stereotyping will only be a vague memory. We will be more than teachers of students as more and more families require two incomes. Many teachers sense a return to a healthier attitude toward work, and there is a growing feeling that vocational training has dignity. Students, as well as their parents, are expressing this attitude.

Change is sometimes frightening and sometimes painful. However, many business teachers, especially those who were involved prior to that 1957 space shot, see change as being full of challenge and opportunity. Business education programs before sputnik did have stability, status, and security, but one must remember how much has been accomplished in business education since then.

Somewhere in business education there are those who will be the specialists and leaders in business education for the handicapped, in business education/career education, in the cashless society, in microfiche systems, and on and on. Perhaps there will even be the day when someone now reading this page will be one of the business educators who pioneers curriculum modification brought about by the use of robots for selected office tasks.

We are not just entering an exciting, challenging time of change in our field; we have been in it for years. All of us must be students of change in order to be teachers of business education. The watchwords in our work must be alertness, optimism, open-mindedness, and adaptability.

CHAPTER 20

Implications for Postsecondary Programs

ELIZABETH IANNIZZI
New York City Community College, Brooklyn, New York

About the only thing we can say with absolute certainty about tomorrow is that it will be vastly different from today.—Ian H. Wilson, Public Policy Research, General Electric Company.

Glance through any issue of a recent newspaper, magazine, convention or seminar program and you are sure to find one commonality—some reference to the future and its implications for those to whom it is addressed. Of course the future as a topic is not new by any means; what is new, however, is the uncertainty that has resulted from the complex and diverse changes occurring daily in business. Perhaps the greatest advantage of such uncertainty is the opportunity it offers business educators at the postsecondary level to develop new concepts and make suggestions as to the directions in which future business education programs should proceed.

THE POSTSECONDARY MOVEMENT—A FORCE
FOR EDUCATIONAL ADVANCEMENT

The community and junior college movement (terms used interchangeably because of the similarities of philosophies and programs) has contributed immensely during the past two to three decades to the educational achievements of our adult population. In the 1950's, for example, of the total civilian population, more than one-third had only eight years or less of formal education; and some 400,000 were attending approximately 600 two-year colleges.

By the early 1970's, however, this percentage of minimally educated individuals decreased dramatically to about 12 percent, as 3 1/2 million attended over 1,000 two-year colleges. By 1990, the Bureau of Labor Statistics estimates that 80 percent of all workers will have completed 12 years of formal education, 16 percent will have completed one to three years of college, and almost 24 percent will have completed four years or more of college. Although statistics are not available at this time, it would appear that the number of two-year colleges will either remain the same or lessen.

A profile of postsecondary students would reveal that they are male and female, of high-school age and older, attending full and part-time, self-supporting and financially assisted, single and married, with and without

212

children. Urban postsecondary colleges would add to this profile a description of varied ethnic backgrounds, since a large percentage of their students are from minority groups and foreign countries.

Postsecondary colleges presently offer these students a variety of program choices: the first two years of a four-year program (transfer in career or liberal arts areas); career programs (specialties relating to business, industry, government); community-oriented programs (courses for the deaf, the homebound, labor unions, criminal institutions); and student-oriented programs (early admissions, dual enrollment, alternate format for adults, credit by examination). A major challenge confronting postsecondary educators is to consider the ways in which the changing office environment will affect these programs, their content, and the students enrolled in them and then develop programs for the future that will not only meet the needs of such students in a cost-effective manner but will also encompass the expanding and changing needs of business.

THE CHANGING OFFICE ENVIRONMENT — A PERIOD OF UNCERTAINTY

Change within the office environment is certainly nothing new or unusual. If you were to compare the office of today with the office of the past, the vast differences between them would come as no surprise. Neither would you be surprised to find that the educational environment had kept pace with the changes required in its programs so that its graduates were successful in business. Why, then, the widespread uncertainty that has led to intensive evaluation, projection, planning, and revision of current business education programs?

One major reason, perhaps, is the great acceleration in the rate of change. Marla S. Batchelder, manager of education and training for Union Carbide Corporation, notes that one of the problems business people face is the need to speculate about what tomorrow will bring while at the same time attempting to keep up with what happened yesterday. Tom Jackson, in an article for the February 1979 issue of *Working Woman* entitled "Forecast for Your Future," projected that changes that would take place by 1980—which could not even be anticipated in 1979—would combine to produce job opportunities only few business people could even conceive as future possibilities. Ian H. Wilson, quoted at the beginning of this chapter, describes the effect of this acceleration by depicting the essential character of management as changing from one of administering continuity to one of managing uncertainty.

Another contributing cause for uncertainty may be the multibillion-dollar race by manufacturers of automated office equipment, each of whom would like to be the leading producer of equipment for the automated office of the future. A December 29, 1978, article in the *New York Times* reported that even the 70 or more companies involved in this race cannot determine exactly what offices of the future will be like: what they do know, however, is that the future market for office-related equipment (e.g. high-speed printers, phototypesetting machines, long-distance facsimile, communications gear, word processing terminals) will reach approximately $15 billion annually.

The need for improved productivity may be yet a third reason. While industrial productivity has risen nearly 90 percent in the last decade, office productivity has risen only 4 percent. Much of the equipment now being produced and introduced almost weekly may be tied together by means of plug-compatible mainframe (PCM) communications lines. Therefore, what you have now is a set of building blocks, according to Sanford J. Garrett, a securities analyst with Sanford C. Bernstein & Company. The challenge then becomes one of linking the blocks together to improve the transfer of information and thus improve office productivity. This challenge and others brought about by a period of uncertainty and flux combine to mandate major changes in educational directions for the future.

THE CHANGING OFFICE ENVIRONMENT—A FORCE FOR NEW DIRECTIONS AT THE POSTSECONDARY LEVEL

Despite the perplexities encountered in projecting future office requirements, the essentials that follow appear with sufficient consistency to be considered indispensable for the future:

- Career titles that reflect nonsexist, more diversified responsibilities
- Increased emphasis upon decision-making and analytical abilities, adaptability, communication abilities, and interpersonal relationships
- More extensive interrelationships among business, education, and community groups
- Offices that incorporate microfilm records, integrated data processing and word processing systems, computer conferencing, and electronic mail
- Administrative managers who are change agents; educators who are managers of learning resources
- A knowledge revolution in which "skilledge"[1] (being fully versed in a particular area of application that includes a background of theory and principle from which to generate answers and, in addition, the pragmatic skills to put theoretical answers to work) is vital to success in business.

Career titles. Changes in career titles are already being proposed by institutions, business firms, and individuals anxious to use terminology that reflects current trends. Two of the titles incorporated into the draft report of the Statewide Business Education Review Committee (New York State Education Department), *Looking Towards the Future,* are *executive office assistant* as a replacement for secretary and *general clerical assistant* for individuals who have positions as tellers, communication specialists, and clerk typists. Emphasis in preparation for the executive office assistant position would be on decision making, management, composition, and proofreading skills and abilities; programs for the general clerical assistant would prepare students to meet the increased demand for office workers who possess not only traditional skills but also display the newer skills

---

[1]Jackson, Tom. "Forecast for Your Future." *Working Woman* 4:34; February 1979.

demanded, for example, by the credit-card age, by facilities within banks for bill payment, and by the interlocking of telephones with computer terminals for banking and credit transactions.

When word processing first became popular, the titles *correspondence secretary* and *administrative secretary* were used to differentiate responsibilities. Current references to these titles substitute the word *specialist* for secretary—a change important not only because it lacks sexist implications but also because many nonsecretarial or administrative functions are assumed by individuals with the latter title.

Other possible titles, suggested by Harold T. Smith in his article, "What's in Store for Tomorrow's Business Grads" (*Management World*, August 1977), are *administrative assistant* for secretary, *communication specialist* for stenographer, *information specialist* for file clerk, *data-entry specialist* for keypuncher, and *administrative systems analyst* for machine operator. Responsibilities for these positions are on a higher level than previously. For example, the former business machine operator, now an administrative systems analyst, will have such increasing responsibilities as developing and improving administrative systems under the direction of the administrative manager, keeping informed about new technologies and new systems theory, and anticipating future problems and solutions to them.

As job titles and responsibilities change, career titles at the postsecondary level will also have to change to reflect both program content and career-ladder opportunities that will be available to graduates who complete these programs.

Decision-making, analytical, and interpersonal skills. If only *one* consistent thread were to be found among all the literature about requirements necessary for the office of the future, it would be that individuals must possess the ability to analyze data and make decisions based upon these analyses. Training in these areas, therefore, must be included in all course offerings, regardless of geographic or program area. If core competencies are to be established for the programs being offered, decision making should be at the top of the list of competencies. Without this ability, success is impossible. Individuals must be able to weigh alternatives, make sound decisions based on the information available, and set priorities.

The need for this ability has been recognized in the past by such groups as the Institute for Certifying Secretaries, which has included for many years an in-basket to test these skills as part of its certifying examination. Increased emphasis is being given to decision-making skills by the business community as the changing office environment focuses more and more attention upon this need. A January 21, 1979, *New York Times* article entitled "A Test to Uncover Managerial Skills" notes that more than 2,000 companies and government agencies are using assessment centers, which use simulation management exercises, to identify and groom managerial talent in their own ranks. The author cites as one example a test devised by the director of human resources research for American Telephone and Telegraph, which consists of six exercises to test the qualities deemed important in management—problem-analysis, judgment, leadership, decisiveness, initiative and organizational planning, and interpersonal sensitivity. Typical exercises within this text include in-basket items. The advantage of this strategy is that it can be used for both training and testing, but it is imperative to remember that in both instances the methodology used and the reasons for the individual's decisions are far more important than the decisions themselves.

In addition to the in-basket, minicourses and minisimulations should be used to expose students to a variety of experiences that demand the ability to gather and analyze data. Opportunities for decision making will then become a part of the student's daily routine.

Role-playing in a leaderless group can also be used to require students to assess situations and make decisions based on their perceptions. It provides, too, opportunities for them to display their leadership strengths or weaknesses. These activities can take place in club- and work-experience related activities as well as in classroom settings. An added advantage of these instructional strategies is that they offer, in addition to decision-making activities, opportunities to develop and evaluate interpersonal relationships.

Interpersonal sensitivity has become a major key in successfully implementing the changes that are necessary if businesses are to keep pace with technology. Many individuals still react to change as a threat to their future and to their job security. The ability to understand and allay these fears will become a vital skill for successful management personnel to possess.

The use of excellent instructional strategies, such as role-playing, minicourses, simulations, in-baskets, case studies, and seminars, will give students ample opportunities to develop analytical, decision-making, and interpersonal skills. They therefore must become a major component of instruction at the postsecondary level.

Communication skills. Whenever business personnel evaluate graduates, they invariably cite as a major deficiency the ability to display mastery of communication skills. Educators also bemoan the lack of these abilities in their students, many of whom have had numerous courses in English. Obviously, then, the approach to teaching these skills in the past has not been successful in terms of carry-over into other areas of study. A major problem has been that the content and focus of the courses offered have not related to the application of these skills in business or other settings. A link must be established between the creative compositions written for English classes and the reports or letters written for business. Closer working relationships have to be established between those teaching English and business courses so that overlapping of instruction is minimized, if not completely eliminated. The current trend towards competency-based education should facilitate this relationship, one that has been discussed frequently in the past but that has been difficult to implement.

The expansion of communication skills to include more than writing ability will force educators to work together to build upon the competencies students already possess and to move them in new directions. Students must possess—in addition to writing ability—the ability to read, speak, listen, translate, and understand business terms and acronyms. As the telephone becomes literally the lifeline of business, students will need to be able to use communication skills to ask for information, hear what should be recorded, discuss work-related problems, and write whatever correspondence or reports are the logical outgrowth of these communications.

Interrelations among business, education, and community groups. In the past, even when changes in the office environment came about more slowly, a time lag existed between business requirements and educational outcomes. As the speed of office changes accelerated, the time lag increased even more, which accounts to a large extent for the great proliferation of internal training programs that businesses have instituted to bridge the gap between the training received in school and the competencies and levels required by employers. A January 7, 1979, article in the *New York Times* reported that corporations are spending more than $2 billion on educational training programs. In an effort to foster closer cooperation and to minimize the need for supplementary training, 200 community colleges have established relationships with unions for joint apprenticeship committees to oversee the training of new employees.

Other alternatives for cooperative ventures between educators and business people are work-study or visitation programs that permit students to have at least limited hands-on experiences with the types of office equipment not found in postsecondary colleges and business advisory commissions. Advisory commissions are not new to the educational scene, but too often they have not been fully utilized. Specific goals and responsibilities will have to be established so that these commissions function more effectively and more meaningfully. Use of these commissions should not be limited to formal meetings only; informal exchanges through telephone conversations, luncheon get-togethers, facilities tours, and other similar activities may prove even more beneficial than large-group meetings.

Technological changes. Changes in the office environment that will take place as a result of technological improvements are staggering to the imagination. The question now before those engaged in computer technology, for example, is not so much whether a particular feat *can* be achieved, but whether it *should* be attained. So rapidly are the technological improvements being conceived that they frequently become outdated before they can be produced in sufficient quantity for marketing. For this reason, V. E. Henriques, vice-president, Computer and Business Equipment Manufacturers Association, describes the changes that will take place as evolutionary rather than revolutionary, purposeful rather than random, and the result of choice rather than dictation.

Technological innovations will make it easier for users to interact with systems not only in businesses and educational institutions but in homes as well. The use of television sets in the home for more than just viewing programs is but one small example of interaction. Pushbutton telephones will serve as input devices; television sets as output mechanisms. It will be essential, in view of current trends, for postsecondary colleges to provide opportunities for their students to interact with computerized information systems via input/output terminals for such activities as generating files needed for producing documents, editing materials, seeking information from additional sources, and formulating necessary decisions.

Project DELTA is one such example that was developed by the Department of Occupational Education and the University of Delaware. As an outgrowth of this experiment, seven instructional modules were developed to teach the use of the computer within an office operation. The format and software developed may be used at all instructional levels because the variable used was the degree of difficulty in formulating data bases for use or development. No matter what careers students may be interested in, they must understand the basics of computerized information systems, how employees or individuals fit into such systems, and why accuracy is essential to proper utilization. When studying and performing office procedures, one of the ways in which computer maturity in a nontechnical program can be achieved is through simulated experiences.

Since systems concepts, logic, verbal expression, and the ability to adapt to changing configurations and job requirements will become far more important than hands-on training in the future, the emphasis in teaching will also have to change so that strategies and methods being used are considered merely examples rather than standards. Students will have to explore other media available, for example, to become aware of alternative procedures and machines and thus be able to make decisions as to which are more appropriate than others in given situations. Items that must be studied or handled for editing, for example, might best be conveyed through hard-copy systems; quick-reference materials, however, could be paperless and produced through cathode ray tubes (CRT's) or telephones.

Word processing trends include the use of minicomputers and microprocessors; breakdown of large centers into smaller, satellite groups; and incorporation of word processing into the larger entity of information processing under the direction of a vice-president of information. Thus the future office will incorporate integrated data processing and word processing centers, microfilming, computer conferencing, and electronic mail. The newly developed computer input microfilm/computer output microfilm (CIM/COM) system and others will increase the importance of microfilming in the office of the future. Facsimile equipment can currently be combined with microfilm and can also be used advantageously with electronic mail systems. Work-study programs and field trips will be necessary so that students may see such systems in operation. Colleges should build upon this initial experience by providing opportunities for students to use a computer terminal for an in-basket project that would require them to produce on the screen a list of reference documents, memorandums, and letters; determine which of the items should be read and what actions should be taken on them; file appropriate items in an electronic filing cabinet; and press a button to activate a printer or copier that will produce a hard copy. Materials for this project and others would be readily available from businesses as a result of the close relationships previously established.

Educators as managers of learning resources. The traditional role of business teachers has been that of diagnostician, motivator, and transmitter of knowledge. To this role must be added that of manager of learning resources, for it will be their responsibility to select from the wide variety of strategies, materials, supplies, equipment, and resources that will be available to assist them in preparing students for changing office occupations those alternatives that are best suited for each student. This selection should depend upon the cluster of competencies needed within specific occupational and geographical regions. A universal core, however, should be a part of all programs, regardless of occupation or geographic region. Rather than duplicate the efforts of others, educators should evaluate and use materials already available (such as the DELTA modules mentioned previously) and then develop additional projects or modules that may be needed as supplements.

Business educators should also engage in self-development programs to keep themselves up to date. Among the choices are such approaches as working in businesses during leaves of absence, spending a part or all of their summers working in offices, visiting businesses, setting up faculty/ business exchanges, participating in business-oriented associations, reading business literature, and attending workshops and seminars conducted by business administrators or managers. Their intention should not be necessarily to become specialists and systems analysts but rather to become familiar with terminology used in business, knowledgeable about the availability and functioning of office equipment, and conversant with the relationships of systems and interactions of their parts.

In the process of becoming managers of learning resources, instructors should serve as models for their students. Students would then see the professional at work: analyzing daily situations; making appropriate decisions based on the analyses; reevaluating and reenforcing or changing directions; demonstrating flexibility; understanding interpersonal relationships and needs; using appropriate communications systems; setting meaningful, realistic goals; motivating self as well as students; displaying a sense of self-worth and adaptability; managing, planning, and organizing time; coping with conflict and stress; listening to others; focusing on the economic environment; and striving for productivity.

SUMMARY

Although not all of the areas mentioned here have been discussed previously, it may be possible to summarize the implications for postsecondary colleges by looking first at the composition of core competencies and then at the additional responsibilities of postsecondary colleges to provide education beyond the core. Core competencies appear to fall into three categories: basic skills, basic understandings, and basic attitudes.

Basic skills. Of critical importance are the skills of decision making, language arts, keyboarding, and computing. Since they are critical, they must be incorporated into as many learning experiences as possible. Again, this need highlights the importance of close working relationships among all educators as well as with management personnel. Of major (but not critical) importance are the skills of shorthand, records management, machine transcription, and reprographics. Inclusion of the skill of shorthand—despite the tendency of many to forecast its demise—is based upon a number of factors. One consideration must be job-market predictions. *U. S. News & World Report* (December 27, 1976/January 3, 1977) and other sources report an increase of approximately 1,597,000 secretarial positions in 1985, as compared with positions available in 1974. Although the position of secretary will undoubtedly not be the same in 1985 as it is currently, the ability to take shorthand will most likely remain one of the criteria used to distinguish this position from other clerical titles. Additionally, business people report that even though the shorthand skill itself may not be used frequently once the individual has been hired, they often use it as an employment criterion because it is one of the skills that may be tested and because they know, too, that the applicant will have some measure of required English skills.

Basic understandings. Critical to this area is a knowledge of self-worth and business literacy; of major importance is a knowledge of business terminology and computer literacy.

Basic attitudes. Critical attitudes are those of intelligent use of time, adaptability to change, and the ability to work well with others.

Additional competencies beyond the core. Once basic skills, understandings, and attitudes have been achieved, it then becomes the additional responsibility of postsecondary institutions to build upon the core to provide students with those skills required for the specialties in which they are interested (legal and medical terminology and shorthand, accounting, marketing distribution, management, to name a few) and to provide a learning atmosphere in which students also acquire the ability to adapt to change and thus be able to function in a business environment not yet possible to envision.

Educators must believe that in today's world nothing is impossible. They must also believe that once they fulfill the responsibilities outlined here, they will be secure in the tomorrow that will not be the same as today. In the educational process, business teachers at the postsecondary level will have provided for all the known and unknown contingencies their students will have to face in the transition from school to the world of work; and they will have provided their students with the skills, understandings, and attitudes necessary to enable them to function with ease, confidence, flexibility, and adaptability in the business world. In addition, teachers will have finally closed the once ever-widening gap between the competencies needed by business and those provided by the postsecondary colleges.

CHAPTER 21

Adult and Continuing Education Curriculum Considerations

ALFRED L. KAISERSHOT and PATSY A. DICKEY

Illinois State University, Normal

Adult and continuing education programs across the nation hold a position that is unique and peculiar. These programs are often housed within the building of another educational institution and are administered and often taught by a staff and faculty unrelated to and entirely apart from the building tenant. The students enrolled in adult and continuing education are likewise unique, being at all levels of learning as well as widely divergent in age, learning ability, and personal needs and goals.

The sole purpose of adult and continuing education is perhaps impossible to state to the satisfaction of all interested in the subject. No attempt will be made here to propose one adoptable definition nor an example of a sole, specific purpose. Most writers on the subject do clarify through a descriptive definition what they consider adult and continuing education to represent. As one example, Hoffer believes that

> . . . a basic purpose of adult education, as of education in general, is to help equip the individual with the knowledge, insight, and skills which will enable him to make the wisest decisions in his social, health, economic, and political life, as well as to contribute to his personal enrichment.[1]

While a great number of the existing programs today carry the title "Adult and Continuing Education," there often is confusion between the two terms and their correct usage. Some people and writers use the two terms interchangeably, while others sharply define both. Those who work closely in the actual programs have tended to apply the term "continuing education" to the programs at the college and university levels and have reserved the term "adult education" for all other activities for adults. There has also been a philosophical distinction that continuing education represents an ideal—a deliberate attempt to learn throughout life—and that adult education represents the means to realize that ideal. Still others, and often educational centers themselves, classify any programs held after five o'clock on their own campus or any courses taught off campus as adult and continuing education.

Needless to say, adult and continuing education covers a very broad spectrum, and very little writing on the entire scope of the subject appears

---

[1]Hoffer, Joe R. "Health and Welfare Agencies." *Handbook of Adult Education.* New York: Macmillan Co., 1970. p. 349.

to be based on sound research. However, all the literature seems to point out that adult and continuing education programs have been, are today, and will continue to be extremely viable programs partially due to the diverse methods of implementing these programs and the fact that they are largely locally controlled.

This chapter is primarily an extrapolation of ideas, findings, and recommendations from numerous readings and interviews and from a survey of adult and continuing education centers across the nation. The chapter includes a brief history of the origins of business education as a part of adult and continuing education; a description of current thinking concerning the activities and types of programs most popular; a delineation of curriculum offerings at present; and finally, a projection, according to the best available data, of those trends, changes, and types of business education programs in the adult and continuing education curriculums anticipated in the years ahead. With the office environment changing so rapidly to accommodate the day-to-day technological changes, it is apparent that business education programs in adult and continuing education will be required to likewise change and otherwise adapt accordingly in order to keep pace with the increased demand for better educated, better trained office workers.

EMERGENCE OF ADULT BUSINESS EDUCATION PROGRAMS

While the origin of adult education can be traced to the 1600's and 1700's, it was in the early 1900's that adult education programs began changing direction from that of citizenship and idealism to other broader subjects, with special emphasis on vocational subjects and realism. Business educators were quick to take advantage of the existing opportunities.

With the passage of the vocational education legislation in the early 1900's, business educators were able to obtain funds for some of the vocational programs which had been established after the Civil War. Returning veterans from that war and from the next two wars were able to take advantage of federally approved courses to provide themselves with marketable skills with which to make a living at jobs other than farming. In these early days of business education, such courses as accounting and math were taught at evening schools as part of the adult and continuing education programs. Students were prepared for entry-level jobs and for promotions in existing jobs. Those who had academic degrees learned job skills when they found that their original training had not prepared them for available positions. The business education program in adult and continuing education has been of primary importance throughout its relatively short history and remains so today.

Continuing education today is often regarded as that education taken advantage of by those who already possess a high school diploma and perhaps even a college degree. Those who complete continuing education programs often receive credit hours, but just as often the courses are listed as noncredit. Continuing education frequently goes by other titles such as "Lifelong Learning," "Recurrent Learning" (especially in European countries), and "Adult Higher Education."

The future of continuing education (lifelong learning) seems very bright. Among those who have taken a special interest in lifelong education and have further studied the implications of the trends in birth decline is Cross, who states:

> The hottest new movement in higher education is generally called lifelong learning in the United States and recurrent education in countries abroad. Those terms refer to an emerging worldwide interest in adult learning. For a number of reasons, the vanguard of the lifelong learning movement in the United States consists largely of women between the ages of 25 and 45.[2]

Cross goes on to state that as a result of the birth decline in recent years, it is expected that the number of 18- to 24-year-olds will grow approximately 8 percent during the 1970's, while the 25- to 34-year-olds are expected to increase up to 44 percent. Furthermore, if the birthrate remains as low as it is today, we may find that by the year 2000 there will be a 30 percent decrease in the number of children under 16 which will be counterbalanced by a 40 percent increase in the number of adults over 16.[3]

That continuing education is today and will continue to be a most important component within our societal structure is without question. Bender and Stair make the statement:

> Continuing education is today being viewed in administrative circles as the untapped market area that will help revitalize sagging higher education enrollments. A report by the Commission on Nontraditional Study estimates that 80 million adults, age 18 to 60, are "would-be" learners, provided they can get what they want, when and where they want it.[4]

Accurate statistics on enrollments in both adult and continuing education programs are difficult to ascertain. Reporting of enrollments, it seems, is not as controlled nor as mandatory as it is for elementary, secondary, or postsecondary educational institutions. Rauch believes that the enrollments are very high and that the possibilities for continuing education programs will remain at a high level when he explains:

> No one really knows how many adults participate in some kind of continuing education program each year, because it is hard to formally identify everything that provides a learning opportunity for an adult. But we do know that the need for well-planned educational opportunities for adults is increasing rapidly, and . . . already are more adults participating in continuing education programs than the combined total of all children and young people in schools and colleges.[5]

The Kellogg Foundation, through the several Kellogg Centers for continuing education located on various university campuses, plays an important role in furthering the cause of continuing education through the conduct

[2]Cross, Patricia K. "Cross Reviews Lifelong Learning Movement." *Illinois State University Alumni News* 11:1; December 1978.

[3]*Ibid.*

[4]Bender, Barry, and Stair, Ralph M., Jr. "Continuing Education: The New Market for Business Schools and Their Faculty." *Collegiate News and Views* 30:21; Winter 1976-77.

[5]Rauch, B. David. *Priorities in Adult Education.* New York: Macmillan Co., 1972. p. ix.

of various seminars, workshops, institutes, colloquiums, and programs offered to adults and young people. No attempt will be made here to further portray the function of this type of continuing education arrangement.

Perhaps for most people continuing education is viewed as the upgrading of skills already learned, retooling for current types of jobs, enhancing one's knowledge in new areas, and simply brushing up through certain courses for improvement and advancement on the job.

CURRICULUM DETERMINED BY NEEDS ASSESSMENT

The functional purpose of adult education must be associated with the evident *needs* and/or *wants* of people within a given community. Since adult education is aimed toward the fulfillment of identified needs of people ranging in age from, say, 16 to 60 and even beyond, these needs reveal considerable diversity and, therefore, create monumental administrative decisions when determining adult education curricular offerings. In this regard, Lumsden states:

> Fundamental to the curriculum development process in adult education is the awareness of needs, social and educational, as they exist within the community context of the educational institution. The institution must be aware of the "urgent wants" requisite for individual self-actualization (sic) and social progress if the organization's (sic) existence is to be justified and its purposes realized (sic).[6]

Who, then, actually determines the needs which will be fulfilled by curricular offerings through an adult education program? One could well expect that organized neighborhood groups would have a voice in the determination of school policy, as this certainly is an evident part of the urban scene today. Adult education is no exception in that it must face the same challenge from its clients in all communities it serves. When explaining ways of determining needs, McMahon states:

> There are many methods for getting information about individual and community educational needs. The methods include surveys, community study, checklists, interviews, questionnaires, suggestion boxes, community representatives, advisory committees, contacts with community leaders, listening, and the use of available data such as census reports. Unfortunately, the determination of community need is a complex continuing process which does not lead to instant and lasting solutions.[7]

It must be borne in mind that adult education is a relatively broad term encompassing the needs and goals of diverse groups of people. Adults who need or desire a high school diploma often enroll in (ABE) Adult Basic Education courses designed to help them prepare to pass the (GED) General Educational Development examinations. Other adult prospects are motivated to enroll in selected ABE courses in order to learn how to speak, read, and write the English language. This is referred to as the (ESL) English as a Second

---

[6]Lumsden, D. Barry. "The Curriculum Development Process in Adult Education." *Adult Education* 49:280; January 1977.

[7]McMahon, Ernest E. "The Needs of People and the Needs of Their Communities." *Priorities in Adult Education.* New York: Macmillan Co., 1972. Chapter 2, p. 40

Language program in ABE. Still others are primarily interested in the (APL) Adult Performance Level program of ABE. Rather than emphasizing purely academic knowledge, this program tends to focus on the functional skills that are highly relevant to everyday living.

Another method of determining need is the prescriptive process through which some designated person decides what another person needs. Adult school directors often adopt this method of determining need since they believe they are best qualified to do so. As arbitrary as the method may be, it frequently proves quite accurate.[8]

The question, then, is: Does the educator prescribe the curriculum or does the client determine both the need and the solution? Atwood believes the client must have a direct voice in the determination of adult education curriculums when he says:

> It is not enough, usually, for the adult educator to determine the educational needs of his client. The client—an individual, members of a group, members or representatives of an institution or a community—must recognize the existence of the needs. Unless this condition is brought about, the adult learning opportunities based upon the results of the diagnosis probably will not be meaningful to the client. In fact it is quite unlikely that the client will be concerned enough to participate in these opportunities.[9]

Regardless of how the adult education curriculum is developed, people cannot be expected to automatically flock to adult education programs. No matter how good the programs are or how great the institution's reputation may be, each program must be sold to those for whom these programs are intended. The people within the community must be motivated to participate and take advantage of the opportunities afforded them. Thus, creating a positive image of the adult education programs is part of the public relations with which an adult education center must concern itself. Creating an image should not be an artificial attempt to simply persuade people to enroll in existing educational opportunities but rather should "tell it like it is" and truly reflect what actually exists and is available for satisfying those discovered needs and wants which had in one way or another been determined. As someone once said, a little learning is fine, more learning is better, but a considerable amount of learning is greatest.

Function of adult and continuing education centers. In this rapidly changing, challenging technological business world, it is apparent that adult and continuing education centers are being referred to more and more when some new idea, machine, procedure, or device affecting office occupations has been introduced. These centers more than any other educational institution are being asked to provide the necessary knowledge, skill, and training required for successful operation of the new equipment and implementation of proper procedures. It is undoubtedly due to the very purpose, nature, and/or organization of adult and continuing education centers that they be requested to offer the appropriate skills and training for most new techno-

---

[8]*Ibid.*, pp. 40-41.

[9]Atwood, H. Mason. "Diagnostic Procedure in Adult Education." *Adult Education: The Diagnostic Procedure*. Bloomington: School of Education, Indiana University, 1973. p. 4.

logical changes affecting offices—especially machines and equipment—since frequently a training period need not exceed a few hours, days, or weeks. While most secondary schools, community junior colleges, colleges, and universities which tend to offer similar training organize their programs in quarter or semester modules, the adult and continuing education centers have proven somewhat more flexible in scheduling and can easily offer adequate training and sufficient entry-level skill in less time. For those reentering the job market or retooling for the office occupations, this type of flexible scheduling appears more favorable and is most often selected.

Who enrolls in adult and continuing education programs? Programs in adult and continuing education, through an open-door policy, are open and available to anyone interested in the offerings at any particular time. Most often, however, the clients served (the students enrolled) are made up of people—mostly women—who wish to reenter the job market after having taken time off to rear a family or for some other reason; those who wish to learn a new skill or otherwise prepare themselves for newly created jobs; those who wish to brush up on their skills, knowledges, and various business concepts; and those who simply wish to take courses for personal use. At times, responsible personnel in business and industry either require or recommend some of their employees to get additional training in certain areas in order to step up to a higher-level job within their establishments. Word processing, keypunch operations, and computer programming are but three examples of this type of request.

It is quite evident that there is no single mission with which adult and continuing education centers are charged but rather that the centers are in existence to enhance the learning in a wide breadth of areas from adult basic education to higher adult education.

THE ROLE OF AN ADULT BUSINESS EDUCATION TEACHER

Adult and continuing centers are known to seek advice from business and industry as to what type of courses, training, and programs are either lacking or necessary in the community and are, in many cases, further engaged in seeking instructors from these very same businesses and industries. If instructors from these sources are not available, the business education departments within the local secondary schools, community junior colleges, colleges, and universities are contacted for interested, qualified instructors to fill any available teaching positions. On occasion, retired business teachers, unemployed business teachers, or employed office workers are asked to teach certain basic, refresher, advanced, or new courses requested by the public. Seldom is there a lack of qualified business teachers willing to teach adult and continuing business education courses—especially the more basic and popular courses.

In order for an adult and continuing education curriculum to succeed and satisfy the needs and wants of the population enrolled in these programs, the teachers employed to carry out the instruction within these programs must not only be knowledgeable within their subject matter but must also possess a perhaps more difficult characteristic—that of understanding the adult student and how adult students often differ in the way they learn and retain what they had previously learned.

The role of an adult educator should be one of a diagnostician. The adult educator should be able to help the client, through needs assessment, to translate the needs identified through diagnosis into program objectives.[10] Moreover, when considering needs assessment, the diagnostician must often make the distinction between (1) the needs of individual persons and (2) the needs of such social systems as organizations, institutions, selected groups, and communities.[11]

In further describing the role of the adult educator, London states:

> If adult education is going to be creative and meaningful , we must strive to find teachers who can make learning exciting. Hence, the role of the adult teacher is not only to convey significant material for study but to present it in a fashion that exhibits the joy of learning when it relates to one's life and experiences.[12]

Whenever secondary school, college, and university teachers are called upon to instruct within adult and continuing education programs, the teaching methodology employed to enable the adults to reach their educational and/or occupational goals must be more sensitive to the ways these people are accustomed to learning. These methods frequently differ from those adopted for students in secondary schools and universities. Among the varied important elements to remember when teaching adult students, the adult educator must bear in mind the constant need for encouragement, the extreme pressures the adults feel from everyday life problems, the impatience and self-criticism on the part of the learner, the fixed living and thinking patterns which may unconsciously affect learning, and the lack of a sufficient attention span, which is required of long evening, once-a-week courses.

A SURVEY OF ADULT AND CONTINUING EDUCATION CENTERS

In order to acquire current data concerning the administration, operation, curriculums, and changes in adult and continuing education a survey was made of selected adult and continuing education centers located in various states. A 16-item questionnaire was developed which would elicit the type of information believed required for a chapter of this type. A cover letter accompanied the questionnaire and was sent to 38 adult and continuing education centers in 25 states. Because no directory of such centers was readily available (even though several attempts were made to locate one), the letters were sent to "Center for Adult and Continuing Education" in care of the public school system in selected cities over 30,000 in population within the 25 states. Of the 38 questionnaires mailed in late October 1978, 18 were

---

[10]Stubblefield, W. Harold. "Teaching Diagnostic Skills: Procedures and Problems." *Adult Education: The Diagnostic Procedure.* Bloomington: School of Education, Indiana University, 1973. pp. 61-62.

[11]McKinley, John. "Perspectives on Diagnostics in Adult Education." *Adult Education: The Diagnostic Procedure.* Bloomington: School of Education, Indiana University, 1973. p. 69.

[12]London, Jack. "The Social Setting for Adult Education." *Handbook of Adult Education.* New York: Macmillan Co., 1970. Chapter 1, p. 20.

received by early December for compilation of information. Of these 18 received, 3 had been returned with the notation that they had no such programs available. The information obtained through this survey is presented below.

The adult and continuing education centers responding to the survey had been in existence anywhere from 6 to 50 years. Most of them (eight) had been in existence between 10 and 25 years.

When describing the changes in the business education curriculum since the inception of their programs, these comments were made: added new courses and equipment, specialized the program, keypunch had come and gone, expanded existing courses, started with only two courses but now have six, individualized the instructional approach, and started giving seminars and workshops in plants and industrial sites when requested by management to do so.

Asked about the growth of their programs, the schools responding replied that they had either doubled in size (seven), increased by 25 percent (three), increased slightly (three), or had no noticeable change (two). Not one of the schools indicated a reduction in the size of its program. This was contradicted somewhat by a responding California school which indicated no reduction in its program and also stated that two courses were deleted due to lack of funds under Proposition 13.

Courses added since 1975 included strategies for personal finance planning, introduction to data processing, business machines, calculators, basic civil service, speedwriting, investments, income tax, secretarial review, basic computer programming, speed typing, medical and legal office practice, insurance designated courses, PBX receptionist, keypunch, fashion merchandising, and office accounting. The reasons for adding these courses ranged from a demand by students to a test offering to see how the course would be received. The most frequently given reason was "an identified need."

Courses deleted since 1975 included strategies for personnel finance planning, keypunch, secretarial review, income tax accounting, grocery checking, real estate tax law, Gregg shorthand, RPG programming, and machine shorthand. Reasons given for deletion of courses were as follows: no interest, machines too expensive to rent, no demand, and new materials too hard to get, as well as Proposition 13 cutbacks.

The centers responding stated they publicized their programs via newspapers, brochures, television, radio, posted schedules, special announcements, direct bulk mail, catalogs, newsletters, and through the employment security division.

The changes most often seen in students in adult and continuing education programs since 1973 were as follows: an increase in middle-aged women seeking skills for additional family income, more younger people, more high school dropouts, more older people, an increase in students whose ages are between 18 and 28 years of age, and an increase in CETA and vocational rehabilitation students. Six respondents indicated no changes or very little change in the type of students.

228

When asked about trends in the business education area of their adult and continuing education program they expected to see in the 1980's and beyond, the respondents listed the following trends: more classes offered to train students on new machines, greater need for classes for adults, increased demand for competent office workers, increased use of electronic equipment, need for word processing training, more short special programs, more computer emphasis, more women workers, increased demand for shorthand skills, increased emphasis on typing skills and accounting knowledge, more data processing classes, and more demand for in-plant seminars and workshops by business and industry.

When asked to rank the most popular business education courses in their adult and continuing education programs, the list of courses mentioned was quite extensive. The results indicated, however, that the five most popular business education courses were typewriting, shorthand, bookkeeping/accounting, office machines, and office/secretarial practice and brushups, in that order. Other courses which were mentioned more than once and which ranked quite high in popularity were real estate, business communications, investments, income tax, keypunch, and filing.

An attempt to describe the length of time in weeks or clock hours allocated to each course within the business education programs would prove too cumbersome. There seemed to be no agreement in time allocation to these courses—either in weeks or clock hours. Most of the highly popular courses met anywhere from 12 to 18 weeks for a total of at least 33 to as high as 50 clock hours. Some of the less-frequently mentioned courses met for as little as eight to ten weeks for approximately 18 to 20 clock hours.

According to the survey, the comments and complaints most frequently heard from adult education students taking business courses were as follows: equipment was inadequate or not up to date, job aspirations were too high, not enough courses were offered, meeting once a week was too infrequent to achieve shorthand or typing skills, too much material was covered at one meeting, and the hours were too long per night after having worked all day. Some of the centers surveyed did not have any comments or complaints to report.

Among the more favorable comments often heard from adult business education students were these: helped update positions; teachers were helpful; good, helpful instructors, equipment, and opportunities; liked the individual approach; excellent and quality instruction; and good, meaningful business education subject offerings.

The centers for adult and continuing education surveyed indicated that, for the most part, they did not experience a shortage of business teachers available or willing to teach their courses. The results of the survey further indicated that, by far, secondary teachers comprised most of the personnel employed to teach the business education courses in the centers. Local business persons were next in order of teachers employed, with postsecondary teachers ranking third in this category. The survey further revealed that nonworking certified persons were occasionally asked to teach business courses; retired teachers were seldom asked to teach courses; and elementary teachers were never asked to teach any of the business education courses in the adult and continuing education programs. This data should have some impact on the necessity for business teacher training institutions to give their graduates a knowledge of the adult learner, the way he/she learns, and methods which are most helpful in allowing him/her to achieve educational goals.

The minimum qualifications which were required of business teachers wishing to teach adult and continuing business education courses were rather diverse in nature. Most of the qualifications described, however, had to do with teacher certification, experience, and proper credentials. Other qualifications listed were ability, five years of work experience or the proper certificate with two years of work experience, basic knowledge, and degree with major or minor in business education.

The means through which the adult and continuing education business education program offerings and course content were determined also brought a variety of responses. Most frequently mentioned for program and course content determination was "students' requests." Advisory committee input, teachers' choices, a system of course rotation, budgetary restrictions, business and industry requests, and proven traditional demands were other means through which business education programs and courses were determined.

Surprisingly few business education courses or programs were being planned for addition to the existing adult and continuing education business education offerings. When asked what new course or program offerings were being planned in the near future, the responses were typing—two levels, shorthand—two levels, accounting, bookkeeping, business law, office machines, medical secretary, legal secretary, office management, word processing and memory typewriter, and computer language programmed courses. Five centers indicated that they did not plan to add any new courses or programs, and the comment was also made that Proposition 13 in California would not allow for any new courses or programs to be added.

A respondent from one adult and continuing education center perhaps summarized it for all centers in expressing the opinion that the center was available to provide through its facilities and expertise the type of instruction, brushups, workshops, and the like for whatever new developments might be forthcoming which would affect business offices and the students who had a need for an education or training of that type.

It was evident that the administrators within the adult and continuing education centers who took the time to complete the questionnaires were not able to project much beyond their immediate course offerings and programs when it came to predicting what the future business curriculums within their centers would be. It appeared—as might be suspected—that it is next to impossible to forecast or predict with any degree of confidence what changes or alterations the business education curriculum will undergo in the immediate years ahead. It was evident through this survey that the function of these centers is to provide whatever educational experiences are required, requested, or necessary at that particular point in time.

CONCLUSION

Centers for adult and continuing education are serving a nationally recognized function in the educational structure of our country. These centers are well established and designed to fulfill an identified need of a divergent group of people which has existed for more than 50 years. Their programs have increased in popularity, and it appears as though the centers will continue indefinitely. Numerous considerations must be taken into account when designing a business education curriculum within these centers since the potential enrollment is not clearly identified sufficiently far in advance. Adult and continuing education centers are most willing and able to design a course, sequence of courses, workshops, or programs in a relatively short period of time when requested to do so by the general public or an interested organized group. While such perennially popular courses as typewriting, shorthand, office practice, and skill brushups are most likely to attract a sufficient enrollment to warrant such course offerings, other business courses such as income tax accounting, real estate, CPS review, word processing, data processing, keypunch, computer programming, filing, and the like are less certain to attract sufficient enrollments and, therefore, may be offered less seldom or perhaps upon special request only.

It is safe to assume, then, that the business education curriculum within an adult and continuing education center is basically governed by those considerations which include budget, demand for such a program of courses, popularity of certain courses, individual and group requests, location of the centers, available facilities and instructors, and the ability of the administration to organize, publicize, and carry out such programs to the satisfaction of the community. It is also safe to say that centers for adult and continuing education will continue to stand ready to accommodate the business education curricular needs and requests of the population served by the respective centers.

CHAPTER 22

Business Administration Curriculum Recommendations

SUSAN I. BRENDER and MARVIN A. CLARK
Boise State University, Boise, Idaho

The world of business today utilizes vast amounts of information. The raw materials for the production of information are words and figures—facts and data necessary to describe daily business activities. In order to provide the highest quality of management information, the production of words and figures and the media on which they are recorded must be properly managed.

Business organizations are now beginning to recognize the importance of viewing records management, data processing, word processing, and administrative services as integral parts of information management. In most schools, business administration curriculums as yet do not reflect any integration of these activities. They are treated as completely separate curriculums. A consequence of this separation is that data processing is considered a business administration subject and is usually found in the business core requirement, while the other three subject areas are studied only by secretarial or office administration students.

Information management is a concept that encompasses the total business organization; it actually is the foundation for the operations of the entire business as well as a separate business function such as marketing or production. The business administration curriculum must reflect the importance of managing information—it already recognizes the importance of information itself.

INFORMATION MANAGEMENT IN TODAY'S BUSINESS ORGANIZATION

In a business organization a great deal of emphasis is placed on management of the organization's functional areas such as personnel, production, marketing, finance, and accounting. Management of the information that supports these functional areas, however, is frequently ignored. Information processing is often fragmented into four different areas—data processing, records management, word processing, and administrative services. Business is only beginning to recognize the overlap in these areas.

While each of these areas does have a separate function to perform, the procedures are much the same. In many cases, the machinery is similar, if not identical. Careful analysis of the technological developments in the last few years would reveal that a new development or innovation in one area often has considerable effect on the other two. Jack Gilmore, of Digital Equipment Corporation, states that "word processing and data processing are simply two logical subsets of information processing."[1] Separation of these areas simply is no longer a feasible approach from either the results or the economics point of view.

The following diagram illustrates the nature of input, processing, and output in records management, data processing, and word processing. Note that the information processing steps involved are strikingly parallel.

**Organizing the Input, Processing, and Output
of Information Through Data Processing,
Records Management, and Word Processing**

	Data Processing
Output	Distribution and Use of Reports
	Reproducing Reports
	Report Preparation
	Security of Files
	Retrieval of Data
Processing	Storage of Data
	Arithmetic Manipulation of Data
	Classification and Sorting of Data
Input	Origination of Data
	Records Management
Output	Use of Records by Authorized Individuals-Retrieval
	Security and Vital Records Protection
	Disposal of Obsolete Records
Processing	Transfer of Records from Active to Inactive Storage
	Maintenance and Purging of Records
	Classification and Storage of Records
Input	Creation of Records
	Word Processing
Output	Retrieval and Use of Documents
	Maintenance and Purging of Files
Processing	Storage of Documents
	Document Revision
	Power Typing Document Preparation
Input	Origination of Words-Dictation

The ultimate goal of each of these areas is quality reports and documents that management can use in the decision-making process. This, of course, is also the ultimate goal of information management, which it naturally must

---

[1]Flato, Linda. "Merging of Data Processing and Word Processing Impacts Users and Vendors Alike." *Datamation* 24:182; September 1978.

be since these four areas collectively constitute information management as it currently exists in the business world.

When information processing is unmanaged, the quality requirements for information are not determined beforehand nor evaluated afterward. As a result, reports and documents that management uses in decision-making may be of lower quality than is desirable, more expensive than necessary, and/or untimely.

Organizations are spending millions of dollars on information processing without the benefit of management. Some of these dollars are expended because duplication occurs. Records management, word processing, data processing, and administrative services are performing very similar functions. With this approach, common business information needs are usually fulfilled, although the process is frequently more expensive and time consuming than necessary.

Unexpected information needs, however, result in a different type of problem. Because information processing is not well managed, a data base sufficient to meet unexpected information needs may not exist. Information needs are not foreseen; therefore, firefighting techniques are necessitated. This approach may well result in incomplete or inaccurate information on which management then bases its decision. If information needs are not determined prior to the time that information should be available, just the time required to collect the data may preclude actually collecting it. Occasionally, it may no longer be possible to obtain the data. In any case, this approach can be expected to add to the cost and decrease the quality of information. The consequences of the lack of planning and management can be severe.

Business organizations are now beginning to recognize the necessity of developing information management programs that maintain information in the proper formats so it can be used to solve common problems. This requires coordination among the procedures used in data processing, word processing, records management, and administrative services. This coordination can also result in providing a good data base for use in solving the unexpected or unusual problem. Business now recognizes the value of avoiding firefighting approaches and is beginning to manage information. Information is no different from any other resource, and it may be the most important resource any manager has available.

There seems to be a tendency for business to identify information management as a responsibility of the office. The appearance on the market of sophisticated and expensive information processing equipment is causing management to take a much closer look at the office and its function in the business organization.

Wohl reports that the integration of information functions is, in some instances, resulting in a reorganization of office activities and, "In some companies, a new department—call it information systems, information processing, administrative services, or whatever—has been formed, which may include such previously disparate functions as word processing, data processing, reprographics, information retrieval (paper files and microfilm), and perhaps in-plant printing."[2]

INFORMATION MANAGEMENT IN CURRENT
BUSINESS ADMINISTRATION CURRICULUM

Business administration curriculums are giving slight attention to information management by sometimes including a section on management information systems in a data processing course. This course is frequently the only contact a business administration student has with the concept. The inclusion of this concept in a data processing course is seldom related to records management, word processing, or administrative services.

Secretarial and/or office administration students can sometimes avoid data processing, and many do if possible. They do, however, usually come in contact with records management, word processing, and administrative services, although records management is often more processing than actual management.

In all four areas, the requirements seldom consist of more than an introductory course. Experience has shown that if courses in these subject matter areas are not required, students tend to avoid them.

Even if students avail themselves of the opportunity to study records management, data processing, word processing, and administrative services subjects, the courses are so structured that they emphasize the machinery used rather than the procedures required. Certainly, they do not emphasize the management of information. There is also heavy emphasis on the *how to* approach rather than the *why* or systems approach in all four areas— records management, data processing, word processing, and administrative services. In records management, emphasis is on records creation and storage systems rather than management. In data processing, emphasis is on programming computers rather than on an organized approach to managing the information processed by computers. In word processing, emphasis is on machinery and how to operate it rather than on managing the word processing function. In administrative services, emphasis is on actual performance of procedures rather than on planning and management.

Additionally, one must not lose sight of the fact that the typical business administration student never comes in contact with the subjects of records management, word processing, and administrative services. Therefore, those students do not even become aware of the technological developments in these fields, not to mention the management procedures.

Any information management approach must concern itself with input, processing, and output. Careful management of these three functions will result in high-quality information which can provide a sound base for good management decisions.

The business administration curriculum must address the concept of information management by recognizing that integration of records man-

---

[2]Wohl, Amy D. "Experiencing the Link Between Data Processing and Word Processing." *Administrative Management*, October 1977. p. 43.

agement, data processing, and word processing is the logical way to achieve a complete picture.

PROPOSED BUSINESS ADMINISTRATION CURRICULUM IN INFORMATION MANAGEMENT

It is clear, then, that the changing office environment and the office of the future will demand more attention from schools of business. In schools of business where work in office administration, office management, administrative management, etc. is offered, an opportunity for that department to make additional valuable contributions to collegiate education for business is at hand. Two obvious ways to deal with this opportunity are:

1. Offer a single introductory course in information management for all school of business students.
2. Offer a major in information management.

Introductory course in information management. Because of the importance of information to the management of businesses; because of technological developments in equipment used in word processing, data processing, records management, telecommunications, and electronic mail; and because of significant changes in office procedures, there is a strong need for all business employees at all levels of management (as well as nonmanagement) to understand information processing and to acquire an ability to manage information. This need can be fulfilled in the professional education of business personnel by including a required course in information management. This course would include much of what is usually taught in an introduction to data processing class and would replace it as a business core course with the following catalog description and course outline:

Management of Information—3 semester hours
This course includes the fundamentals of the data processing cycle, the records life cycle, and word processing procedures. Emphasis is on the determination of management's information requirements and the design and management of systems to meet those needs. Both manual and automated procedures are studied as they relate to the management of personnel, procedures, and equipment.

COURSE OUTLINE. Major attention is given to integration of word processing, data processing, and records management as it applies to the following areas:
> Origin of data
> Records creation
> Classification of data and documents
> Sorting of data and documents
> Storage and retrieval of data and documents
> Calculation
> Maintenance and purging of files
> Maintenance and protection of permanent files
> Disposal of obsolete files
> Security procedures

Preparation of reports

Distribution and use of reports.

Major in information management. Overwhelming evidence points to increased efforts by business and government to increase office productivity. With enormous increases predicted in dollars spent on information resources in the United States ($150 billion per year in 1975 and estimated to increase to $350 billion by 1985),[3] it is readily apparent that schools of business must respond to the need for preparing managers of this enormous resource.

Education for business must acknowledge the technological developments in recent years which have resulted in equipment that will change the nature of information management. Computer technology is now a common base of almost all information processing.

There seems to be an increasing number of business managers who view information as a major *functional* area of business—along with marketing, finance, production, etc. The areas included in information—word processing, data processing, records management, reprographics, and telecommunications—would be included in the information management major.

Beyond the business common body of knowledge (business core), the following business courses are suggested to complete the business administration course requirements:

Records Management—6 semester hours
   a. **Managing the Records Life Cycle—3 semester hours**
      This course includes management techniques involved in the creation, use, storage, transfer, and disposal of records. It also includes classification systems, equipment, automated procedures, microforms, and forms design.
   b. **Records Retention and Maintenance—3 semester hours**
      This course includes retention decisions and procedures, legal requirements, security systems, operation of retention centers, operation of archives, and vital records protection.

Word Processing—3 semester hours
      This course includes organization and structure of word processing in business input systems; discrete and continuous media; output systems including text editing, display, and computerized equipment; reprographics and records management; and creating and managing a word processing system.

Data Processing—6 to 9 semester hours
   a. **Introduction to Data Processing—3 semester hours**
      This course briefly introduces the entire field of data processing including manual vs. machine data processing, the data processing cycle, structure of input and output, processing procedures, computer programming, and applications.
   b. **Information Processing Systems—3 semester hours**
      This course includes the determination of information processing needs, requirements for information processing systems, personnel and computer requirements, batch and on-line computer applications.

[3]Kleinschrod, Walter A. "Information, Yes, But How Much and in What Form?" *Administrative Management.* January 1977. p. 23.

c. **Programming for Information Management** (optional)—3 semester hours
   This course includes the design, preparation, and maintenance of software for information management systems using the computer. Emphasis is on design of procedures.

Other courses:
   Systems Analysis
   Human Resource Management
   Personnel Administration
   Other business electives

Programs and majors related to information management. Other related information management majors could be offered either as separate majors or as options under information management. For instance, a major in data processing (or business data systems, or another appropriate title) would continue to be offered as would office management or office administration. Other options or separate majors might be two-year and/or one-year programs in office systems directed toward the preparation of word processing and administrative support secretaries.

These suggested majors allow for a broad information management major with more specialized options available (data processing, office management, and office systems) for interested students.

Role of office administration in information management. Many schools of business presently offer majors in the office management area, although the exact name of the major may vary. Whether it is called office management, office administration, administrative office management, administrative services, or something similar, the objective of such a program is usually to prepare graduates for positions in which they will handle, process, and/or manage certain kinds of business information. With the advent of new technology in data and word processing (microcomputers, electronic mail, and telecommunication equipment) and records processing (computerized indexing, computer output microfilm, etc.), new relationships and new procedures are appearing in the changing office. The office administration curriculum must address these changes.

New relationships are occurring between word processing and data processing. As a result of the introduction of newer microcomputers, much of computing is being transferred from the computer room to the office, a trend that emphasizes the dramatic changes taking place in information processing. Word processing applications, as well as accounting and inventory control, are some of the applications possible on the same piece of equipment. The office supervisor will probably have responsibility for providing both word processing and data processing support required by principals. Similar new relationships between records management and data/word processing are occurring.

New office procedures using new technology are also occurring. With regard to the office worker's function, Greenblatt states:

With the DP/WP integration the secretarial function will be operating in an environment surrounded by new technology and new concepts in office pro-

238

cedures. Administrative and correspondence secretaries will assume additional responsibilities.

The administrative secretary, more than likely, will take on a paraprofessional role and absorb more delegated management responsibilities. This stronger management support position will probably call for the administrative secretary to be the main interface between management and the computer.

The position of administrative secretary will probably be structured into a number of levels, with junior administrative secretaries responsible for the more routine tasks such as filing, messengering, and telephone answering, and the senior administrative secretaries performing the more critical management support functions. The senior level positions will most likely attract candidates with college degrees and/or significant experience because of the expanded scope of responsibility and increased opportunity for growth and advancement. As the concept gains acceptance, it will probably be recognized as an effective management training program.

The correspondence secretary will also have a changed and exciting role. DP/WP integration will place correspondence secretaries in the mainstream of office activities. Assignments will vary between word and data processing. Basic typing skills will still be mandatory, but less emphasized when teamed with the speed and flexibility of computer-supported word processing machines. The correspondence secretary will be able to utilize a broad range of skills.[4]

Departmental organization. Integration of information functions in business might lead one to ask whether these functions should logically be integrated within the business administration curriculum. Assuming that office administration curriculums now address the areas of word processing, records management, and reprographics, the addition of data processing courses would complete the integration of the areas commonly included in the information management concept.

If data processing offerings are administered in another department of the school of business, consideration should be given to a reorganization which would bring the information functions together in one department. A departmental name change may be appropriate and provide impetus to such a reorganization. Some possibilities might be department of administrative services, department of business information systems, department of information management, or department of information services.

As is the situation in many schools of business, business teacher education is also included with office administration. With a name change, business education would, of course, appear in the departmental name—such as department of administrative services and business education.

The restructuring or reorganization of information functions would strengthen both the school and the department. The school of business would be stronger because it would be addressing a major area of concern to business, one that business now considers a "functional area." The department of office administration (or whatever the title happens to be) would be stronger because it would be contributing to an even greater extent to the goals of a school of business. Benefits could also accrue in some situations

---

[4]Greenblatt, Robert. "Forecast for DP/WP Integration." *Word Processing* 3:11; October 1976.

wherein inclusion of data processing would increase the number of credit hours produced in the newly reorganized department, while taking pressure off the department where it was formerly administered. Another benefit not to be overlooked is that the reorganized department can contribute more to the reality that both males and females can enter business careers through any of the information functions of word processing, records management, data processing, reprographics, and even administrative support.

CONCLUSIONS

The professional preparation of business personnel at the top management level and below must include the concepts of managing information resources. Timely and accurate information is a product of the office of today.

Dramatic changes in equipment technology and office procedures to provide even more information to management will characterize the office of the future. Office costs are alarming. Doolittle states that "during the last decade, the cost of the office has doubled or is now 40 to 50 percent of total costs."[5]

Productivity, on the other hand, has been largely ignored in the office: "While we invest an average of $40,000 per factory worker to ensure high productivity, we only invest $2,500 per office worker."[6]

As in other functional areas of collegiate business education, an introductory course in information systems should be available and required of all school of business majors. For those who wish to specialize in information management or related areas, a major program should be provided. Implementation of the majors suggested may not, for some schools, involve the establishment of new courses. The reorganization of courses presently offered may be sufficient.

Most certainly, information processing and information management will receive much more attention in schools of business curriculums. The opportunity now presents itself for office administration departments to acquire increased acceptance through a broadened as well as a specialized approach to the information function of business. If office administration departments do not accept the responsibility, without a doubt there are other departments in schools of business that must.

---

[5]Doolittle, Harold F., Jr. "What Management Should Know About Word Processing." *Infosystems* 25:74; October 1978.

[6]*Ibid.*

CHAPTER 23

Business Teacher Education Day After Tomorrow

GORDON F. CULVER
University of Nebraska, Lincoln

Inherent in the changing office environment is the need for office personnel with the necessary technical skills and personal qualities to discharge efficiently the responsibilities for which they are employed. Future employment opportunities for office personnel appear to be unusually good. Because the secondary and postsecondary schools of the country are the major sources of new office personnel, educational institutions are presented with a tremendous opportunity—and challenge—to prepare competent personnel for tomorrow's office. The extent to which this challenge is met will be determined largely by the quality of business teachers provided by the business teacher training programs of the country.

Teacher education has always been subject to the influence of such forces as accrediting agencies, state departments of education, and professional associations. Teacher certification requirements are influenced by contemporary forces which prevail at any one time. However, it is doubtful that there has ever been a time when so many forces have been operating to influence the status and direction of teacher education. Many of these forces have little to do with accrediting and certifying agencies but result, instead, from political, social, and economic influences and conditions.

Because the products of our teacher training programs must meet minimum criteria of the agencies that certify them and certain expectations of the publics that will employ them, it is essential that teacher education programs be sensitive to those criteria and expectations; it is imperative that graduates of those programs be equipped to compete successfully for teaching positions.

The demands being made of teacher education programs today are monumental, and this can be expected to continue into the foreseeable future. Besides having a teaching specialization, today's secondary teacher must also be knowledgeable about such subjects as sex equity, mainstreaming, multicultural education, remedial reading, and career education, to name only a few. In addition, a teacher's employment is very likely to depend on his/her willingness to coach one of a number of athletic activities or to sponsor some other extracurricular activity, such as a business student organization.

Business teacher education has always provided an attractive educational opportunity for persons completing such a curriculum. The multiple employment options provided by such preparation—to teach or to enter business in a variety of situations—have been advantages associated with only a few other curriculums in higher education. In recent years when the supply of business teachers has exceeded the demand in some parts of the country, business has been the beneficiary of the talents and abilities of many of these individuals. Unemployment is not a common condition for graduates of business teacher education programs.

Business teacher training programs of the future will continue to provide graduates of those programs with numerous advantages that are unique to this field of preparation. The ability to move with ease between the classroom and business will continue to be a major advantage. The opportunity to make personal use of the foundational business skills and understandings needed to function effectively as consumers increases in importance as our lives become more and more entwined with governmental and business regulations; this aspect of a business teacher's preparation can greatly influence the quality of the teacher's life. The opportunity to update occupational skills periodically through employment in business will also continue as an advantage of persons completing a business teacher education curriculum.

But the business teacher education curriculum of the seventies will not be adequate to prepare business teachers for the eighties. Secondary business education curriculums of the eighties will require teachers with different kinds of personal qualities and different kinds of technical skills and instructional competencies. It is the purpose of this chapter to consider some of the changes that are taking place on the national scene and to indicate how these changes are likely to influence the preparation of secondary business education teachers in the future.

THE EDUCATIONAL PENDULUM

Because business teacher education must function within the total framework of higher education and must be in harmony with the needs of secondary schools, it is important to review briefly the educational climate that prevailed throughout the period of the seventies. During this decade, the higher education pendulum swung a frenzied course. During the early seventies, when postsecondary vocational-technical schools were expanding rapidly, the four-year colleges and universities continued their emphasis on general education. However, by the mid-seventies, when enrollments in four-year institutions were beginning to decline and the nation's economy was showing signs of stress, the entire educational spectrum was espousing the virtues of a practical education for everyone by the time of graduation from high school and certainly by the time a college degree had been completed. In recent years the value of a college education for everyone is being questioned, and an increasing number of four-year liberal arts colleges are modifying their requirements in order that students might prepare for a vocation while acquiring a liberal arts education.

In secondary education, such matters as high school graduation requirements and student control were undergoing change. Permissiveness in program development in secondary schools—begun during the latter part of the sixties—continued throughout much of the seventies. Graduation requirements were relaxed and course requirements eased so that graduation from many high schools became simply a matter of endurance on the part of students. Many schools placed restrictions on the amount of homework teachers could require of students; the study habits of students deteriorated noticeably as did their mastery of subject matter and their attainment of basic skills.

With the greater permissiveness in program development came a proliferation of courses in many different time and study packages from which secondary school students could choose. Students were encouraged to *explore* new fields of study and areas of possible interest. Students even designed their own courses and determined their own progress in some secondary schools. A "cafeteria approach" to course selection and program development for students became a reality in many schools. Although a number of these procedures were commendable, all too often they resulted in the high school graduation of students who did not have the basic skills needed either to continue in programs of higher education or to secure suitable employment and were not even equipped to handle their personal business activities intelligently.

As the decade of the eighties begins, the secondary education pendulum gives an indication that it will probably swing back to a more conservative position. Evident on the educational horizon are the measures being taken by secondary schools to assure that all students achieve minimum levels of competency in language arts and computational skills. Also evident are adjustments to see that students have competent teachers and counselors available who can provide accurate and up-to-date information concerning career development, vocational options, and continuing education. Finally, a higher quality of student discipline seems to be developing in the secondary schools; this should lead to greater self-discipline on the part of individuals in the future.

CONTEMPORARY SOCIETAL CONDITIONS

Curriculums must be sensitive to the forces of change. Future business teacher education curriculums will be shaped by the forces at work today and modified by situations that will prevail in the future. Consideration will be given to some selected prevailing social forces or circumstances that are likely to have an influence on future business teacher education curriculums.

The economy. With inflation and a discouraging economy interacting to diminish real incomes, lifestyles of American families are changing dramatically. Average family income has risen substantially in recent years, primarily as a result of two-income families. Today a majority of women work outside the home at some time during their adult lives. It is estimated that a female graduating from high school today can expect to work an average of 25 years in some form of employment outside her home; and this situation will not change if she marries or has children. For various reasons, the two-income family is probably here to stay.

Employment situation. Graduates of business-related programs, whether high school or postsecondary, enjoy a decided advantage in the struggle to secure employment. Graduates of such programs experience little difficulty in locating suitable employment. However, a recent *Kiplinger Letter* reported that business and industry are experiencing unusual difficulty with their efforts to attract and keep good employees. The reasons cited for this situation were that many of the workers don't really want to work; some cannot be loyal to their employing firm; others are not willing to give a good day's effort for a day's pay; and still others are unwilling to adapt to change brought on by new technology or by shifting market needs.

In the area of business education, numérous studies show that the schools do an excellent job equipping office education students to handle clerical, stenographic, and secretarial tasks. But an alarming number of these office workers are discharged because they have poor interpersonal relationship skills and poor attitudes, are troublemakers in the office, or exercise poor judgment.

Employment outlook. The future employment picture for students with a business education appears to be exceptionally bright. Labor Department reports indicate that a number of business-related jobs will offer excellent employment prospects through the mid-1980's. Among these are accountants, secretaries and stenographers, typists (especially typists familiar with power typewriters and word processing equipment), and computer programmers and system analysts. Accounting-related jobs have provided excellent employment opportunities for the past several years, and it is anticipated that this situation will continue.

The Labor Department makes particular mention of the need for secretaries with shorthand skill. The market for skilled shorthand-writing secretaries is so great today—and the supply so short or nonexistent—that some employment agencies look upon this occupational classification as an endangered species.

Tax limitation measures. As inflation mounts and continues to take its toll on the purchasing power of the dollar and as energy and other shortages in the area of consumer goods continue to add to a spiraling increased cost of living, we can expect governmental bodies to respond to the urgings of consumers by legislating ceilings on taxable money that can be used for specific purposes. A recent Gallup poll involving a cross section of citizens indicated that concern over taxes will rank among the top two or three national issues well into the 1980's. It can be expected that people will become more discriminating about how their tax dollars are spent and that financing all levels of public education will come under closer scrutiny in the future than ever before.

Sex equity. Title IX of the Education Amendments of 1972 has had a tremendous impact on American education—perhaps the greatest impact of any federal legislation during the decade of the seventies. The reverberations from this legislation can be expected to continue for many years and can be expected to be reflected in greater educational opportunities for both men and women.

With passage of the Equal Employment Opportunity Act of 1972, provisions were made to protect citizens from all kinds of employment discrimination based on race, religion, color, sex, or national origin. Women have found this legislation particularly welcome because it removes many of the limitations placed upon their career aspirations. As women's career horizons expand and as they participate more fully in the world of work, their educational aspirations are also extended in order that they might be competitive in the employment market.

As efforts are effective in reducing sex-role stereotyping and sex bias in employment and in educational and training programs, the makeup of student populations in certain subjects and activities in the schools has changed remarkably. For instance, high school accounting and marketing classes now enroll a larger percentage of females.

Other social changes. It is estimated that more than 51 percent of all married women are in the work force today. This percentage can be expected to grow as the economy tightens. Current Census Bureau reports indicate that a majority of working mothers remain employed througout their childbearing years. Women are also assuming greater responsibility for the management of family finances, and this situation prevails to a great extent even in families where the husband and father is present.

CONTEMPORARY EDUCATIONAL CONDITIONS

A number of educational conditions has also developed within the past few years that are likely to affect secondary business education in the future. Because of the impact these conditions could have on business teacher training programs, a selected few will be identified.

Economic education. The quality of an individual's life in a private enterprise, business-oriented society is tied inextricably to his/her ability to make intelligent decisions on numerous personal business and economic matters. In recognition of this fact, increasing concern is being expressed that schools should do more to provide students with a basic foundation in personal money management and consumer business skills.

Several states have already mandated that *all* high school students complete work or demonstrate minimum competencies in such courses as economics, consumer economics, personal finance, money management, or basic business prior to graduation. An increasing number of state boards of education are also requiring comparable kinds of basic business and economics competencies for high school graduation.

Back to the basics. Following the permissive years of the sixties and early seventies, the educational pendulum has once again swung in the direction of increased emphasis on the basic skills. As indicated earlier, employers, parents, postsecondary institutions, and students themselves became concerned that many graduates of our secondary schools could not read and could not solve problems requiring simple arithmetic skills; neither could they communicate intelligently—either in writing or orally.

Today, a concerted effort is being made by boards of education and state departments of education to assure that graduates of secondary schools will have achieved minimum levels of competency in the 3R's. Increasingly, *all* teachers are expected to help with identifying students who have reading problems, to teach remedial reading, and to help students develop adequate communication skills.

Student enrollments. Because of a declining birthrate, enrollments in elementary and secondary schools are declining rapidly. Many colleges and universities are also experiencing declining enrollments. However, other phenomena are at work causing enrollments in numerous postsecondary institutions to record all-time highs.

For one thing, a higher percentage of high school graduates are enrolling in some form of postsecondary education. Much of this increase can be attributed to female enrollments. It is not unusual to learn of freshmen enrollments in colleges of business administration in which the class is almost equally divided between male and female students.

Another cause for the stabilized or increasing enrollment situation in postsecondary institutions is the influx of older students—large numbers of them women—who are returning to the campus or starting college for the first time after raising a family. Many of those returning to college are "stop-outs" who previously had interrupted their education in favor of a period of full-time employment. An increasing number of women and men are also returning to the campus to learn new vocations or to explore new intellectual interests.

Another phenomenon influencing college enrollments today is the large number of part-time students, who are often employed full time and continuing their education in evening classes. Many business firms today provide released time for employees to continue their education—oftentimes with the employing firms paying the tuition. An increasing number of part-time students are enrolled in courses which prepare them for one of several professional certification programs: for example, the Certified Professional Secretaries exam, the Certified Administrative Manager exam, and the Certified Public Accountant exam.

However, the major cause for the large increase in postsecondary enrollments is the growth of the two-year college. The two-year college is regarded by many as the most powerful single phenomenon to appear in higher education during the past two decades. Increasingly, the two-year school is being regarded as the bridge from the community to the senior college.

Mainstreaming. With the passage in 1975 of PL 94-142, the Education of All Handicapped Children Act, *all* teachers have need for an understanding of how to counsel, teach, and work with students with various degrees of handicaps. Popularly referred to as "mainstreaming," the intent of this law is to move handicapped children from their segregated status in special education classes and integrate them into regular classroom situations with "normal" children. The law does not apply to youngsters whose handicaps are so severe that education in the regular classroom with the use of supplementary aids and services cannot be achieved; these students will continue to receive their education in special education classes.

Career education. Whether encouraged by the unfavorable economic conditions of recent years, by efforts to reduce sex-role stereotyping, or some other factor, the importance of work in the lives of *all* individuals is now recognized. Because career education is concerned with values, the entire education spectrum is affected by this movement. Educational programs must help individuals develop personal value systems concerning all aspects of human activity in a work-oriented society. Included in these educational efforts will be such varied concerns as choice of a vocation, use of leisure time, money management practices, civic responsibilities, and continuing education plans.

IMPLICATIONS OF SOCIETAL AND EDUCATION CONDITIONS FOR BUSINESS EDUCATION

The kinds of social and educational conditions described earlier have definite implications for business education and for the preparation of secondary business teachers. Work and careers have become concerns of *all* people, not just men. Female students are now preparing for careers and vocations in areas previously considered the exclusive domain of men. Business education programs can expect to enroll a large percentage of these students, but much of the enrollment will be in areas not previously attracting large enrollments of females: i.e., accounting, business administration, management, marketing. Business teachers will need to be knowledgeable about career opportunities in business and the educational preparation needed to prepare for such careers.

Greater efforts will be needed to establish cooperative, continuing relationships between business teachers and high school guidance counselors. Business educators have a responsibility to keep well informed about employment opportunities in the business and office occupations and the educational preparation needed to prepare for those occupations. By all means, this information must be shared with guidance counselors.

Vocational business education programs must give greater attention to the human relations skills and personal traits needed for successful employment. It is not enough to equip future office workers with only the technical office skills needed to secure employment; they must also be given the opportunity to develop decision-making skills and the cooperative, helpful, interpersonal relationship skills that contribute to a productive and pleasant work environment.

Personal lives and jobs affect each other. The manner in which individuals handle the consumer-business aspects of their lives affects everything they do—job, family, personal happiness. Basic business-economic education must become a part of every business student's preparation. Teachers in this area of instruction should be able to make the subject matter interesting and challenging and should conduct their own personal business in a manner that is worthy of being emulated. This aspect of a person's educational preparation for the future must not be left to chance. With females assuming more and more responsibility for the money management of families, business education programs should actively recruit female students into the basic business-economic education classes.

Business education teachers need to be broadly prepared in business in order to be as flexible as possible in their teaching assignments. Every business teacher should be prepared as a vocational teacher, with a record of occupational employment and an orientation to vocational education. Every business teacher should also be certifiable in the area of basic business-economic education.

With the growing emphasis on co-equal opportunity in athletics, business teachers should cultivate an interest in some of the athletic activities that are usually found in secondary schools. Increasingly, employment of new teachers is dependent on their ability and willingness to coach one of several sports. A majority of states do not require a coaching credential.

Business teachers should be able to identify students with reading and communication problems. All business teachers need to accept as one of their major objectives that of helping students develop good language arts skills. In fact, every teacher has a responsibility to help develop the communication skills of students.

With handicapped students now being enrolled in classes with "regular" students, business teachers must know how to provide for their special needs. Some states now require all teachers applying for initial certification to have had training in how to work with handicapped students.

OTHER CONDITIONS AND TRENDS AFFECTING BUSINESS EDUCATION

In addition to the conditions and trends cited previously, business teacher education curriculum specialists must also weigh carefully the effects other innovations and conditions are likely to have upon the preparation of secondary business teachers. Advances being made in office technology remain one of the biggest challenges to business teacher training programs. With more and more high schools having access to highly sophisticated office equipment for instructional purposes, business teacher training institutions must provide prospective business teachers the opportunity to develop the skills needed to instruct students in its use.

The multimedia resources available in many schools today for instructional purposes are awesome. Future business teachers must be aware of the contributions these resources can make to a successful education program. The possibilities for individualizing instruction are greater today than at any previous time. As a director of learning, every teacher should have some degree of expertise in the multimedia possibilities for instruction.

Today's emphasis on competency-based education will continue. Business teachers will need to develop skill in writing behavioral objectives and designing instruments for measuring student progress toward meeting those objectives.

THE POSSIBLE CURRICULUM OF THE FUTURE

With the foregoing discussion as a foundation, let us consider what the undergraduate curriculum is likely to be for high school graduates who aspire to become secondary business education teachers in the eighties.

General education. With the kinds of demands being made on teachers today—for broader teaching fields and additional professional education competencies—it is highly unlikely that the present level of general education can be maintained. In the past, the general education component of a student's undergraduate business teacher education program could be expected to approximate about one-half the total program. It would appear that future programs will do well to reserve 40 percent of the total program for general education studies. The National Association for Business Teacher Education in its *Guidelines for Business Teacher Education* recommends that the general education component constitute from 40 to 60 percent of the undergraduate program. In a 125-hour program, this would require that at least 50 semester credit hours be in general education studies; this will be difficult to maintain in the future.

Area of concentration. The area of concentration—or teaching major —for secondary business education teachers of the future will, in all likelihood, be substantially increased. With emphasis today on broad teaching fields, the comprehensively prepared secondary business teacher has a decided advantage in the job market.

With unanimous support from the business education professional associations that the objectives of business education at all levels of instruction are to prepare people *for* and *about* business, every business teacher training program has an obligation to prepare teachers to meet these instructional goals. To accomplish this, it may be anticipated that the teaching major will require between 50 and 60 semester hours. Included in these hours will be courses that constitute the business core and the office education skills. Whether located in a college or department of business administration or education, it is likely—and desirable—that *all* business teacher education majors will complete the core of courses required of business administration students.

The teaching minor lost credibility some time ago. Teacher education institutions—and school administrators—are reluctant to have instructors teaching in subjects for which they are only half-prepared.

Particularly in the area of office education, more and more courses will be completed by students demonstrating that they have attained the necessary competencies. It might also be anticipated that college-level office education classes will be highly accelerated to accommodate and encourage students who wish to meet competency requirements on an individual basis.

The occupational experience requirement for vocational certification will be increasingly fulfilled by undergraduate students through carefully structured and coordinated practicum programs administered by the business teacher education units.

Professional education. Because of the increased demands placed on all secondary teachers (in the area of mainstreaming, coequal and multicultural education) and on vocational teachers (vocational certification, special vocational needs), the professional education component of the undergraduate preparation of future business teachers will probably increase. To minimize that increase as much as possible, a number of teacher education institutions are redesigning existing courses in professional education in order that the new content areas might be treated without increasing the number of courses or credit hours required. In business teacher education, the content of special methods courses and the student teaching component are being carefully evaluated and restructured to meet some of the new requirements: for example, providing for the handicapped student.

Some of the more noteworthy changes in teacher education in recent years have involved the use of competency-based programs in the professional education sequences, particularly in general and special methods courses and in student teaching. The emphasis on competency-based education can be expected to continue.

Components of the undergraduate program. In meeting the requirements for graduation and initial certification, business teacher education majors of the future may anticipate that their undergraduate programs of 125 semester hours will approximate the following:

General Education	40-50 semester hours
Area of Concentration (business teaching major)	50-60 semester hours
Professional Education (including general and business)	20-25 semester hours
Electives	0-10 semester hours

In order to retain greater emphasis on general education in their undergraduate programs, a number of colleges have moved all professional teacher education and some of the work in the teaching major to a fifth year. In many instances, completion of a fifth-year program at these colleges results in completion of certification requirements as well as requirements for a master's degree.

THE BUSINESS TEACHER OF THE FUTURE

Business teacher education institutions have a proud heritage of outstanding accomplishments. Many of the practices and procedures in business teacher education have been good and will be retained in future programs. However, all indications are that, perhaps for the first time, business teacher education programs can become more concerned with developing quality programs that will produce quality business teachers.

The business teacher of the future will be a better educated individual, more broadly educated in business administration and economics, better prepared by formal training and occupational experience in the business and office skills, more knowledgeable about and skillful in the use of educational media and instructional procedures, more sensitive to the individual needs of student learners and more skillful in providing for those needs, more attuned to classroom experimentation and action research, and more highly motivated to continue education and professional development. However, as important and commendable as these qualities and abilities are, perhaps the greatest asset the business teacher of the future can have will be *adaptability*. To produce this business teacher of the future is the responsibility—and the challenge—of our business teacher education institutions!

NBEA EXECUTIVE BOARD

OFFICERS

President: DORIS Y. GERBER, Office of Superintendent of Public Instruction, Olympia, Washington

President-Elect: CALFREY C. CALHOUN, University of Georgia, Athens, Georgia

Secretary-Treasurer: CARL E. JORGENSEN, State Department of Education, Richmond, Virginia

Past-President: ROBERT POLAND, Michigan State University, East Lansing, Michigan

Executive Director: O. J. BYRNSIDE, JR., NBEA, Reston, Virginia

EXECUTIVE BOARD MEMBERS

Eastern Region: JOHN S. NIGRO (EBEA President), North Haven, Connecticut; MARY B. WINE, Washington, D.C.; WARREN T. SCHIMMEL, Little Falls, New Jersey; MILDRED F. JOHNSON, Cheyney, Pennsylvania

Southern Region: JOHN M. BUNCH (SBEA President), Charlotte, North Carolina; CHERYL M. LUKE, Columbia, South Carolina; MARGARETT A. HUGGINS, Clinton, Mississippi; BASIL O. SWEATT, Hammond, Louisiana

North-Central Region: ADALINE J. EASTMAN (N-CBEA President), Muncie, Indiana; DAVID J. HYSLOP, Bowling Green, Ohio; THOMAS B. DUFF, Duluth, Minnesota; D. SUE RIGBY, Marquette, Michigan

Mountain-Plains Region: JOHN F. KELLER (M-PBEA President), Valley City, North Dakota; OSCAR H. SCHUETTE, Denver, Colorado; MARCELLA MOUSER, Emporia, Kansas

Western Region: KENNETH McDONALD (WBEA President), Seattle, Washington; ROBERT J. THOMPSON, Los Altos, California; MONA NOBLE, Mountain Home, Idaho; HOWARD L. JONES, Gresham, Oregon

NABTE Representatives: THOMAS E. LANGFORD (NABTE President), Kingston, Rhode Island; JAMES ZANCANELLA, Laramie, Wyoming

Ex Officio: ARTHUR H. RUBIN, New York, New York

PUBLICATIONS COMMITTEE

OSCAR H. SCHUETTE (Chairman), Denver, Colorado; DORIS WILLIAMSON (Secretary), Cedar City, Utah; THELMA C. HOYLE, Weston, Massachusetts; EDNA SCHIFFERNS, Ariba, Colorado; GORDON A. TIMPANY, Cedar Falls, Iowa; ANNE L. MATTHEWS, Columbia, South Carolina; DORIS Y. GERBER, Olympia, Washington; and O. J. BYRNSIDE, JR., Reston, Virginia